How to Help a Friend

PAUL WELTER

LIVING STUDIES
Tyndale House Publishers, Inc.
Wheaton, Illinois

ACKNOWLEDGMENTS

Two grants from the Faculty Research Services Council at Kearney State College made it possible for me to do the necessary research and studying to put together the approach to helping people which is described in this book. I am indebted to the Council and to the college administration for encouragement and help in carrying out what I saw as a mission.

The examples used in the book are drawn from interaction with many friends and counselees. In most examples details were changed to insure confidentiality.

Three chapter contributors are specialists in their areas, and are effective helpers as well. Dr. Vic Cottrell, who contributed chapter five, "Helping a Friend Through Appropriate Modeling," is President, Ventures for Excellence, Inc., Lincoln, Nebraska. Vic has been an effective model to me in the intensity of his helping mission. He has found new ways of calling forth people's strengths, and has shared these methods with thousands of people in workshops throughout the United States.

Mrs. Anita Norman, who contributed chapter thirty-four, 'How to Use Books in a Helping Way," is reference librarian at Kearney State College. Throughout her career as a librarian, in a number of different settings, she has had a quiet, effective way of helping people finding books that speak to the whole person. She has worked hard, as her chapter shows, to become knowledgeable concerning the rapidly increasing resources available for bibliotherapy. She is recognized by students and faculty as an effective helper.

Dr. Marvin Knittel, contributer of chapter thirty-six, "Imagine That! The Use of Images," is Vice-President for Academic Affairs at Kearney State College. He is also a counseling psychologist, and is one of the two or three most effective counselors I have known. In the last few years he has developed a growing interest and special skills in the powerful and unique method of using images in counseling.

Karen Diestler obtained the structured interview material used in chapter thirty-eight, "Divorce—Finding a Way to Help." Jeanette Pekarek, Kathy Welter, and Carol Echtenkamp typed the numerous revisions of the manuscript. Readers of various parts of the manuscript included John McNeill, Floyd Butterfield, Dick Smith, and Vic Cottrell. Lillian, my wife, provided constructive criticism throughout revisions. She has a keen sense of what is helpful and what is not. Victor Oliver and Virginia Muir at Tyndale House both have the gift of encouragement. Drawing courage from them at critical times has helped me to complete this task.

Third printing, Living Studies edition, November 1984
Library of Congress Catalog Card Number 83–71014
ISBN 0-8423-1505-5

*This book is
dedicated
to my friends
who have helped me*

Contents

Section One
Preface

THIS MANUAL ON HELPING IS INTENDED FOR people in all kinds of vocations—homemakers, accountants, cosmetologists, taxi drivers, secretaries, and machine operators, to name a few—who have friends turning to them for help. It is for "laypersons," those without professional counseling training. (Being a layperson is not uncommon. There are an estimated 40,000 occupations. Each of us is a layperson in 39,999 and a professional in only 1!) It is also for nurses, teachers, ministers and other persons in the helping professions who may have received only a limited amount of counseling training, but who are heavily involved in counseling every day.

1

What
I Learned
About Helping

As we sat among the barrels of "2-4-D" pesticide eating our brown-bagged lunches in an industrial section of Los Angeles, I decided we made a rather strange pair. Jim was referred to around work as "The Wino." He was a small, dark-haired man of about sixty. His face was tanned and lined, with a rough, friendly appearance. I was a tall, skinny young man. It was my first day at work at the insecticide plant in Los Angeles, and I had gotten acquainted with Jim that morning. Before the morning was over I was quite aware of his hangups. I was not yet aware of my own. As I looked at Jim, I realized he needed help. For a starter, he needed help to stop drinking, although I wasn't at all sure how to help him do that. As I think back on it, the hangup *I* had was seeing myself in a helping, "good-guy" role. I'm sure this made me come across in a condescending, arrogant way. It was as if I had a neon light on my jacket flashing on and off with the word "HELPER."

After I became a Christian at nineteen, I stayed in college for another year or so and then dropped out because college had no meaning for me. I had several jobs; then I was drafted and spent two years in the army. During this time in the service I married Lillian and we began our family. When I got out of the service, I finished college and then decided to go to a seminary to pursue a personal quest. I wanted to study the Bible to learn more about God, and about me. Also, I thought that I might later teach in a Christian college and I wanted this preparation.

During my middler year at seminary I found this part-time job at the insecticide plant and worked every weekday afternoon after finishing my classes, and all day Saturday. Jim worked full time at the plant, that is, when he wasn't at home with a hangover. We worked together for nearly two years and came to be friends. I worried about him because he often came to work with his hands shaking. When he carried sacks of powdered pesticides, he often stumbled. But as we glued five-pound boxes of pesticide, he was somehow able to keep his fingers from going through the gluing rollers.

When we got better acquainted, he began to tell me his story. He grew up in Pittsburgh, Pennsylvania. He remembered an influenza epidemic that occurred when he was fifteen years old. His father had given him some whiskey and told him to drink it—it would keep him from getting the flu. Since that time he had been drinking whiskey and wine and about anything else with alcohol in it that he could get his hands on. When he got old enough, he began working in a steel plant in Pittsburgh and was able to keep that job until he was about forty. By then, his alcoholism was interfering so much with his work that he was fired. Then he came to Southern California and started out in a steel plant there. However, he held that job for only a year or so, and then he "just bounced around" for the next twenty years.

He never talked much about his first family back in Pittsburgh. Apparently, his wife had divorced him because of his drinking, and he seemed to want to forget those days. He did talk some about the woman he had been living with for twenty years. They had never married and neither of them seemed to be concerned about this. She was, in fact, his common law wife. I could tell he loved her by the way he talked about her. He always called her "Mom," even though they had no children. He helped her get around. She could move about only with the aid of a walker.

I shared out of my life with Jim—told him about Lillian, and about Steve and Kathy, our children. I told him about the time I had found new meaning in my life when I received Jesus Christ. But I don't remember sharing with him my struggles with pride and selfishness and grumpiness. In general, I think I regarded myself as the person up here with the answer, and Jim as the person down there with the problem. Still, he listened intently when I spoke about Jesus Christ. I don't know what he decided to do about Jesus.

During the second year we worked together, I noticed that his work became harder and harder for him. His hands were shaking more now. He sometimes came in late to work and was absent more. Our boss appeared gruff, but actually he was pretty understanding and allowed Jim to continue work.

I was still trying to do something *for* Jim—trying to "straighten him out." I remember asking him one time if he would like to stop drinking. Not knowing anything about alcoholics, I was not prepared for his answer, which was "No." When I heard this response, my blinking neon light dimmed a bit.

Down inside I thought he and his "wife" really should get married, although fortunately I was able to keep that bit of advice to myself. I began to become frustrated as a helper, because he didn't *want* help. He did seem to like to spend time with me though, and we talked about everything under the sun as we worked, and as we had our lunches together.

Then came a time when Jim was off work for two consecutive days. When he came back the third day he said to me, "I'm really worried about Mom. She's been sick the last two days. She's a little better today but I hate to leave her home alone." He was preoccupied the whole day and left work the minute the work day was over. He didn't come back to work for the next three days. The evening of the third day I got a telephone call from a man who told me, "I'm Jim's neighbor. He told me your name and asked me to look you up in the phone book and give you a call tonight. He wants you to come over."

I went over, and when nobody answered my knock at the door, I opened it and walked in. Jim was running through the house, drunk, yelling, "Mom, Mom!" I went over to him and put my arm on his shoulder and walked with him a little while until he could talk in a fairly coherent way. He told me his wife had died two days ago and had just been buried. Her walker looked lonely standing in the corner by itself. Periodically as we talked he would yell out, "Mom, Mom!" I talked with him an hour or two and then went home feeling helpless.

The next morning I went over to see Jim again before my first class. I walked in without knocking and saw Jim and another man sitting on the couch, both drunk. The other man had his arm around Jim's shoulder. They looked at me without saying anything and I sat down in an old overstuffed chair near Jim. Finally Jim said, "My buddy here came over last night and spent the night." The men had never gone to bed. They had stayed up talking and drinking.

I fixed some coffee and as we sat around a little dinette, drinking the coffee, his friend said to me with slow, slurred speech, "I'm just an old drunk like Jim, but I thought the least I could do was to spend the night with him."

Before I went to class, I had to sit for awhile on a bench outside the school building. Jim's friend's word "with" kept echoing inside me. I had worked very hard to do something *for* Jim. His friend had understood that Jim needed someone to be *with* him. At that moment some of the "professional helper" started to shrivel inside me. I began to realize that the night before when I went home from Jim's house, it was not just to be with my family; I went home because I could not stand my own helplessness. I had failed Jim earlier because I had tried to help him without getting involved. I failed him at his time of greatest crisis, because the crisis had stripped me of my helping role. What I didn't realize was that now the front of my jacket didn't flash on and off with the word "HELPER." I was in a position to help for the first time. Instead, I fled.

Jim never came back to work. He died that day. Apparently the alcohol level got high enough in his blood, coupled with the shock of his wife's death, to kill him. It may have been, too, that he felt as if he didn't have anything left to live for.

I had tried to do something for Jim—and failed. But he and his friend had given a gift to me. They taught me that it is more important to do something *with* another human being than to do something *for* him. I had always thought how much Jesus did *for* his disciples.

However, I began to see that Jesus' primary reason for calling the disciples together was not to do something for them. "And he appointed twelve to be *with* him . . ."

So I failed in my attempt to help a friend. This failure caused me to begin a lifetime quest to find a better way of helping—a way that would build on the involvement I already had with a friend, and a way that would permit me to be with my friend person-to-person, not "helper-to-helpee."

In the years that have followed since Jim's life—and death—touched my life, I've been putting into practice, little by little, the idea of "withness." I put on the old helper's uniform now and then, but more and more I'm aware that it gets in the way. Sometimes now I don't run away when I feel helpless. Instead, through the power of the Holy Spirit, I find myself moving forward to be with my friend in the time of crisis.

2 I Believe

This manual is the result of several beliefs I have which are based on my experience with Jim (mentioned in chapter one), and with others. The first belief is that effective helping requires far more than just gaining insights and skills. It involves on a deep level the kind of persons we are, and our willingness to invest time, energy, and sometimes suffering. Effective helping is: a mechanic who stops on the way home from work to help a stranded motorist repair his car. It is sharing our lunch, or maybe even giving blood for a transfusion. I believe it costs us something to help another person.

I believe that most of us get into predicaments and crises because of the way we live—because of our life-style. This is directly contrary to the idea that most of our struggles in life are caused by some deep psychological problem from our past which keeps eluding us, yet renders us helpless, and which requires the expertise of a mental health professional. I believe that although we are influenced by our past, we are not *bound* by it. This means that helpers who are not professional counselors can often assist others in their predicaments and crises. This manual shows you how you can develop the skills necessary to do this.

I believe that helping skills need to be taught to and shared with persons in non-psychological professions. Most professions have walled themselves in and others out with unnecessary technical terms. I've tried in this manual to use terms and language that will be meaningful to persons in all vocations and professions.

I believe this method of helping works best with friends. It is not a method for helping people generally, implying that we must look around for many people to help. Rather, this method requires that we have built an involvement with another person, and that he/she wants help. It is, in short, a way to help a friend. If you study the manual carefully and use this approach to help two or three friends a year, you will have accomplished a great deal.

I believe that effectual interpersonal helping requires the use of both human and spiritual resources. Scripture teaches that Christians are persons of two ages, the present age and the age to come.[1] As persons of this age we need to take advantage of all the human resources available to us in the findings of the behavioral sciences, such as psychology and sociology. We can spend a lifetime putting these findings together in a way that will make us more effective helpers.

THE TWO AGES

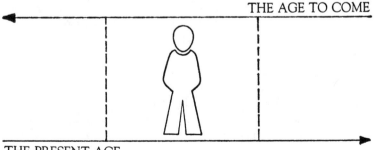

THE AGE TO COME

THE PRESENT AGE

Also, we have a second resource. As shown in the drawing, the power of the age to come has backed up into this present age. So the Christian has access to the redemptive power of Christ, the redemptive community of the church, and the redemptive insights of the Bible. The most effective helpers are those who add to their repertoire all the insights they can from *both ages*.

We tend to work with another person based on what we know about ourselves. The difficulty with that approach is that all persons have their own particular points of view and interests. Therefore, if we use only our own intuition and what we know about ourselves in trying to help a friend we may find that what we are doing is not helping. I believe the method shown in this manual will aid you in setting up an approach to helping your friend that takes into account the way he or she learns and lives.

I believe this method can aid you in helping a friend in that it can provide you with a direction for helping. This is a crucial aspect of helping because in most helping relationships there comes a time when the helper feels like he and the person he is trying to help are just going around in circles and neither person knows how to get out of the circle. If you have a method to refer to you can often find the next step that will move you along significantly in a helping direction.

I believe there are many other effective methods of helping besides the one shared in this manual. It is advantageous to follow some method, whether it is this method, one of many others that are available, or best of all, one that you put together yourself. A method also provides one with a greater sense of confidence in working with another person. This is important because your friend will lean on you for strength during the helping process. The confidence that you will feel will provide you with a greater sense of strength. At times of crises, the weak person draws his strength from the strong person. Another advantage of having a method to follow is that when things aren't working we can "read the directions" again. Actually, of course, helping someone is much more complex than this. However, it is important to have a reference that you can go back to for help. This will provide you with a source to consult to see if you are moving in the right direction, or maybe even help you find where things went wrong. In addition, having a method to follow helps keep us from doing harm. This is the first consideration of the helping professional and it should be the first consideration in *any* helping relationship.

I believe that a person who follows this method begins to see helping as a process rather than just a single encounter with another person. Your friend will be helped probably not so much by a single flash of insight that he gains from you, but rather by the way your life touches his over a sustained period of time.

Finally, I believe that gaining information is not enough when it comes to helping friends. We must develop skills through practice. This presents some difficulty because books are generally strong on insights, but weak on skill-building. Therefore, this book is presented in manual form with a "how-to" format. The Table of Contents permits use of the book as a reference manual. Also, the format will permit the manual to be used as a source for small group study. Chapter forty-two, "Finding Strength in an Action Support Group," tells you how you can bring together a group of friends and use this manual as a source for building helping skills. You can enjoy this combination "Action Support—Study Group" approach for almost a year if you go at the rate of a chapter a week.

The fact that you are reading this manual means that you are willing to invest a significant amount of time in preparing yourself to become a better helper. You are doing this at a time when friends need all the help they can get. I commend you for your interest and your work.

REFERENCES

1. "And whoever says a word against the Son of man will be forgiven; but whoever speaks against the Holy Spirit will not be forgiven, either in *this age* or in *the age to come*" (Matthew 12:32, RSV, italics mine).

   I am indebted to Dr. George Eldon Ladd, Professor of New Testament at Fuller Theological Seminary, Pasadena, California, for the notion of the Age to Come backing up into our present age.

Section
TWO
Let's Begin with You

3 The Need for More Helpers

Imagine yourself in the following situations:

1. There is an elderly woman living next door whose husband died a month ago. At first she had many friends and relatives who came by. However, the callers have dwindled over the weeks and now you have not seen anyone come by for the last several days. You know she is lonely and needs to talk. You think about going over to see her now and you wonder what to say and how to help.

2. You go to the lounge in your office for coffee and a man comes in and sits near you. You have heard that his thirteen-year-old boy was diagnosed last week as having leukemia. The two of you begin to talk

first about the weather and then about how things are going in the office. You both sense a need to talk about the topic that is foremost in your minds. You wait for him to bring up the topic and then you get a sudden insight that he may be avoiding talking about his son because he thinks it might make you uncomfortable. You realize this is true.

3. A good friend is getting a divorce. She told you last week that it would be finalized today. You know that she will be especially lonely and needing to talk today. You wonder how to reach out to her. What should you say or do?

4. You and your husband are good friends of a couple who are having some stormy times. Last time when you dropped by, the man was gone and his wife explained that he was out drinking. Thinking she needed to explain further, she said, "Oh, he's not an alcoholic, he just has a drinking problem." But she goes on to say that now she's scared when he comes home drunk. She is fearful of the future. She looks at the two of you and says, "What can I do?"

You have probably had one or more experiences of this type. As you read through the above situations and saw yourself as the helper or the potential helper, how comfortable did you feel in that role? How confident did you feel about your skills? Would you have taken the initiative in helping? Would you see your intervention in these situations as meddling or a demonstration of your caring?

To illustrate what is meant by loving one's neighbor, Jesus told a story involving a crisis intervention situation between strangers.[1] A priest and a Levite passed by an injured man, and a Samaritan "having compassion" came by and chose to get involved in another person's crisis. The fact that the first two chose to pass by *on the other side of the road* suggests that they felt uncomfortable, if not afraid. It appears that part of what it means to love our neighbor is that we choose to intervene when people need help. This requires caring and courage, as well as competence.

THE NEED TODAY

There are many evidences to support the need for more persons with helping skills. Many American families have chosen to self-destruct, or at least one person in the family has made that choice. There has been an increasing number of articles in periodicals in the last several years on the general theme, "Can the American Family Survive?" The destruction of the family is not entirely an inside job. Dr. Robert S. Mendelsohn, a pediatrician who was national director of the medical consultation service for Project Head Start from 1967-1969, puts it simply, "Society is out to kill the American family."[2] He says that symbolic of this situation is the obstetrician, who upon the birth of the infant, gives the infant to a nurse to be washed and handled. Thus he initiates an immediate separation between the child and the mother.

There are other, everyday evidences for the fact that the family is in trouble and needs help. Recently I held a Crisis Intervention workshop for a group of public school teachers. We happened to meet on Valentine's Day. One of the first grade teachers told me about an experience that had happened with a child in her class the previous day. He brought two valentines to school and said to the teacher, "This one is for you and this one is for the man you are living with." The first grader came from a family situation in which his mother lived with a succession of men, and he saw this as the norm.

Another evidence of the need for more counseling help today comes from a group of about three hundred psychiatrists who form the Group for the Advancement of Psychiatry. The Committee on Research of this group has issued a book-length report on the use of drugs and psychotherapy, *Pharmacotherapy and Psychotherapy: Paradox, Problems and Progress.* [3] They found the results of a survey in California on the use of psychotropic drugs (drugs that alter moods or behavior by their effects on various regions of the central nervous system) showed that about 17 percent of the adults sampled had used such drugs and that the incidence of use by women was almost twice as high as in men.[4] They also found:

> Among men, stimulants are used most commonly in the 30-year age group, tranquilizers in the 40's and 50's, and sedatives from age 60 on. About 30% of a random sample had used a psychotropic drug in the preceding 12 months.[5]

This group of psychiatrists is quite concerned about findings such as these because they indicate "a very high incidence of emotional distress in the population at large."[6]

Indeed, the problem is so severe that, according to the research done by this particular group of psychiatrists, "probably 25% of all prescriptions contain psychotropic drugs."[7] Dr. William Glasser, the psychiatrist who formulated Reality Therapy as a way of helping, has reported that of all the people who consult physicians, only about one half have physical ailments which can be diagnosed, while (just as the above research indicated) about one-fourth of all prescriptions are for mood modifiers—mostly tranquilizers.[8] Obviously, many people are hurting and are seeking relief.

NOT ENOUGH PROFESSIONAL COUNSELORS

There is a relatively small constituency of professional counselors. Moreover, counseling, measured in time allotted per person, is far more time consuming than medicine, for example. A general practitioner may see more than forty patients a day because his average time-per-person probably would be only a few minutes. He may be contrasted with the professional mental health worker who is able to see only perhaps six persons per day individually for an hour each, and conduct one small group of eight to ten persons.

Besides the problem of a relatively small number of professional mental health workers, who each can carry only a small case load, we have the problem of many persons who will not see a professional counselor even when they need help. Some refer to psychiatrists and psychologists as "head shrinkers," or simply "shrinks." These terms are usually used by persons who have not been to psychiatrists and psychologists. Most of the professional mental health workers I know are persons who have spent a great deal of their lifetime getting prepared to help others, and who genuinely care.

Others will not consult professionals because they do not want to reveal parts of their private life, in much the same way that many people resist going to a physician for a complete physical because they would have to take off their clothes. Still others refuse to go because they believe that seeking a professional counselor is an announcement to relatives or friends that they are mentally ill.

Ministers meet the counseling needs of many persons. But nearly all ministers have a preaching ministry and administrative work in addition to their pastoral ministry, so they are limited in the amount of time they can spend in counseling. Moreover, while pastors have had instruction in counseling theories, many have not had extended supervision in counseling practice. Therefore, some pastors lack confidence in their counseling skills, and this lack of confidence reduces the amount of time they choose to spend in counseling. Also, there are some persons with religious hangups who refuse to see a pastor for counseling.

For whatever reasons, there are many persons who need help desperately, but who refuse to see a professional counselor, or who wait so long that the professional counselor finds it difficult if not impossible to help.

THE NEED FOR A HELPING PERSON IN THE MAINSTREAM

Let's say Phil is a twenty-three-year-old man, who is married and has a job. He is involved in a predicament right now because he is having difficulty adjusting to the responsibilities of marriage, and he doesn't like his job. The chances are that he may not have a person with helping inclinations and skills among his daily associates. Because people are more mobile now, he is less likely to have parents and grandparents readily available than used to be the case. And because a minority of persons attend church regularly, he may not have an ongoing relationship with a pastor. Phil, therefore, is left without help from persons in the mainstream of his daily life. And until his predicament reaches crisis proportions, he is unlikely to seek help from persons he doesn't even know.

There is a need today to prepare more people so they can help their friends. We need to have competent persons "at the scene of the accident." To carry the medical analogy further, helpers can provide psychological first aid, but they can do far more than this—they can make a *long-term* positive difference in the lives of the persons they help.

A person who reaches out to help someone who is psychologically close already has met the first prerequisite of successful caring—a friendly relationship. Whether it is referred to as involvement,[9] the therapeutic relationship,[10] or respect,[11] it is something that good friends have been doing for a long time.

There are some who believe that a friendly relationship actually precludes one person from providing help to another. The early psychoanalysts who sat behind the reclining patient and maintained a social and psychological distance were examples of this point of view. This point of view said the helper had to be inscrutable, distant, mysterious, and functioning more in a role than as a person. Fortunately, the contemporary helper is much more likely to want to get involved and to let the other person see him or her not just as a minister or psychologist, for example, but as a *person*. In fact, it is becoming clear that in the real crisis of life, we help best when we mentally shed our helping labels and roles and simply allow one life to touch the other. This does not mean we put aside our skills, which are very necessary for helping. Rather it means that we have integrated these skills into our way of living, so they have become a part of us rather than just a way of behaving we adopt to help someone.

Counselors-in-training often report that their wife or husband or children say to them, "Don't counsel me," or "Now you're talking like a counselor." There are usually two reasons for these reactions. First, the person who is learning counseling skills may be changing significantly the way he talks. Perhaps he needs to. And because he talks in a different way, he sometimes comes across as unnatural. A second reason is that beginning counselors feel artificial about the skills they are learning. This does not mean the skills are not real and helpful. For example, when we are learning a new physical skill, whether it's a tennis serve or a golf swing, it feels artificial at first. Later it becomes automatic.

As you learn, through practice, the skills that are taught in this manual, you may feel clumsy and artificial at first. But don't give up. If you keep working at incorporating them into your life-style, they will become natural and automatic. If we efficiently achieve any skill, it means we have learned it and "forgotten" it.

When I enter into a helping relationship, I automatically go through the three-step sequence presented in this manual. First, I assess the urgency of the other person's need—whether he or she is involved in a problem, predicament, crisis, panic, or shock—and if the urgency is great I try to respond in some way that will meet the immediate need. If the situation is not so urgent, I work to understand that person's life-style, if I do not already. Then I move to the third task, an understanding of how he/she learns. Along with these kinds of understandings, I am automatically responding in the Listening and Resonating and Tender-Tough kinds of ways described in later chapters.

There is no substitute for patience and determination in your quest to acquire helping skills. But the outcome is worth it. Gaining greater insights and skills in this area can serve to positively change your own life-style. And it will enable you to become a far more effective helper to your friends.

REFERENCES

1. Luke 10:29-37
2. From the column "Can the American Family Survive?" Field Enterprises, Inc., *Omaha World-Herald,* February 18, 1976.
3. Group for the Advancement of Psychiatry (New York: Brunner-Mazel, Inc., 1975).
4. *Ibid.,* p. 18
5. *Ibid.,* p. 18
6. *Ibid.,* pp. 18, 19
7. *Ibid.,* p. 18
8. William Glasser, *The Identity Society* (New York: Harper & Row, 1971), p. 72.
9. The concept of involvement is discussed by Dr. William Glasser in *Reality Therapy* (New York: Harper Colophon Books, Harper & Row, 1965), pp. 21-27. He notes on page 22 that it is a *personal* involvement: "The title psychiatrist means little to a patient; he will test him for the kind of person he is, and if the patient finds him lacking, there will be no involvement."
10. Dr. Carl Rogers discusses the nature of the therapeutic relationship in chapter three of his book, *On Becoming a Person* (Boston: Houghton Mifflin, 1961). He notes that this relationship has a personal basis: "I have long had the strong conviction—some might say it was an obsession—that the therapeutic relationship is only a special instance of interpersonal relationships in general, and that the same lawfulness governs all such relationships" (p. 39).
11. Robert R. Carkhuff and Bernard G. Berenson discuss respect as one of the "primary core dimensions" of effective counseling, in chapter two of their book, *Beyond Counseling and Therapy* (New York: Holt, Rinehart and Winston, Inc., 1967). They see respect as a "positive regard" for others which is communicated through the expression of warmth (pp. 27, 28).

You Can Acquire Helping Skills

One of the most exciting developments in counseling today is that professional counselors are beginning to give away their skills. For many years there had been a controversy over the question, "Can nonprofessional counselors acquire and use counseling skills?" Then with the emergence of drug use in the sixties, personal crisis lines came into existence across the country. There were not enough professional counselors—psychiatrists, psychologists, social workers, and other mental health professionals—to serve on these telephone lines. Therefore, persons in other vocations were given a minimum amount of training, usually around thirty to forty hours, and were put on the telephones. The above question concerning the use of volunteers in counseling has now been answered.

Richard McGee, who has served as the Director of the Center for Crisis Intervention Research at the University of Florida, made a careful study of crisis intervention in various communities in the United States. He has discussed the practice of using volunteers in crisis intervention.

> The practice needs no further justification or defense, since the 1972 directory of suicide prevention and crisis intervention agencies published by the American Association of Suicidology shows that 87 percent of the 185 programs use non-professional volunteers as their crisis worker personnel. Further, the ratio of volunteers to professionals engaged in crisis work, as reflected in this directory, is three to one. There can be only a continuing increase in the utilization of trained volunteers in local programs.[1]

Further support for the use of the lay volunteer in crisis intervention has been given by Louis Dublin, one of the pioneers in crisis intervention.

> The lay volunteer was probably the most important single discovery in the fifty-year history of suicide prevention. Little progress was made until he came into the picture. The lay volunteer had the time and the qualities of character to prove that he cared. With proper training he can make a successful approach to the client, and by his knowledge of the community services available for useful referral he can often tide the client over his crisis.[2]

For me, a compelling factor concerning the use of lay counselors has been my own observations of their effectiveness. I live in a city which has had a personal crisis line functioning for six consecutive years, and have served the line in various ways. For two years, I served directly on the line for two or three nights a month. Then I helped train volunteers, and more recently I've served as a referral source. Through these years I've observed that selected lay persons who have appropriate training have been able to function effectively in serious crises.

You may be wondering, "Do *I* have what it takes to acquire effective helping skills? Do I truly love and have a desire to serve others, or is helping just a 'head trip'?" You may determine the answer to these questions by responding as honestly as you can to the following queries.

HOW EFFECTIVE IS MY OWN LIFE?

We cannot help at a higher level than we live. Stated in a slightly different way, we can be no more effective in helping a friend than we are in our own daily living. We can't give what we don't have. This does not mean that we have to have life completely figured out nor that we should be happy twenty-four hours a day. It does mean that we need to have our own life reasonably well together if we are to be of the most help to others.

For one thing we need to have a good sense of our own identity. A friend of mine says he does not understand why some people have trouble knowing who they are. Whenever he has a question about that, he says he just takes out his billfold and looks at his driver's license. I respect what he's saying—that for him a quest for identity has not been a problem. He has always had a good sense of who he was. For many others the quest for identity is an urgent one.

A nineteen-year-old college student came into my office one day and asked me, "Was there ever a time in your life when you didn't know who you were?" I could see that she was troubled and that she was searching. So I told her my own story. I also happened to be nineteen years old when I was engaged in the same search she was. The big question for me that whole year had to do with who I was, what life was about, and where I was going. I came to know who I was when I became acquainted with Jesus Christ and received him as my Savior. I was no longer isolated but now I belonged. I belonged to the family of God by faith in Jesus Christ. Now this didn't solve life's problems and not all my questions were answered. But it did enable me to discover who I was.

We should be mentally healthy ourselves, if we are to become effective helpers. We can check this out by applying Freud's simple, yet profound criteria: We are mentally healthy if we love well and work well. To meet the first criterion, we need to be able to give and receive love—warmth, caring, affection—from those around us. If we feel loved and if others close to us feel loved by us, then we pass this part of the test. To meet the second criterion, we need to be productive in whatever work we are doing, whether it is as a homemaker, office manager, student, factory worker, architect or farmer. Check with those close to you to get their evaluation of your productivity. It is not important that you be the *most* productive person in your setting, or highly competitive, just that you are efficient in getting work done.

WHAT ARE MY REASONS FOR HELPING?

It's very difficult to get at our intentions. But in this case, it's worth the effort. Our reasons for helping make a considerable amount of difference in our effectiveness as helpers. One way to start is to look at some *poor* reasons for helping.

Some "Helpers" Who Are Not Helpful

The Curious Helper

A person who begins a helping venture with someone else just in order to satisfy his curiosity is usually unable to help. Such a person has considerable difficulty establishing an atmosphere of trust because he is usually unable to keep confidences. Also the curious person comes across as pushy because he often interrogates and seeks further information. For these reasons most people back off from the curious helper.

The Lonely Helper

The lonely person is usually unable to help another person because he lacks a sense of roots, a sense of community. Everyone is lonely now and then, but I'm speaking of the person whose life-style is *characterized* by loneliness. This may not be a person who is living alone, because, of course, there is a difference between aloneness and loneliness.

We made an interesting discovery in working with teachers in a program to reduce drug use among youth. The intent of the project was to get teachers to reach out to alienated youth. We found that a number of teachers were simply unable to do this. When we began to figure out why this was the case, we found that those teachers were ones who had no roots of their own. In many places teachers are not seen as permanent members of a community. They come and they go. They may not even be expected to buy a home. So, many teachers who do not have a sense of community do not find it possible to reach out to an alienated youth who also lacks a sense of community. Teachers are no different from anyone else; they cannot give what they do not have.

Questions which get at the motivation of loneliness for helping include, "Are my needs for friendship and belonging fulfilled well enough that I don't require this need to be met by people I'm trying to help?" "Am I reaching out to help that person just so I won't be so terribly alone?" If we find ourselves in the predicament of extreme loneliness, then we should *seek* help.

The Bossy Helper

The authoritarian person goes around looking for people to "straighten out." Most people don't want to be bossed and those few who do are perhaps in a larger predicament than they are aware of. If first base in helping is careful listening, this helper never makes a single. This helper also relies heavily on advice-giving, even when it is not requested.

The Rescuer Helper

This helper is one of those who has the best of intentions but leaves the other person worse off for being "helped." The rescuer takes the responsibility away from the person being helped. It is as if we would say to a person, "You can't handle this at all; let me do it for you." This has the same effect as doing something for a child he could have done for himself with some guidance—it leaves him a little more helpless and considerably more resentful.

A Good Reason for Helping

There are probably many other kinds of helpers who really don't help. However, the above four show a common pattern—if I help someone in order to meet some nagging inner need I have because *my own life* is not together, then I am not really helpful to that person, because I'm actually focused on me.

A valid reason for helping is that someone reached out to help us, and we pass this on to a friend. This involves the concept that helping is a swinging door. We may even be helped by a person we help. If we have a clear understanding that helping works both ways, we are much more likely to be able to help others. On the other hand if we believe when we enter into a relationship where another person needs help that it is all going to be one way, we come across in a condescending manner. We tend to put on a helping role, sort of like Superman going into a phone booth to change into his special uniform. This tends to scare people away. Furthermore, it keeps us from growing.

A number of years ago the National Education Association produced a film called "A Desk for Billie." The film tells the story of the school days of Billie Davis, the daughter of migrant workers, who seldom stayed in one community very long at a time. It is a true story and I have heard Billie speak at a convention—a talented, articulate lecturer and author. The film focuses on Billie's encounters with adults. One observant elementary school teacher noticed that Billie kept changing her focal length as she read. The teacher made an appointment, had her vision checked, then purchased the glasses which were prescribed. When she gave them to Billie one day after class, Billie said, "I can't take these; we've got no money." Her teacher then told Billie how she herself had needed glasses as a child and *her* teacher had purchased them for her. Her teacher had told her that someday she would buy glasses for another little girl and in that way repay the debt. Then Billie's teacher said, "So you see, you can take the glasses; they were paid for a long time ago."

HOW MUCH TIME AND ENERGY AM I WILLING TO COMMIT?

Everyone functions as a helper at one time or another, but there is a difference between using counseling skills and using only intuition and common sense as the bases for helping. The person using counseling skills, in addition to intuition and common sense, works hard to get *training* in helping. This training, while not necessarily in a school setting, involves learning a systematic method of giving help to another person. It requires an investment of time and energy to gain as many understandings and skills in the counseling area as one's circumstances will permit. This is important because some persons with the best of intentions, but without these understandings and skills, go about "helping" in a way that leaves their friends worse off than before. So, if you want to gain effective counseling skills you need to realize that this commits you to learning and hard work. It will mean putting your interpersonal skills to work in your own life with your family and friends. It will mean reading as much as you can, perhaps attending workshops, and making every effort to upgrade your helping skills.

Some people seem to be able to help without really having worked at it. It is true that some persons are gifted in interpersonal helping. On the other hand, persons who do anything very naturally are often people who have worked very hard at a skill. For example, the skilled golfer looks very natural, whereas the beginner looks fairly mechanical. People often work hard and then what they do looks easy. Lord Byron wrote beautiful, "natural" poetry. As a matter of fact, however, he kept a rhyming dictionary on his desk.

The "natural" helper, then, is one who is effective in his own life, is motivated by love, and is willing to work hard enough that helping skills become automatic. And he reaches out, not down, to help someone. (This method was demonstrated very clearly by the life of Jesus. He didn't reach down to help, he *came* down, and reached out.) Perhaps the most important way the "natural" helper helps is that he serves as a model for his friend.

REFERENCES

1. Richard K. McGee, *Crisis Intervention in the Community* (Baltimore: University Park Press, 1974), p. 285.
2. This reference is from page 45 in the chapter by Louis Dublin, "Suicide Prevention," pp. 43-47, in the book edited by Edwin S. Shneidman, *On the Nature of Suicide* (San Francisco: Jossey-Bass, Inc., 1969).

5 Helping a Friend Through Appropriate Modeling *by Vic Cottrell*

Have you ever given much thought to those people in your life who have been most helpful to you? I'm certain all of us can pinpoint individuals in our lives who have been especially helpful to us by serving as effective models.

Whenever I think of persons who have been especially helpful to me, I cannot help but think of Daryl. Daryl is probably the finest counselor I ever had. I first met him when I was about twelve or thirteen years old. He was a farmer in the community in which I lived. He was a very tall, well-built man with a fine wife and two lovely children. Daryl was one of the few adults in my childhood who stood out as truly being a helper and friend.

Although I came from a family of five children, he seemed to see me as an individual whenever he entered our home. He sought me out to determine what my interests were and how he might be of helpful assistance to me in whatever I was undertaking. He soon asked me to come over to his farm and help him with jobs he had to do. As I entered the home I always felt as though I was a good and valuable human being. His wife, Dorothy, always seemed so excited to see me, and it seemed as though she always knew the exact food to fix which would get to a young boy's heart. Through their questions and excitement, I always felt as though I was making a contribution to them as well as enjoying their contribution to me.

As I came to know Daryl better, I soon found that he perceived himself to have some real inadequacies in his own life. I found, for example, that he had not completed high school, and he had always felt his lack of formal education was a disadvantage to him. I also soon found he was not the best reader I'd ever heard as an adult, and I'm certain his spelling had much to be desired. I found in Daryl a person not always informed by specific knowledge of the world or the universe, but I found in him a person who knew what it was to be a friend. He could convey love, warmth, companionship, understanding, and always a sense of appreciation for who I was as a person, regardless of how much knowledge he might have in this world.

Daryl also saw me as a person capable of learning, and he was anxious to be a part of my development. He always seemed to know the next step I was ready to take in my own development and before very long I had moved from pulling mustard weeds to driving his new W-C Allis Chalmers tractor. He seemed so happy and proud of every new venture I took, and of the new learning that resulted. He knew me as a person. He knew me in terms of my strengths and my goals, and he knew what brought joy to my life. Yes, Daryl was able to take me where I was and through a gradual, tender, loving process was able to help me to become. I want to be a helper like Daryl.

I would like for you to list some of the Daryls in your own life. I would encourage you to list ten or fifteen people who have made a very significant contribution to your own growth and development as a person. After you have done this, I would like to have you think about them in terms of their unique contribution to you, as well as the kind of personality each of them has. I would encourage you to use three words to describe the basic essence of the kind of persons you perceive them to be.

If your list is like mine, I'm quite certain it will include such words as understanding, caring, supportive, loving, affirming, knowing, empathetic, listening, and freeing. Yes, it seems that those people in our lives who have been most helpful to us are indeed ones who understand and know us, yet allow us to grow and to become at our own pace. These persons are nurturers and supporters, not controllers. As a result of the many Daryls in my life, I have gradually been able to model myself after their behavior and therefore become more effective as a helper.

A few of these basic ideas are as follows. I believe very strongly that a helper must also be willing to be a helpee. For me to always be in a helping relationship with friends is to rob them of some of the growth that they are so entitled to as persons. To allow your friend to help you is one of the greatest things you can do for your friend.

Let me share with you an experience a friend of mine, Rev. Hal Edwards, shared with me a few years ago. He had been seeing one couple for a number of months and had made seemingly no progress whatsoever. One day he had been counseling intensely with couples in marital predicaments, and he felt drained as a human being. He felt as though he really could not be of any more help that particular day.

He was beginning to think of home and a nice time of relaxation and enjoyment when he glanced at his calendar and realized he had one more appointment for the day. Yes, it was the couple he had been counseling in a futile manner for months. His first thought was, "What shall I do? How can I ever be a counselor and helper to this couple today?" As he explored his own feelings and spiritual state, he came to the conclusion that it would be impossible for him to really be of help to this couple.

As he was trying to contemplate what to do next, the couple arrived for the appointment. They immediately began to cast animosity and conflict toward him. He told me that somewhat out of desperation he stopped the conversation and informed them of his own poor state of emotional well-being. He said he really felt that he had nothing he could offer of himself to them and it would therefore be impossible for him to minister to them. Instead he said, "You are going to need to minister to me today." This was somewhat of a shock to the couple since they had never thought of themselves as ever being able to minister to anyone, let alone their counselor. Within a few minutes, almost unknowingly, they began to relate to his feelings and concerns. Yes, they began to help their friend.

Within a half hour of their ministering to Hal's needs, he found they had been extremely helpful to him. Through this act of desperation on his part, he had somewhat unknowingly become a tremendous helper to his friends. He had made himself open and vulnerable to them as they had been to him. They began to meet his needs and probably for the first time in many years they were helping another person in a cooperative manner. The couple had actually been able to put into practice the helping behaviors modeled by Hal.

Hal said this became a real turning point in his counseling with his friends. From that point on, they did believe they had something which could be helpful to other people and that they could work together in that effort. From this meager start, they began to be able to serve each other rather than serving themselves. My friend, through the example of his openness, was able to teach all of us a very important lesson, that one of the finest ways in which we can help a friend is to also be in need ourselves.

This experience helped to trigger something in my own mind which also helped me to understand that I had experienced this principle in my life before. I was in my second year of teaching and had a very difficult boy to work with. Earl seemed to be capable of doing absolutely the opposite of everything I wanted him to do as a student. Whenever I wanted him to listen, he talked; whenever I wanted him to sit, he stood; whenever I wanted him to keep his hands off other classmates, he pulled their hair; it seemed as though he was plotting to do everything counter to what I believed to be correct or good behavior within the classroom. I remembered that as a young teacher trying to cope with such adverse behavior I found myself very frustrated. I had tried everything I knew, from kindness, to scolding him in front of all his peers, to removal from class, to having his parents talk with him. Nothing seemed to work. One day out of sheer desperation, I asked him to see me after class. He came to me and appeared ready to accept another scolding. But much to his surprise, I began to talk about myself. I shared with him what I had done to try to make a change in his behavior and I said that I had been a failure. I shared with him my deep sense of anxiety, guilt, and frustration over the way in which I had dealt with him, all to no avail. I said to him, "Earl, it must be my problem. I know I have a problem. I become angry with you, I become frustrated, I become upset, and I exhibit behavior to you and before the other students in the class—behavior which I am not proud of." I asked him if there might be a way for him to assist me with my problem.

Such a request must have come as a very startling experience to Earl. I'm not so sure any adults had ever asked him to help them with their behavioral problems. In that encounter, he was able to recognize that I did not consider myself perfect either, and he certainly must have picked up my concern for him in that I wanted my behavior toward him to become more of an example of what it should be.

During the weeks that followed, he began to help me very much with my problem. In helping me with my problem, he in turn became responsible in terms of his own behavior. Indeed, he not only assisted me, but he also found that positive relationships with another person can be a very rewarding experience.

I worked with him for two more years and we became excellent friends and helpers to each other. Yes, I learned from this experience that through allowing myself to be open and having a sincere desire for Earl to help me, I had also helped him. Since that time I have applied this principle in many situations. I have found that through allowing people to become helpers to me, we have both grown immensely in the process. We became helping models to each other.

A second principle I have discovered is that in entering into a relationship of mutual helpfulness, there is a strong need to identify very clearly what is good in that relationship. We need to clarify with each other, for example, that it is very good to be a listener. We need to identify that it is good to try to enter into the shoes and world of that other person. We must recognize that it is good to be objective and to seek as many different dimensions on a given problem as possible. We must recognize that it is good to continue the dialogue until both of us feel very confident that we have clearly defined the problem. We must recognize that it is good to take specific action upon some new insight or understanding which enables us to move in a positive direction. It is critically important to reach some understanding of what is good in the relationship. I have found that, in working with people, if we can clearly identify and help each other become aware of our perceptions, it is a tremendously powerful aid in the relationship. People know when they have been heard, and to identify clearly with their thoughts and feelings, in a way in which they know they have been heard, can be tremendously affirming.

I cannot help but think of Sue, a college student of mine, who came from a divided home. Her mother deeply resented the fact that she was going to the college at which I was a professor. Her mother was also very upset that she was dating a person of whom she disapproved. The hate and anxiety between the mother and daughter were so intense that it was impossible to know how to unravel the situation. I did become a strong listener with her, however, and worked very hard to identify with her feelings in every session we had together. Just the fact that she knew that I had had some very intense negative feelings about my parents and that I was also struggling to overcome some of my negative anxieties was a tremendous help to her. She found that I was able to identify with her frustrations, and she no longer felt alone among the adult world. By clearly recognizing that such dynamics were good in the relationship, we were able to move toward being extremely helpful to each other.

A third basic principle I have come to understand about relationships is the fact that both of us must move toward a clear definition of good values. We must come to recognize that there are many values we share in common and that we can find unity in terms of our need to live out these values. This concept was brought home to me so clearly in my relationship with Glenn.

Glenn came to the college primarily because his parents expected him to be there. He had been living in a commune for several months before coming to college and had had a great deal of experience with drugs, including LSD. His parents and some friends of the family were doing everything in their power to reform him. I believe he came to the college with the intent to be thrown out as quickly as possible. He saw the best way to accomplish his goal would be through alienating as many of the adults in the college setting as possible. Every time I would make a statement in class, he would attempt to contradict the statement. Every time I would assign some reading, he would attempt to tell me why the readings were of no benefit to himself or others. He came to class in bare feet and made a point to try to get other college students to do likewise.

I readily became aware that in order to work effectively with this student, I would need to relate to him in a listening manner. I made special attempts to listen to him as carefully as I could. Before many days had passed, he was a regular visitor with me after the class session. I soon found that his favorite topics for discussion were drugs and communes. I found that probably the most meaningful experience of his life had been his experiences at Woodstock. My first thought was, what do I really have in common with this person?

I have found that as we search for common values, one of the most important questions I must ask is a very open, nonjudgmental "why?" I began to ask Glenn why he used drugs and he informed me that he used drugs because it provided him a tremendous opportunity to be an associate with his friends in "very heavy conversations." He informed me that he never took drugs when he was alone, but always made sure he was with very good friends. He found that all his experiences on drugs had been enjoyable and that he and his friends had been able to discuss and deal with issues which he felt were of great significance. I began to discover through the conversation that one of Glenn's values was friends, and another value was the opportunity to relate with them on a very meaningful and personal level.

I began to ask him why he liked to live in communes and he informed me that he valued the intimate relationships and closeness he could have with a wide variety of people of both sexes. I soon realized that close companionship and intimacy were very important to him. I asked him why he liked to come in bare feet and he told me that he found it felt good and brought a lot of pleasure and laughter to others. I found that, indeed, he did like a good time, and he enjoyed positive recognition from others. Yes, there were many values Glenn and I shared in common; the only difference was that the way in which he worked them out in his life-style was radically different from my way.

I began to share with him my perceptions about those areas of life which brought meaning to him and that these areas of life brought meaning to me as well. I shared with him that I, too, liked my relationships with people and always felt very fulfilled in meaningful conversation with them. I shared with him how important a very close, intimate relationship was in my life, and shared that I found my family to be my most prized possession. I shared with him that I, too, liked recognition and enjoyed very much bringing happiness to others. Yes, Glenn and I had found some common ground. We had become friends. We established a relationship in which we shared many things in common. In fact, we shared some very basic values in common. This provided a tremendous base for understanding of each other.

I invited Glenn into our home and allowed him the opportunity to meet my wife and daughters. He soon found that the quality of relationship we had in our own home was very radically different from that which he had experienced in his own. Over a period of time he began to realize that indeed there was a quality to our relationship as a family which was superior to that which he had experienced in the commune. He also began to realize that there were ways of having in-depth, meaningful discussions with others without the use of drugs. Glenn and I shared many values in common, but the way in which we worked out our values in our behavior was radically different. As we began to love and appreciate each other for our shared values, it provided an opportunity for him to determine in a clear way what kind of behavior he would like to exhibit in finding fulfillment of his basic values.

A few years later I had the pleasure of going to a beautiful wedding in which Glenn and his young bride made a commitment to each other before God regarding the quality of life they were choosing for their marriage.

Glenn and I had developed a deep and trusting relationship with each other. We found things we could converse about, and we worked very hard to help each other to understand the other's world. We shared our values in common and affirmed each other for having good values. I did not have to tell him how to behave in a way in which those values could be worked out to their fullest. He was provided some alternatives through my modeling and came to know what was right for him. He already knew what was right. All he needed to do was to find that such behavior led to the fulfillment of what was important to him.

I believe the *relationship* we establish and maintain with our friend is the most important dynamic in the entire helping venture. The quality of relationship I am sharing with you, I believe, is precisely that which Christ wants us to have with him as well as with our fellowmen. Christ was able to enter into these types of relationships with people on this earth. When I think of biblical characters such as the woman at the well, Zacchaeus the tax collector, and Martha, I find that the distinction is very difficult to draw between the helper and the person being helped. In these cases, Christ allowed himself to be one who had needs, and saw these people as very capable of assisting him with his needs. He was willing to make himself vulnerable before others. He was able to look beyond the behaviors and see the essence of what a person valued and desired to become. He established a mutually supportive relationship in terms of the essence of the person, with limited focus in terms of the behavior. In this type of a loving and supportive relationship, these individuals were able to see that they could more effectively achieve what they really wanted out of life through better behavior. To enter into a mutually loving and trusting relationship requires that both parties become vulnerable. This indeed is a risk to both parties, yet the rewards are beyond measure. I believe as we are willing to take as our model the Humble Servant, to be open, to serve and to be served, we indeed become a model, the helper as well as the helpee.

Daryl was a helper to me, and I was a helper to Daryl. The couple coming to counseling with Hal helped Hal, and he was a helper to them. I was a helper to Sue, and Sue a helper to me. I found it difficult to be a helper to Earl, but Earl found it easy to be a helper to me and therefore both of us grew. Glenn did not want me to become a helper to him, but we became a helper to each other as we searched and found a common bond of friendship, based upon our mutual values. Christ was a helper to me, and he allows me to be a helper to him. We need each other and therefore one of the greatest things we can do for each other is to enter into a relationship which enables us to become all we are meant to be—to become Christlike models.

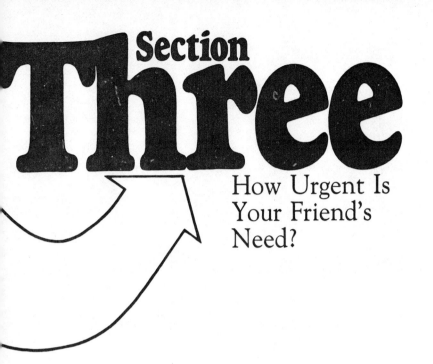

Section
Three

How Urgent Is
Your Friend's
Need?

6 Levels of Need

When I begin a helping relationship, the first thing I want to discover is the level of need of the person I am working with. The level of need is important because it determines the urgency with which the help must be given. If the person is in panic or shock, then the urgency is very great. On the other hand, if the need is at the milder level of problem or predicament, or even crisis, a slower approach can be used which will take into account the person's life-style and learning style.

LEVELS OF NEED

To become an effective helper, you should be able to *recognize* the level of need of a friend who wants your help. These levels are described in the accompanying chart, "Levels of Need." We will

LEVELS OF NEED

LEVEL AND DEFINITION	CHARACTERISTICS OF THE PERSON IN NEED	EFFECTIVE HELPING RESPONSES
PROBLEM Has a solution.	Asks specific question; wants immediate advice or information.	Supply information or advice.
PREDICAMENT No easy or satisfactory solution.	Often feels trapped; is not helped by information or advice.	The helper must get involved; use "tender-tough" caring approach.
CRISIS A very large predicament; usually short term.	Has a sense of urgency; may both want and not want help.	Often requires a high degree of perceptiveness on the part of the helper to sense the state of crisis; helper needs to intervene; get in touch.
PANIC A state of fear in which the person sees only one way out.	Does not listen to others; the mind is caught in a fantasized, dreadful future event; behavior often appears nonrational.	Helper needs to move the helpee from the "panic button" to the "hold button"; use touch, eye contact.
SHOCK A numbed or dazed condition.	Fails to take necessary action; mind may lapse for minutes or hours; is unable later to account for lack of action.	The helper may need to act for the person in shock. Stay with the person. You may need to get medical help.

examine these levels in detail later; for now it will be enough to look at them briefly to provide an overview of the way they fit into the method of helping taught in this manual.

The term "problem" is often used as a catchall to describe every kind of difficult human situation. However, it is used in this manual in a *precise way* to refer to the easiest level of need to provide help for. As the dictionary points out, a problem has a solution. Let's suppose you have a friend, Pat, who moved to town recently. She calls you saying she doesn't feel well, and she asks for suggestions for a family physician. As the chart points out, often information is all that is needed in a problem situation. You suggest several names to her, and she sets up an appointment with one of these physicians. Thus, you have solved her problem.

Pat comes over for coffee one morning during the following week. She tells you the doctor could find no physical cause for her discomfort. He believes she is suffering from anxiety, and he has recommended she take tranquilizers for awhile. She is opposed to taking tranquilizers, yet she feels miserable in her present condition. She is now immersed in a situation for which there is no easy or satisfactory solution. Giving suggestions and advice, which worked in her previous *problem,* does not help her now because she feels trapped. She is now at the *predicament* level. You will need to shut off advice-giving and seek a deeper involvement with her. Let her know you care by your attentive listening. By just being a friend to her and providing her a listening ear, you may help her reduce her level of anxiety.

Let's suppose, however, that her predicament deepens. Later you are at a lunch counter in a downtown department store with her. She cries as she tells you that things have gotten worse during the last week. Her family is tired of her edginess, and she is sick of their yelling—and she is afraid. She doesn't know what will happen to her. Pat is now in a state of *crisis.* You will notice on the chart that this is a difficult, usually short-term situation, a very large predicament with a sense of urgency. The most helpful thing you have to give in a crisis is your presence. The caring presence of a friend may help a person slow down, avoid rash decisions, and seek professional help, when necessary.

Again, for the purpose of illustration, let's suppose the situation worsens. Pat calls you at nine o'clock the next morning. Her husband has gone to work and her children are at school. She tells you she is holding a full bottle of sleeping pills in her hand, and she says, "I'm sick of all the hassles I'm going through." She is now in a *panic* situation. You as a helper may also feel a twinge of panic. If you do, some deep breathing may help you get back in control. Remember that she has called you because you are a person who cares and who offers hope. You will want to listen to her and to get with her personally as soon as you can. You will use some of the special skills you learn in this manual to help her move from the "panic button" to the "hold button."

We seldom see a person in a state of *shock,* but when we do, it is imperative that we recognize it. Rather than try to create a hypothetical situation with our Pat, above, it would probably be better to refer to a real situation. When Senator Edward Kennedy drove off the bridge at Chappaquiddick, and the young woman with him was drowned, he was unable to account for several hours of lapsed time before reporting the incident to the police. It is possible that psychological shock may account for his dazed condition during some or all of those hours. If you are with a person who is in a state of shock, you will need to act for him because he usually will be unable to care for himself or others.

In the following chapters in this section, you will discover some ways to help a friend at each of the above need levels.

7 Problem— There Is a Solution

Earlier in this manual we referred to Pat, who wasn't feeling well and called for suggestions in selecting a family physician. She was fairly new to town and didn't want to limit herself to the yellow pages for information in making such an important decision.

Pat had a *problem*. We are using the term in the same limited way the dictionary uses it—a situation which has a solution. Most "problems" that require counsel are not problems at all, but predicaments or crises. It is absolutely crucial for the helper to distinguish between a problem and a predicament or crisis. Otherwise, we will "help" in a way that is neither desired nor helpful.

RECOGNIZING PROBLEMS

A Person *Asks* You for Advice

One clue that the situation may be a problem comes when someone asks your advice. A problem is the only one of the five levels of need that can be remedied by advice. Advice will usually help move the person toward a solution in a problem situation. This is true, for example, in the illustration of Pat, above.

It is not always true that one who asks for advice has a problem. If a friend asks you what he should do in a certain situation, when he knows what he needs to do, but wants you to take the responsibility for the decision, he is really involved in a predicament rather than a problem. This predicament has stemmed from a deficiency in his life-style (a weak choosing channel). Advice given in this situation would tend to weaken your friend further because it carries the message, "You really *aren't* able to make your own decision."

Your Advice Meets No Resistance

Suppose your friend says to you, "I have this problem. I'm overweight. Nothing seems to work in helping me lose weight. What would you suggest?" In reply you give three or four ideas which you think might be helpful. If your friend accepts these as worthwhile suggestions to think about, then he probably really wants advice. On the other hand, if he meets each suggestion with a "Yes, but—" then the chances are he may not really be seeking advice. Also, if you find yourself urging someone to do something or to take some suggestion, this is an indication that there is defensiveness or resistance in the other person, showing this to be a predicament rather than a problem situation.

Involvement Is Not Required

Anyone with accurate information can help a person who has a problem. One chain of service stations has used the motto, "As you travel, ask us." And people who are lost can stop in and ask directions. They, thus, receive help in their problem from a person they don't even know. However, most of us prefer to get information from a friend, if possible.

Someone may have difficulty starting a car and you stop and give a suggestion which helps that person get the engine started. You have solved his problem for him. One person can solve a problem for another person. This is the only one of the five need levels at which one person can take care of the situation for another person. However, when a person is in shock, we may need to *act* for him.

A situation can be severe and still be a problem rather than a predicament. For example, if I fall and break my leg on ice as I go to work, this would be a problem. An ambulance can come and take me to the hospital where an orthopedic surgeon could "solve the problem." But if I were backpacking in northern Canada and broke my leg on the ice, then I would be involved in a crisis, because help would be inaccessible. Or if for some reason I had a bone deficiency so that my bones did not mend well, then breaking my leg on the ice near home would result in a deeper level of need than a problem.

THE FIRST HELPING STEPS

Although a problem situation is the easiest need level to work with, it's still possible to "blow it." By using the approach shown here, you can increase the chances that your interaction will be genuinely helpful. First, be sure you understand the problem and the specific nature of the help being asked for. This requires very careful listening on your part and probably some dialogue between the two of you until you are *sure* what the person wants. Then, if you have the information, provide it. If you don't have it and are willing to do the necessary research or work to get it, let the person know when you get back to him. If what you are giving is an opinion rather than a fact, label it that way.

Let's suppose at work you have noticed that another person who is fairly new on the job typically does things "the hard way." One day he says to you, "I'm always beat at the end of the day, but you seem to get through the day in pretty good shape. How do you manage that?" At this point you can share your observations and suggest more efficient procedures to help him with his problem of fatigue. If you can give this information in a brief, easy, matter-of-fact way rather than "laying it on him," he will, of course, be more likely to use it.

FOLLOW-UP

If you are giving advice or information to a person whom you know and whom you will be encountering again, it is a sign that you care if you ask later how the situation worked out. This follow-up will also help you because you will begin to put together a set of experiences that show when advice is helpful and when it is not.

The concept of follow-up is a key concept in helping. It is a logical outgrowth of a point of view that we *can* make a difference in a friend's life as our lives flow together over a period of time. It is a much different point of view than looking around for persons to help in a single encounter with no thought of seeing them again. This idea of continuity is discussed in a recent essay on "The Modern Imagination of Death."

Whereas life once appeared to be a pilgrimage and like a journey, it now seems to be very much like one of our major airports on a busy holiday week end. And thus it is indeed that the time which modern men characteristically experience is very much like that of the cinema.[1]

In a movie, time is episodic rather than continuous. We see isolated events and flashbacks. However, in the shared journey of friends, it is not only the giving of help in times of need that is significant, it is also just being together when neither person needs help.

In summary, it is important to be able to differentiate a problem from the other levels of need. Once you have identified that it is a problem, the approach is a relatively simple one—you work to solve it. This is the only one of the five levels of need that you can solve for another person. It is also the only need level at which giving advice is helpful.

REFERENCES

1. N. A. Scott, Jr., "The Modern Imagination of Death," from John D. Roslansky, Ed., *The End of Life* (Amsterdam: North-Holland Publishing Co., Fleet Academic Editions, Inc., N. Y., 1973), p. 41.

8 Predicament— There Is No Easy or Satisfactory Solution

Imagine that you are locked in a dark room and that you have been calling for help. You have been unable to get out, and no one has responded to your calls. You sit down, discouraged, then get up and call out again. Finally you hear an answer to one of your calls. The person who has heard you checks the door but finds it is locked from the *inside*. The presence of another human being encourages you, and the information that the door is locked from the inside provides some insight. You get down on your hands and knees and feel on the floor with your fingers for a key. Finally, you find it; you rush to the door, unlock it, and regain your freedom.

Who got you out, you or your friend? Well, you unlocked the

door. On the other hand, you were unable to get out before your friend came along. This situation illustrates a saying that is used by Integrity Therapists, "You alone can do it, but you can't do it alone."[1] This is a saying that generally holds true for predicament situations. The person involved in the predicament is the only one who can get himself out. However, he needs a helper who will be with him, get involved with him, and talk with him.

RECOGNIZING PREDICAMENTS

No Solution Is Apparent

A predicament is a situation with no easy or satisfactory solution. In an earlier chapter a situation was posed in which Pat, a neighbor, tells you she has seen her physician who could find no physical cause for her discomfort. He has recommended she take tranquilizers. She is opposed to this; however, she feels very anxious and "edgy." So she doesn't know what to do; there is no good alternative apparent to her.

A Feeling of Being Trapped

Because she can see no way out, Pat becomes aware of something that is happening to her emotionally—she is beginning to feel trapped. The trapped feeling brings with it some twinges of hopelessness. The situation may look to you more like a problem than a predicament. But the level of need is a function of *how the situation looks to the person in the middle of it.* Therefore, to determine the level of a person's need, you will have to look at the situation through the other person's eyes.

Uncomfortable, But Not a Sense of Great Urgency

People generally feel quite uncomfortable in a predicament. It may last a long time or only a short time. It differs from a crisis in that a crisis, although usually of shorter duration, is much more threatening and therefore produces a sense of dire urgency. In a crisis the involved person knows that something *has* to be done right away. The person in a predicament knows that something *needs* to be done, but he usually does not feel the pressure of time so keenly.

TAKING THE FIRST HELPING STEPS

Get Involved

I'M WITH YOU

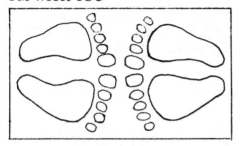

An important way to work with persons in a predicament is to get involved with them. This means we talk with them, listen to them, and do some activities together. So with Pat, for example, the helper would need to get involved with her when she finds that there is no physical cause for her misery. She may be plagued by anxiety or loneliness and she needs a friend who is willing to invest time in her.

```
TAKE
MY ADVICE;
I WON'T
BE
USING IT!
```

Avoid Giving Advice

A student in the middle of a predicament came into my office and opened the conversation by saying, "I came to see you because I knew you wouldn't give me pat answers." Most people in predicaments do not want advice, perhaps because nearly all advice is from the giver's, not the user's, point of view. Advice works with a problem because it has a solution that does not depend on a point of view. But a predicament is a vastly more complex situation than a problem.

Have you had the experience of urging someone to do something and feeling his resistance? If we come up behind someone and push him, the chances are that he will dig his heels in right away. Most people don't want to be pushed. Newton's Third Law of Motion applies here, "For every action there is an equal and opposite reaction." When we advise somebody to do something, or push someone toward some action, that person will usually push back and resist. The helper therefore must find some other way to help than by giving advice.

Work for Openness Rather Than Closure

One reason we often give advice is that we want the other person to get the matter settled, to get on with it, to make the decision. Psychologically, we push for closure in many things. If we see a partially formed geometric design, we tend to close it in our minds. This tendency works well for us sometimes, and rather badly at others. Giving help is one venture in which working for speedy closure is usually nonproductive and sometimes even counterproductive.

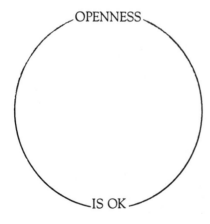

Suppose your friend is involved in a predicament concerning her elderly father who has been living alone but is rapidly losing the ability to care for himself. There are two or three options open as a place for him to live. It is tempting to help your friend get all the information regarding each option and arrive at a rational decision as rapidly as possible. After all, the decision cannot be put off indefinitely. We often tend to see a person like this as being in a predicament regarding a *decision.* However, the predicament may be much deeper than the rational decision-making process. It may involve a psychological journey for your friend in which she moves from a "child" position in relation to her father to a position of care-giver or guardian of her father. To bypass this tremendous psychological need in a push for closure would do your friend a disservice.

Therefore, if we go into the helping venture without a personal need to arrive quickly at a "solution," we will listen much more carefully and will be far more open to where our friend is psychologically. Usually as we adopt this position, we help our friend to make the personal growth and necessary changes in points of view so he can begin to make decisions.

RESPECT   THE BIG R

Show Respect

It is unlikely that we will be able to help a person whom we do not respect. If we feel our friend is "making a mountain out of a molehill," then this impatient attitude of ours comes across as a lack of respect. If we "can't understand" why it takes a person so long to make a decision, our arrogance may be taken as a lack of respect. Jesus demonstrated his respect for persons in the incident regarding the rich young ruler. He answered the young man's questions, and even told him what he would need to do to achieve his quest, but he didn't push him to do it.

GETTING
TO THE
POINT

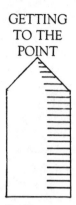

Be Concrete

One of the characteristics of effective helpers is that they get to the point, they are specific. The helper is able to share his own actual feelings. He avoids abstractness and favors concrete, substantive communication. Instead of saying, "I can see where this situation with your family has you in a dilemma," he may respond, "It looks as if you don't know what to do next because you and your husband don't agree on how to discipline your youngest child." As the helper becomes concrete, he enables his friend to talk more concretely and think more concretely. Thinking in concrete terms makes the predicament much more manageable.

The barrier to concreteness is usually not a lack of language skills, it is rather that we are purposely vague. We pull our punches because we think we may hurt the other person, or because we lack courage to risk possible misunderstanding. Actually, most people are quite resilient and we can say the truth in the plainest way possible without harming them. The exception to this occurs when we *want* to hurt the other persons. If this is the case, the chances are we will hurt them no matter how much we disguise the truth. If we feel any need at all to get revenge or to "teach them a lesson," of course we need to back off fast and not pretend to help.

A lack of courage was mentioned above. Sometimes we convince ourselves that the other person is fragile and cannot stand the truth, when the fragility is within *us*. It is not that the other person can't bear the truth, but that we *won't* bear it. God has made the human personality strong—able to bear the truth when it is clearly stated in a loving way.

FOLLOW-UP

The follow-up in a predicament can be done in a more relaxed way than in a crisis or panic. But it is necessary to follow up and see how your friend is feeling and functioning. The example was given above of a friend who was faced with her father's declining health and the need for a different place to live. Making yourself available to your friend at a later time to talk about this predicament again will be important. Along with this, we need to remember that there will be times when our friend does not choose to talk about her predicament, and we need to respect her right to be silent.

REFERENCES

1. O. Hobart Mowrer, "Integrity Groups: Principles and Practices," *The Counseling Psychologist*, Vol. 3, No. 2, 1972, p. 22.

9 Crisis— A Short-Term Predicament in Huge Proportions

A crisis is a special sort of predicament. Therefore, most of the understandings and skills you need to help a friend out of a predicament are applicable also with a friend who is in a crisis. But in addition to these, you will need further abilities because of two special characteristics of crises—size and urgency. A crisis is a very large predicament which requires attention within a relatively short span of time. A crisis may be expected to last from one to six weeks. The *average* length of a crisis seems to be about two to three weeks.

HOW TO RECOGNIZE A PERSON IN A CRISIS STATE

We often tend to be more aware of our own reactions than we are of others' actions. For this reason the following list of reactions is presented from *your* point of view as a friend and helper. Remember that no one or two reactions serve as a sufficient indicator that your friend is in a state of crisis. There may be many other reasons for each of the following reactions. However, if you begin to get a pattern of a number of these reactions, then the possibility is increased that your friend may be undergoing a crisis.

1. *He's not listening to me.* You sense that you're not having a conversation. Your friend is not responding to you. He seems to have lost his ability to concentrate on a train of thought. Thus, a growing irritation inside you may be your first indicator that your friend is preoccupied by a crisis. It is important that you not be offended by your friend's temporary inability to listen to you; otherwise, you will be psychologically unavailable to help him when he needs you.

2. *He's not looking at me.* A person who is in the middle of a crisis may alternately look away from you as you talk with each other and, at other times, may stare at you. In both cases your reaction is that his vision really stops inside his own head. He is caught up in his thoughts trying to figure out ways to extricate himself from his crisis, and he is attempting to avoid a sensory *overload.* To understand the concept of overload, think of a situation in which you were trying to find the answer to a problem, or remember a fact that keeps eluding you. At a time like this you may have closed your eyes to keep visual stimuli from overloading your circuits and interfering with your thought processes. In a situation in which a person wants to use all his mental energy to think of ways to get out of a crisis, he avoids an overload by looking at another person without really *seeing* him, and by looking at things which don't require mental processing. Many persons who are depressed or feeling down, actually *look down,* that is, gaze at the floor.

3. *He doesn't act like he usually does.* At this point, involvement as a *friend* pays off in helping. A stranger would not know whether a person's behavior is unusual or not, *for that person.* But *you* know if you have been acquainted with that person for some time. A quiet person may become talkative; a talkative person may rather

suddenly come across as aloof or very quiet. You may observe a sudden
change in eating habits or note unusual complaints about headaches or
other bodily ailments.

4. *He isn't getting along with people close to him.* Freud said it was a
sign of mental health if we love and work well. The stress that goes
with a crisis often interferes with our ability to continue a loving
relationship with those close to us. If a person suddenly begins to
treat his family and close friends badly, or without consideration,
this may be an important clue to stress.

5. *He isn't getting his work done.* The ability to work well is the
second sign of mental health mentioned in 4, above. Therefore, it is
well to take into account a fairly abrupt decline in productivity. One
fall I noticed a student in one of my college classes rather abruptly
(over a period of a week or two) stop producing. He not only did
not do the required work, but he didn't appear to listen or to look
at me when I was talking, nor at other students when they were
talking. His behavior was unusual in that he slouched and was very
quiet, whereas he had formerly sat in an alert position and involved
himself in the class activities. Also he entered and left the classroom
by himself instead of with other students, as he had formerly done.
In other words, I reacted to him in each of the five ways.

After class one day when he was the last student to leave, I
went over to him as he was getting his jacket on and his books
together and said, "This has been a hard week for you." I said this
not in a "psyching out" kind of way, but in a way that let him know I
understood that he was undergoing stress. He looked at me as if he were
deciding whether to trust me or not. Then he said, "You want to
know what I'm thinking about in this class and all my other classes?"
I replied that I did, if he wanted to tell me. He then described his
anguish as he sat through his classes thinking of his father, an
alcoholic, who was operating a large combine daily, beginning the
harvesting on the family farm. He finished by saying, "I wonder
every day if today will be the day he kills himself on that combine."
After a time of talking, he decided to see his instructors and take a week
out of school (he was so preoccupied he wasn't accomplishing
anything anyway) and go home to run the combine for his father.
He came back able to resume his work at college. He had made it
through his crisis. Obviously, he would have other crises in the
future, given his concern for his father.

THE FIRST STEPS IN HELPING

1. *Take time to be with your friend.* The first step in helping friends in a crisis is to just be *with* them. It means listening to the other person with as much concentration as you can muster. A friend of mine told me yesterday that he went to visit a fellow employee of his who is dying with cancer. My friend said he couldn't think of anything to say, so he didn't say anything for ten minutes. He was just there in the room with the sick man. Then, they began to talk and they talked for two hours. It takes time to "center" one's attention on a person who is in a state of crisis. Job's friends sat seven days without saying anything when they went to be with him in his crisis. They probably accomplished more by their quiet involvement than they did with all the talking they did later.

2. *Expect that you will be able to help in some way.* If you begin to feel panicky yourself because you lack confidence, do some deep breathing while you are listening. This will aid you in relaxing. You will be able to help in most crisis situations if you focus on your friend's needs rather than your own. Count on your *presence* to make a positive difference.

3. *Establish eye contact with the person in crisis.* You cannot interact with your friend so long as he remains in a state of deep thought, fantasy, or daydream. Engage your friend visually. You may need to put a hand on his shoulder, say his name, or use another means of getting him to look at you and *see* you, but the eye contact is crucial. (If you are working with a visually impaired person, touch becomes even more important.) Sometimes it is useful to say to a person who seems to be looking right on through you, "I feel like you are looking at me but not really seeing me."

4. *Bring your friend into the present.* Eye contact and touch help to move the other person out of his despair about the past or anxiety about the future. Some other means of doing this include listening to music, which is a present activity, or playing a game (whether it involves physical skills or is a simple table game), which requires concentration on a present task. Resonating with (verbally echoing) his feelings will help your friend move into the present, because emotions are "now."

5. *When necessary, discuss the way your friend talks.* Some persons in a crisis state increase their rate of speech until it is difficult to understand them. A response here could be, "I want to

understand every word you are saying; please slow down so I can keep up with you." Others may slow their rate, mumble their words, or speak very softly. Request any necessary change, noting as above, that it is very important to you to understand what your friend is saying.

6. *Walk alongside your friend emotionally, rather than leaping ahead to find a "solution."* Remember that while problems have easy or satisfactory solutions, crises usually do not. What looks like a solution to a crisis from the viewpoint of an onlooker usually won't even make sense to the involved person. Your friend has to find his own way, but he can find it better if you stay with him. If you "run ahead" looking for solutions, he may not be able to hear you.

7. *Accept your friend's point of view as being true for him, but be willing to state another point of view.* Pascal has said that when we wish to influence another person, we must be willing to grant the other person's point of view, and then suggest an additional point of view. We thus maintain the cordial relationship, while opening the person to a whole new way of looking at his situation. An example of a helping response using this guideline could be, "I understand that you're feeling helpless right now, and I can see you really are in a tough situation. Several times you have said, 'I can't do it.' Another way of looking at it is you could if you chose to. Could it be that it's more that you *won't* do it, rather than that you *can't* do it?" You have to be involved with a person to say this, but if you *offer* it as an alternative rather than "laying it on him," he may gradually begin to buy the idea.

8. *Use Scripture in a helpful way.* Christians often quote a biblical reference to a person in a crisis. Such a use of Scripture has been of great value in providing comfort and encouragement. Scripture may also be used to confront another person. This (scriptural confrontation) is the primary counseling method advocated by Jay Adams in his books, *Competent to Counsel,* [1] and *The Christian Counselor's Manual.* [2] Confrontation is a counseling skill often overlooked, and these two books provide a useful reference on this specific topic. A guideline on the use of Scripture would seem to be that it is wrong to use Scripture to back us up in trying to convince the person to do something we think he ought to do. It is a right use of Scripture to present it and then let the Holy Spirit use it in the life of the person. Pushiness on our part is counterproductive, whether it is in the use of Scripture or in other approaches.

9. *Suggest church or community resources to the person in crisis.*

Giving your friend several options for further help provides a needed service. Ways to make a referral are discussed in chapter thirty-nine, "Moving Anxious, Depressed, and Suicidal Persons Toward Professional Help."

FOLLOW-UP

Because of the urgency and short-term nature of a crisis, follow-up becomes crucial. When you leave your friend it is important to ask him if he needs help in any other way, or if he has anyone to be with him. This is especially important at night when crises tend to seem overwhelming. A follow-up phone call in the evening will usually be appreciated.

As you make contact on a follow-up basis, look for emotional indicators which will let you know whether your friend is emerging from the crisis or moving into it. If the person is not able to resolve the crisis, then he may move into a panic situation. It is necessary that there be at least one person who says to the one who is in a state of crisis, "If you need me, just call me anytime." Many times just knowing there is one person who is available enables the person to make it through the crisis.

REFERENCES

1. Jay E. Adams, *Competent to Counsel* (Presbyterian and Reformed Publishing Company, 1970).
2. Jay E. Adams, *The Christian Counselor's Manual* (Presbyterian and Reformed Publishing Company, 1973).

10 Panic—
The Wild
Flight

One morning when I was walking to work I came to one of those intersections where drivers from all four directions think they have the right-of-way. An accident had just occurred and a young woman of about twenty with blood streaming down her face (her injuries later proved to be minor) was running around a red Mustang which had one fender and the hood crumpled. Two or three other people were there and were calling to the young woman. She was not responding to anything anyone was saying but was continuing to run and shriek. One of the other persons who was there teamed up with me and we put our arms around her and held her for a moment. This seemed to get her in touch with the present, and while she continued crying she began to talk about what had happened and about the meaning this had for her. She was panicked because she had borrowed the Mustang from her boyfriend and now she had wrecked it. At that point the emergency unit came and took her to the hospital.

Caught in the Future

The panicked person is grappling with a future situation which is clearly imaged on the screen of the mind. This young woman was seeing herself talking to her boyfriend and having to tell him that she wrecked his car. Now the future is seldom as bad as the panicked person fantasizes. But it doesn't help to tell panicked persons this because they aren't listening. The terror of the images in their mind is very real to them.

Duane Schultz has written a small, very worthwhile book called *Panic Behavior: Discussion and Readings.* He deals with this tendency to fantasize the future.

> The panic participant is future-threat rather than past-danger oriented. His attention is focused on what may occur rather than on what has happened. His thinking is not oriented toward such dangers as have already been experienced, but instead is focused on the possibility of becoming blocked off from escaping from an impending threat.... A rapid reaction of some sort is considered necessary in order to survive the quickly anticipated consequences of the threat.[1]

HOW TO RECOGNIZE A PANICKED PERSON

At first it seems ridiculous to spend time trying to figure out how to identify a person in a state of panic. It appears as though it should be obvious—just look for a person running around wildly. What makes it difficult is that some panicked people do their running inside their bodies and they *appear* relatively calm. Therefore, it is important to talk with a person for awhile that you are working with, and to observe him closely.

I was called out one night to work with a young man in a bar who was in an upset condition and requested help. A friend of mine went with me and we got him out of the bar and took him to a restaurant and drank coffee for several hours and talked. He didn't look panicked to me. But I noticed that whenever I would say anything to him, he would respond with "Can you help me?" I realized that he wasn't hearing a word I was saying, so I put my hand on his arm, established eye contact with him, paused for awhile, and then said to him, "What kind of help do you want?" Then he responded to me. The touch and eye contact had made a difference. (As I thought about it later, I realized I hadn't listened to him any better than he had listened to me.)

The Panicked Person Is Frightened

Fear is present in all panicked persons. They are afraid of a dreadful threat to their immediate future. Schultz has made a thought-provoking point here: "However, the panicky reaction is characterized not so much by the presence of fear as by unchecked fear."[2] This corresponds with C. S. Lewis's observation that in battle he noticed, not that men became very frightened and then ran, but rather that they ran and then became more frightened. When the behavior, the flight in this case, is unchecked, the fright increases. The flight is most often an actual running, but it may be a visualization, an image in one's mind, of running.

Look, then, for the usual signs of fear. Begin to observe people you know are afraid (for any reason, not just panic) and build your own list of behaviors which may indicate fear. Sometimes there is a "jumpiness" about the person. There may be some shaking and some sweating. Sometimes the body is in a closed or defensive position. Communication difficulties, such as the failure to listen and the inability to interact clearly, have already been mentioned.

The Person in a Panicked State Runs

As noted above, the running can be an actual fleeing, and usually is, or it can be a mental flight. Flight can be observed in panic buying when persons rush from store to store or from counter to counter to buy up scarce merchandise. The girl with the wrecked car, discussed at the beginning of this chapter, was taking flight when she ran around the car.

About five hundred people died in the Coconut Grove fire of 1942. The death toll was so great because the panicked patrons rushed both sides of the revolving doors, thus jamming them, and others choked a six-foot-wide stairway in their flight.[3] Panic flight is usually without rational direction, and, therefore, is most often counterproductive. It is often antisocial as well. It is well to remember, though, that fleeing from impending danger sometimes makes a lot of sense. Whether fleeing is rational or nonrational depends, as Schultz has pointed out, on the number of escape routes present.[4] To run from the area of a train wreck where poisonous gas is escaping is sensible because there are many escape routes. To run toward the main exit inside a building that is on fire usually does not make sense because of the likelihood of jamming the exit or injuring others.

There Are Limited Psychological Escape Routes

It is characteristic of panicked people that they see only one way out. Then they rush toward that opening. Fire codes require that public buildings have panic hardware on the doors so that as people rush against a door in a fire, the bar will be depressed and the door will open.

This concept of limited escape routes can be seen psychologically with a runaway who sees only one way out of his situation at home. If he can be brought back from his panic condition he may find that there are several ways. The same is true of the suicide who has panicked and has also determined that there is just one way out.

Everyone is subject to panic if the conditions are right. However, the person most subject to panic is the one who has an impulsive life-style. This person tends to panic more often than others and under less severe conditions than others.

HELPFUL APPROACHES TO THE PANICKED PERSON

What you need to do is to move the person from the "panic button" to the "hold button." Until you do this, any other intervention will probably be useless. The most effective way I've found to do this is focusing on the *present relationship* between the other person and myself.

Call Attention to the Present Relationship Between You

Here is the way it works. You as a helper will deal, not with the cause of panic nor even with a solution to the panic, but rather with the relationship between the two of you. You strengthen or call attention to that relationship right here, right now, in the middle of the panic. When the other onlooker and I put our arms around the young woman who was running around the wrecked car screaming, we were establishing a relationship with her. When I placed my hand on the arm of the panicked alcoholic and established eye contact with him, I was strengthening our relationship. This focusing of the present relationship helped both these persons to move from the panic to the hold button.

Therefore, the first thing to do with a person in a panicked state is to get in touch with him. It may be eye contact, it may be a hand on the shoulder, whatever you think the person will accept and respond to (some persons will not accept touch). Remember the person is caught in the future and must be brought back into the present. Eye contact and touch are always in the *present*. So is a verbal response that refers to what is going on between the two of you right now, such as "I'm here with you," or "I'll stay with you." The concept of "withness" is much more powerful than the concept of help. It is the feeling of being with a confident person that enables a panicked person to move to the hold button. The panicked person, as noted above, has a powerful image or visualization of a dreadful event. The intensity of this image is dimmed by focusing on the present.

Working with the Person Who Is on Hold

After you have been successful in helping your friend move away from a panicked state, your work is not yet finished. But you have reestablished a relationship that, although it may be fragile, is real. You can now work with your friend as you would with a person in a state of *crisis.* Don't push rapidly for a solution because usually a person who is panicked is not ready for this. Let him know you are willing to listen to his story of the events that just happened. It is important not to probe. Interrogation is usually not necessary because most people want to tell about what happened. *People often straighten out their thinking by talking.* They become oriented by talking about what they have been through.

Decide whether professional helpers are needed. If there is dizziness, or a change in complexion (e.g., paleness), or any other unusual physical reaction, secure the help of a physician or get an emergency unit. If you cannot get your friend out of the panicked state, this is another reason to get him to a physician, or to a professional mental health worker, such as a psychologist. In the meantime, stay with him.

FOLLOW-UP

Fortunately, panic is not a long-lasting state. People do not have enough energy to remain panicked over a long span of time. Usually panic lasts minutes, or in some cases hours. Therefore, the panicked person needs someone with him until he is through the panicked stage. Then for awhile afterward there needs to be a person who remains there for support so that the person does not move back into a state of panic. If you are helping a person move from a "panic button" to the "hold button," then you need to be sure that there is someone who can stay with him or be available if needed. This is especially true at night when there are fewer helping persons and agencies available.

REFERENCES

1. Duane P. Schultz, *Panic Behavior* (New York: Random House, 1964), p. 74.
2. *Ibid.*, p. 75.
3. *Ibid.*, p. 10.
4. *Ibid.*, p. 7.

11 Shock— The Dazed Walk

Gina Barriault has written a compelling short story, "The Stone Boy."[1] Arnold is emotionally very close to his older brother Eugie. One morning they get up early to pick peas and Arnold takes an old rifle along in case they see any ducks. As they go through a fence, the rifle catches on the fence, discharges, and Eugie is shot and killed. Instead of running home, Arnold goes ahead and picks the peas and then returns home after an hour or two. When all of the details are known, the one incomprehensible fact that confronts the parents and neighbors is the lapse of time that occurred between the time of Eugie's death and Arnold's reporting the accident. Arnold is taken to the sheriff's office and interrogated, with the implication being that he shot Eugie on purpose. Arnold is unable to answer the questions because he cannot understand why he did not run home the moment the accident occurred. Of all the persons who gather around Arnold in the hours after the accident, not one realizes that he is in a state of shock.

Many persons go into a state of shock for awhile after an accident, a near accident, or the death of a loved one. A two-car accident occurred last week in my own state. Two survivors of this accident were found a half-hour later wandering along the road in a dazed condition. The Committee on Civil Defense of the American Psychiatric Association has noted that some persons respond to an accident with a depressed or slowed down reaction:

> In disasters many people will act for a time as though they were numbed. They may stand or sit in the midst of utter chaos as though they were completely alone in the world. Their gaze will be vacant. When spoken to, they may not reply at all, or simply shrug their shoulders and utter a word or two. Unlike the person in panic who seeks physical escape at any cost, they appear to be completely unaware of the situation and devoid of emotional reaction to it. They are unable to help themselves without guidance.[2]

The fact that persons in a state of shock cannot act for themselves is a crucial one. Such persons need someone to act for them, and at times to protect them. Therefore, there is a need for many people in every community to recognize, and be able to help, a person in shock.

Psychological shock and physical shock are closely related. A man suddenly loses his wife of twenty-nine years, and he goes into psychological shock. But there are physical components in terms of his body's reaction to the psychological shock. A woman suffers physical shock in an automobile accident, but there are psychological components resulting from the shock. In fact, to show the similarity even more sharply, it is possible that her *behavior* may be the same whether she is in an accident and suffers actual physical injury or whether she is in a near-accident and suffers no physical injury.

HOW TO RECOGNIZE A PERSON IN PSYCHOLOGICAL SHOCK

There are a number of characteristics and behaviors that will be helpful in identifying a person who is in a state of psychological shock. No one of these symptoms is enough to establish this identification. On the other hand, if you observe a pattern involving a number of these symptoms, then you will do well to assume the person is in shock and begin to provide help.

1. *There is no recognition reflex.* Ordinarily when you approach persons and begin talking to them, you will observe a facial response (and often a response with other parts of the body) that lets you know they are aware of your presence and are responding to your being there. This "recognition reflex" is often missing with the person in shock. He may look "through" you or past you.

2. *True dialogue is not happening.* For a true dialogue to occur, each person has to listen carefully and take into account what the other has said in responding. The person in shock rarely does this. He doesn't "compute" what you are saying to him. Therefore, as in other situations in which there are one or more poor listeners present, there is a series of monologues rather than a dialogue.

3. *There is an inability to recall the immediate past.* Usually persons in shock are unable to give a logical account of the event causing the shock, or of the use of time between that event and the present. It is as if they have blown a fuse on their time line and their short-term memory.

4. *Emotions are shut down.* It is this characteristic that probably most disguises the victims of psychological shock. They *appear,* at first glance, to be rather calm. It is as if the emotions, if expressed, would be so wrenching that the central nervous system pushes a safety which inhibits their expression.

5. *Confusion is apparent to observers.* If the person is walking, the walk appears to be aimless. If he is talking, the same lack of direction is apparent. He is confused in his thinking, his talking, and his physical activity.

TAKING THE FIRST HELPING STEPS

The way you approach a person in shock will determine your effectiveness. Therefore, it is important that your initial contact be a good one. The following steps can be useful:

1. *Show respect.* We need to approach a person in shock believing he is doing the best he knows how.

When a man's thigh is shattered, no one (including the patient) expects him to walk for a time. When a man's ability to cope with his feelings is shattered, many (often including the patient) are inclined to expect him to function normally again almost immediately. "It's all in your head." "Snap out of it." "Pull yourself together." Such goading, scolding types of "reassurance" have no place in psychological first aid.[3]

Psychological limitations, although unseen, are just as real as physical limitations. We allow for these limitations when we show respect for the person.

One time a twenty-five-year-old man had an epileptic seizure in my college classroom. Several of us provided the necessary help of supplying a cushion for his head, removing the surrounding chairs, and assisting in other ways. After he had completed the seizure cycle, he got up with great difficulty, said he was going home, and headed, with shaky steps, for the parking lot. (He commuted from a small town fifty miles away!) I realized he was in a state very closely resembling psychological shock, and should not be driving on the Interstate, or any road, for awhile. I also realized he was bigger and stronger than I was. To have argued with him would have done no good. Besides, I could accept the fact that a disoriented person would want to go home. So I took him by the arm and walked him up and down the hall until he was quite tired. Then we sat down for awhile and talked and he then became willing to go to the Student Health Center which was close by. We walked over there. He rested some more, then gave us the number of a friend to call who would drive him home. I stayed with him until his friend came.

2. *Be confident.* A person at any level of psychological need responds positively to a helper who comes across as strong. Expect that you will be able to help the person in shock. Be willing to get close. Look him in the eye. Put your hand on his arm or shoulder unless you get the feeling he does not want you close. He will draw strength and assurance from your presence. Don't spend a lot of time anticipating what he may do. Just focus on what he is doing. Talk in a quiet, firm voice.

3. *Work slowly.* Don't expect too much too fast. It takes awhile for the mind of the person in shock to clear. In the case of the young

man above, walking, talking, and time seemed to bring about a better awareness and clearer thinking. Your willingness to invest time is very important. An impatient attitude on the helper's part can slow down the recovery.

4. *Do not be alarmed if the person in shock suddenly becomes very active.* Sometimes a person who has been involved in a near accident will seem numbed for awhile, then break out in a sweat, have an increased pulse rate, and start walking around rapidly. This is a step toward recovery that some take and indicates that an awareness of the shock-producing event is being permitted to surface. Just continue to be with the person and talk with him calmly. Treat him as you would a person in panic.

5. *Get help when needed.* If the person has been physically injured, or if there is even a chance that he has been, you will, of course, need to get medical help as soon as possible. If the person is in psychological shock and is not making progress toward recovery after awhile, you should obtain psychological help. Psychologists and most social workers have been trained in this area, as have some ministers and school counselors. Help is harder to get at night. If your community has a "hot line" or personal crisis line, call in. Usually the volunteer on the phone has a list of backup mental health professionals to call in just such an emergency.

6. *Do not assume that the shock is psychological* just because there is no apparent injury. Under certain conditions a diabetic may go into shock. Drugs and medications may bring about shock. If there is no evidence of a psychological shock, nor of injury, obtain medical help on the chance that it is shock in this third area.

7. *Stay with the person* until he is back to normal or until professional help has arrived. Do not leave the person alone as long as the symptoms mentioned at the first of this chapter are still apparent. A person in shock may walk right into traffic or otherwise endanger himself. Or he may flip-flop, as noted above, from a numbed to a panicky condition. When help does come, let the person know that you will be checking back with him later (if you will).

FOLLOW-UP

Follow-up is useful at all the different levels of psychological need. Among other things, it is a sign that you care. Often the person who has been in shock will, upon full recovery, want to know what happened and what he did. You may be the only person who can tell him. It will mean a great deal to him to learn that a friend stayed with him.

REFERENCES

1. Gina Barriault, "The Stone Boy," *Child Development Through Literature* (Englewood Cliffs, N.J.: Prentice-Hall, Inc., 1972), pp. 261-271.
2. Calvin S. Drayer, et al, "Psychological First Aid in Community Disasters," *Journal of the American Medical Association*, Vol. 156, Sept. 4, 1954, p. 37.
3. *Ibid.*, p. 38.

Four

How to Discover
and Fulfill
Life-Style Needs

Part

A

The Four Elements of Life-Style— Feeling, Thinking, Choosing, Doing

12 Developing a "Response-able" Life-Style

If you have determined that your friend's level of need is not urgent, you will have time to discover his strong and weak "living channels." Knowing the strong aspect of your friend's life-style will enable you to build on that strength, and knowing the weak channel will tell you what part of your friend's life-style needs to be strengthened.

Life-style refers to the ways one typically responds to what one has learned. The living channels I have found helpful to work with are *feeling* (awareness of one's emotions, and the ability to express them); *thinking* (the ability to plan and the ability to connect cause and effect); *choosing* (establishing a clear set of values and moral standards,

finding meaning in life and having the courage or will to act); and
doing (performing whatever action is desired or necessary). You
need to know the living channels that are not functioning
efficiently in order to help your friend become more
"response-able"—that is, able to respond to life fully through all four
living channels.

In the chart headed "Living Channels" you will see four ways we
respond to what we learn. If you are a person who is able to "image"
well, imagine four small channels or tributaries flowing into a river.

LIVING CHANNELS

CHANNEL	PERSON WITH STRONG CHANNEL	PERSON WITH WEAK CHANNEL	FORCES ENCOURAGING THESE CHANNELS
FEELING	Aware of own feelings; able to express them.	Doesn't know how to take own emotional pulse; may come across cold or inhibited.	Families, sharing groups, churches (especially where expression of feelings is fostered); coffee break talk.
THINKING	Analytical; investigative frame of mind.	Unaware; impulsive.	Schools, research institutes, games, e.g., chess.
CHOOSING	Courageous; has a clear value structure.	Indecisive.	Politics, religion, advertising.
DOING	Changes behavior when necessary.	Immobilized by deep feelings.	Work, i.e., factories, offices; recreation.

That river is your life. For most of us, these four channels would
not be the same size. Usually we have a wide channel or two and
a narrow channel or two. For example, a person who has a strong
choosing channel, tends to be courageous and to have a clear value
structure. The person who has a constricted choosing channel is
indecisive because 1) He lacks the courage to make a decision on
insufficient evidences (and the evidences are always insufficient); or
2) Because he does not have a value structure that is well organized.
If all his values are equally important to him there is no way for him
to prioritize in order to make a decision.

Now on this same chart notice over in the right column the forces that encourage one of these specific channels. Some churches, for example, appeal more to the feeling channel than do others. An example of a societal unit that focuses on thinking is the school. The school has typically seen children and youth as learning machines. In so doing, they have sometimes overlooked the fact that students have feelings. The human relations movement in the schools is an example of a force that is beginning to fill this vacuum. Also, in the school the growing movement of values clarification is aimed at correcting a deficiency in training for decision-making. Finally, in the schools there is a growing emphasis on learning by doing.

The richness of our lives is dependent on the free flow of each of the above channels. To the extent that all four of these channels are open and strong, our life-style is rich and fulfilling. But sometimes one of the channels is clogged. One woman said concerning her husband, "I wish he'd just once say, 'I love you,' and put his arms around me when he didn't want sex." Her husband had so constricted his feeling channel that the expression of warmth didn't get through. This is not to say that he didn't love his wife, but warmth doesn't mean so much *if it doesn't get through* to the other person. Another woman said concerning her husband, "Oh, he says several times a day he loves me, but I wish he'd show it by doing some of the work around the house." This man had constricted his doing channel, or action channel, and didn't see work as a way to express love. The quality of our love life depends on the openness of these four channels through which we express love.

In the following chapters in this section you will 1) Discover your own strong and weak living channels; 2) Learn how to find a friend's strong and weak living channels; and 3) Learn how to help a friend work toward greater wholeness in his life-style by strengthening his weak living channel.

13

A Way to Discover the Strong and Weak Elements of Life-Style

Let's suppose that you have a friend who mentions to you that the right-hand tread on the front tires of his car is just about gone. At this point you could suggest he buy new front tires, or you could continue to listen. Let's suppose you continue to listen and he says his front tires have only 10,000 miles of wear on them. You now are relatively sure the front end of his car is out of line and this is causing the excessive tread wear. You talk with him about this possibility; it makes sense to him, and he decides to get his front wheels aligned.

It is important that your friend get new tires, but if he did not get the front wheels aligned, he would soon be back in the same old predicament of having unsafe front tires. In the same way, when your friend comes to you for help with some human predicament or crisis, it is almost never enough to help him "solve" the immediate problem. *It is usually the way we live that gets us into predicaments and crises.* Of course, this is not always true. Sometimes there may be disease or an accident over which we have no control that can cause a crisis. But most of us would probably agree that we have gotten into the largest percentage of our jams under our own power.

It is usually the weak component of our life-style that gets us into a predicament. For example, one man lost the respect of his wife and that was his predicament. However, what he discovered he needed to work with was his weak choosing channel. He had gradually moved into a life-style that was marked by indecisiveness. Therefore, his wife had to make all the decisions regarding the children, the home, and sometimes even her husband. He had to discover this weak channel and strengthen it in order to get out of his predicament and to avoid similar ones in the future.

A Look at You

This manual is designed to help you focus on yourself as well as your friend. As a helper, you cannot teach what you do not know. Therefore, you need to have worked through your own living channels in a careful way in order to determine your strengths and weaknesses, so that you can work on necessary growth. The four ways of living that make up your life-style were discussed briefly earlier. Now we will look at them in some detail, because, to work with the life-style approach in counseling, you need to learn how to determine your own strong and weak living channels and the strong and weak living channels of the friend who comes to you for help. It is most important that you be able to determine the *weak* living channel, because this must be strengthened to get people out of present crises and to enable them to avoid future ones.

I find I am sometimes unaware of some important things about me. We need to be reminded of the obvious. Most persons whom I have talked with do not know their strong and weak living channels. Therefore, the "Checklist for Discovering Strong and Weak Living Channels" can be helpful as a starting point in your quest to find your own life-style makeup. The checklist is set up in such a way that the column with the most checks indicates the strong channel and the column with the least checks indicates the weak channel. Now take time to go through and put check marks to the left of each item that is typical of you. No one item means very much by itself in telling you what your life-style is, but taken all together you may find the results helpful. After you have finished the checklist, then total the number of checks in each column. The column in which you have the least checks may be your weak living channel. But don't make a firm decision on this yet. Think some more about it and, most important, talk with those closest to you about how they see you.

Now that you have begun to establish what your weak living channel is, you may wish to strengthen that channel. You will find in this section of the manual some approaches that are effective in strengthening each channel. Remember, it is the helpers who are working hardest at their own personal growth who are most helpful in reaching out to others. You will find that it is no easy task to strengthen one of the channels because it will require you to make a change in the *way* you live.

A LOOK AT YOUR FRIEND

Having worked through the checklist and taken other steps to discover the weak component of your life-style, you now understand the concept well enough to use it with a friend. Also having begun to strengthen your weak living channel, you will realize how very difficult this is and that any help you give to your friend will have to go beyond pat answers and easy advice.

If your friend is in the predicament stage in terms of level of need, you can usually just give the checklist to him and ask him to fill it out. (Remember, we are taking for granted that your friend has come to you for help. It is not a workable thing to see somebody who needs help and try to give it to him if he does not want it. If he doesn't ask you in an outright way for help, at least there should be evidences that he wants help and is open to receiving it.) Just tell your friend that this is an important way to find out how he or she lives, that it helped you (if it did), and it would give the two of you something worthwhile to talk about.

CHECKLIST FOR DISCOVERING STRONG AND WEAK LIVING CHANNELS

I. THE FEELING CHANNEL	II. THE THINKING CHANNEL	III. THE CHOOSING CHANNEL	IV. THE DOING CHANNEL
✓ 1. Someone has told you in the last six months that he/she appreciates your warmth.	✓ 1. You usually consider consequences before acting.	___ 1. You make important decisions early and decisively, rather than spend a lot of time worrying about them.	___ 1. You generally live in the present by forgetting the past and not worrying about the future.
___ 2. You usually are able to express angry feelings.	___ 2. You usually plan purchases well in advance and resist buying on impulse.	✓ 2. You prefer to make your own decisions.	✓ 2. You are involved in life and rarely spend time "feeling miserable."
___ 3. You like to have people touch you.	___ 3. Once you've made plans you usually carry them out.	___ 3. You usually have a clear sense of what is right and wrong.	✓ 3. You typically find it easy to sleep at night.
✓ 4. You find it easy to touch people, especially those who are psychologically close to you.	✓ 4. You are prompt for appointments.	✓ 4. Life has a great deal of meaning for you.	✓ 4. Overall, you feel confident about your future.
✓ 5. It is natural and easy for you to maintain eye contact with a person you are talking to.	✓ 5. You can visualize the results of your actions easily.	✓ 5. You have clear-cut personal goals.	___ 5. You see yourself as a competent person.
✓ 6. You enjoy receiving compliments and react graciously.	✓ 6. You usually plan ahead and avoid predicaments.	✓ 6. You can usually find the courage to make the decisions you need to.	✓ 6. You value constructive criticism.
✓ 7. You've been angry at someone in the last few weeks.	___ 7. When you have a task to do, you typically do it rather than avoid it.	___ 7. You decide which clothes you are going to wear each morning with little hesitation.	✓ 7. You usually feel healthy and full of energy.
	✓ 8. You would classify yourself as dependable rather than undependable.	✓ 8. You like to make moral decisions ahead of time rather than waiting	___ 8. It is easy to concentrate on what you are reading.
			✓ 9. You see yourself generally as successful.

someone within the last week that you appreciate, like, or love him/her.

___ 9. Others see you as a friendly person, easy to get to know.

___ 10. You smile as much, or more, than most people.

___ 11. You rarely use sarcasm.

___ 12. You often share your deep feelings with others.

easier for you than for most to stay within a budget.

___ 10. At a restaurant you rarely order more than you can eat.

___ 11. You find it easy to think through your day tomorrow.

___ 12. You are strong in "sales resistance."

finding it fairly easy to decide which of these areas you're strong in.

___ 10. You could quickly and easily list three or four values in life that are very important to you.

___ 11. Courage ranks high in your value system.

___ 12. You feel confident of your decision-making ability.

what you start.

___ 11. You enjoy beginning the day.

___ 12. You view difficult circumstances as challenges rather than insurmountable obstacles.

(Column with most checks—the strong channel; column with least checks—the weak channel)

STRONG—*Warm*; very aware of emotions and effective in expressing them.

WEAK—*Cold*; low in awareness and expression of emotions.

STRONG—*A planner*; can visualize consequences of actions and can plan effectively.

WEAK—*Impulsive*; has difficulty in planning ahead and in seeing consequences of action.

STRONG—*Decisive*; life is charged with meaning; has internalized moral standards, knows own values, demonstrates courage.

WEAK—*Indecisive*; life may lack meaning, clear moral standards, a value system or courage.

STRONG—*Active*; expends energy in action rather than worrying.

WEAK—*Immobilized*; spends much "head time" in daydreams, fantasies, or feeling miserable.

If persons have gone beyond the predicament stage to the crisis or panic stage, don't bother with the checklist. Rather, begin to work with their immediate need. You will have to use other means of judging what their weak living channel is. If you have reviewed the items in the checklist carefully, you will begin to develop a way of looking at others that will help you understand them in terms of their life-style. You will begin to notice evidences of impulsiveness, for example. Or you may observe that a person may spend a great deal of "head time" in daydreaming activities. These clues will help you understand your friend's life-style.

When your friend's immediate need has been met, begin to talk to him/her in terms of life-style. You may want to see if your friend can decide which are *your* strong and weak living channels. Then you can begin to talk about your friend's strong and weak living channels. If this continues to make sense to your friend, then the next step is to begin work to strengthen the weak channel, as described in the following chapters.

Part B

FEELING—
*Helping
Your Friend
to Respond
More Warmly*

14 Sharing Your Warmth

When we compare a cold, logical person to a warmer, but more impulsive person, we are faced with what C. S. Lewis called "equal and opposite evils." He built his book, *The Pilgrim's Regress*, [1] around the concept of Northerners and Southerners. A Northerner is a cerebral person, cold, analytical, and unfeeling. On the other hand, the Southerner is a visceral person, unthinking and impulsive. Lewis observed that even in the animal world these two kinds of beings are represented by the crustacean and the jellyfish. Lewis noted that for the Southerner, "every feeling is justified by the mere fact that it is felt: for a Northerner, every feeling on the same ground is suspect."[2]

The purpose of this chapter is to provide some guidelines for approaching "Northerners." Let's suppose that a friend comes to us for help, and we have concluded that this friend is weak in the feeling channel, that is, either he comes across as cold or he is unaware of some of the feelings he has, or both. There are some guidelines that will aid us in more effectively helping this friend.

ACCEPT, DON'T CONDEMN

Often the person who seems unable to get in touch with his feelings is not a cold or bitter person. He just comes across that way. Therefore, it is helpful to approach "cold" persons with the idea they are warm *inside*. If they come across as cold, usually they simply have not learned to express the warmth that they have inside. This was true in my own life for many years. When I discovered that I often came across as cold, then I began to work to express for others the warmth that I felt for them.

We have a fireplace which our family built. The chimney is made of an inner and outer tube of metal, with the two-inch circular space between packed with asbestos. Even when there is a roaring fire in the fireplace, the outside of the chimney is cool to the touch. It is possible that many people are so well insulated that the warmth inside doesn't get out to warm the person next to them.

It is good to accept the fact that most people have a good reason for being the way they are in terms of their coldness. For example, one middle-aged man went to see a counselor about several predicaments he was in. One of these predicaments was that the relationship between him and his daughter was a cold one. He wanted to show affection to her but he said he simply could not touch her or show her warmth. As this father continued to talk, he shared the information that in his own growing up days he had observed his father commit incest with his sister. Obviously, to him, physically touching or embracing his daughter would bring back many painful memories and would seem wrong. This dad had to be taught through a series of task assignments to get closer to his daughter and to touch her and finally to get to the place where he would hug her, whether he felt like it or not. But the point is, if the counselor early in the sessions had mentally condemned the father as a person who didn't care about his daughter, then he would not have been able to help him. We have to accept people as they are in order to help them change.

If we have friends who are not in touch with their feelings, then it is probably best for us to assume that they have experiences which have caused them to push their feelings down below the level of their awareness. It is not always necessary for us to know about these experiences. We just need to take the point of view that they have a good reason for doing what they're doing. For example, a man who has difficulty sharing tender feelings with his wife may have been taught by others as he grew up that "macho" men only show toughness. If a person seems unable to share any of his angry feelings, it may be that the earlier expression of his angry feelings has resulted in someone hurting him physically or psychologically, or in leaving him. In other words, that person associates the expression of anger with the rejection or separation of a loved one.

SHARE YOUR WARMTH

Usually friends who come across as cold will begin to express their warmth to others, not when we have succeeded in "straightening them out," but rather when we have succeeded in *warming* them. We do this by being friendly to them and by investing our time with them. The friendliness must be genuine. One time a sixth grade teacher said to me, "I don't know what's wrong with that boy. I've tried everything with him; I've tried liking him..." I suggested that if she had to *try* to like him, he probably got the message.

It is possible to be involved in a "helping" relationship with another person whom we may not like. I remember teaching a senior class in high school and having one of the students tell me he didn't like me and that he wanted out of my class. I suggested he see one of the counselors in the school to obtain a transfer to another class. What disturbed me most when I looked at myself was that I had to admit I didn't like him and hadn't for some time. He saw a counselor who was a very wise person and who began to talk to him about my good points. I went to see the same counselor for help and she began to talk to me about some of the things he had going for him. She also helped each of us to see some ways we needed to grow as persons. So we stayed together that year and by the end of the year we had begun to like each other.

"Cold" people are just like other people: they are looking for a warm place. You can provide that warm place as you spend time with your friend, affirm your friend as a person, and express your warmth.

GIVE STRAIGHT FEEDBACK

People usually don't change unless they see a reason to change. And our life-style is so much a part of us that our awareness of it is usually dim.

The approach of this manual takes for granted that you have built an involvement with your friend. This means that you can be direct with your friend and that you know him well enough, so that you know the best way to provide him or her information without hurting. For example, it may be helpful to say something like, "You seem to me to have a lot more warmth on the inside than you actually express to others." You should, of course, say this only if this judgment is true from your point of view.

If you are talking with a friend and he relates an incident that quite obviously makes him angry just to tell about it, you may wish to point out his anger. If he is weak in this feeling channel, he may deny the anger and say something like, "No, I'm not mad." Then if you have a good involvement, it is possible for you to mention physical evidence, such as, "Your face is flushed, your jaw is clenched, your forehead is wrinkled, the veins on your neck are standing out, and your fists are doubled up." You have to say this in the same way you would say, "Pass the salt." It will not work if you say it with an edge on your voice.

TOUCH THE BITTER PERSON

Sometimes people mention being out in "bitterly cold" weather. Just as cold weather is sometimes so sharp it is bitter, so bitterness in people sometimes goes with coldness, and is marked by intensity, regret, animosity, and unpleasantness. The bitter person is abrasive

to anyone who happens to be around, but most abrasive to people
who are close. As a friend of mine says, "He is the kind of a person
who would stroke a cat from the tail to the head."

The bitter person is often involved in predicaments and sometimes
in crises. There is, of course, a tendency to upset and alienate others.
The biggest predicament is the terribly heavy burden that bitter
persons carry. It is a foul-smelling load from the past that they put on
their shoulders again every morning—if they have been able to lay
it down at night. Every day the load grows heavier because they
are aware that they are hurting people every day unnecessarily.
This has a ring of truth to most of us because at some time or other in
our lives, we have personally known bitterness—our own. Perhaps
someone reached out to help so it did not become a permanent part of
our life-style.

How can you reach out to the "bitterly cold" person, whether that
person has just recently become embittered, or whether the
bitterness is deeply entrenched? The Christian helper, at this
point, has a powerful advantage over the one who does not have
access to the resources of Christ, because what the bitter person
needs is to learn how to FORGIVE. The reminder needs to be given,
though, that Christians are not immune to bitterness.

I remember having a series of conversations with a very fine Christian businesswoman. She was middle-aged, competent, bright—and
bitter. Her predicament was that she was alienating the persons
around her, they were backing off, and loneliness was rapidly
moving in. She was most bitter with her husband and with
herself, but did not know how to shed the bitterness. After trying
many things that didn't work (helpers often experience failure!), I
suggested she use a concordance and do a study of the word "mercy" as
it occurs in the Bible. (For some who are reading this manual and have
not used a concordance, this is a book which lists each time a word
occurs in the Bible and gives the reference so that it can be looked
up. There are a number of good concordances available.[3])

We had two or three more conversations and then I didn't see
her for nearly a year. She volunteered the information that this
word study had helped her find forgiveness toward her husband and
herself. She had studied many passages of Scripture, over a period of
months. One of these was Ephesians 2:4-7:

> But God, who is rich in mercy, out of the great love with which he
> loved us, even when we were dead through our trespasses, made

us alive together with Christ (by grace you have been saved), and raised us up with him, and made us sit with him in the heavenly places in Christ Jesus, that in the coming ages he might show the immeasurable riches of his grace in kindness toward us in Christ Jesus.

Studying such references to mercy touched her life and she experienced again, in a time of renewal, the love of God, and was able to get rid of her bitterness.

Another way of touching a bitter person is through a spontaneous act of love or kindness. There are many examples of a child giving a hug to a cold, bitter man with the result that the "Northerner" begins to melt. A neighbor takes in a cake to a cross, bitter woman next door and she begins to feel a strange warmth taking over inside.

The Life-Style Versus the Medical Approach

Should you as a friend spend time helping someone discover *why* he is bitter? Most of us are tuned in to causes. Physicians spend time diagnosing the cause of an illness, believing that if they eliminate the cause of the illness, the illness will cease to exist. Psychiatrists, because they are physicians, typically use the same analytical approach. Usually this requires making the long trip back to the person's early childhood. This may be why psychiatrists, and some psychologists who use a similar analytical approach, are (unkindly) referred to as headshrinkers. They regress or "shrink" the person back to childhood. There are some persons who are extremely disturbed who need to discuss their childhood in depth. A lay person should not attempt such analysis but should refer to a professional.

The best bit of news here is that for the great majority of people, it is not necessary, in order to change behavior and life-style, that either the person helping or the person being helped know *why* he is the way he is, for example, bitter. There are likely twenty-nine (or sixty-four) reasons why he has this life-style. Nearly all behavior is *multiply* caused. It is usually a myth that one event in the distant past can be uncovered and the person is "OK" again. The truth is that most people change their life-style, not by detective work, but by hard work and courage, and with some help from their friends.

REFERENCES

1. C. S. Lewis, *The Pilgrim's Regress* (Grand Rapids, Michigan: William B. Eerdmans Publishing Company, 1943).
2. *Ibid.*, p. 12.
3. Your local religious bookstore personnel can show you the different concordances that are available.

15 Teaching Your Friend to Take His/Her Emotional Pulse

Can one person teach another person anything? This question was asked by Saint Thomas Aquinas in the thirteenth century. When I first ran across the question, I thought *"Of course,* one person can teach another person something." As I thought more about it, I became more skeptical and decided that the question had considerable substance.

My reaction now to this question is, "Yes, provided both the teacher and the learner have the very important characteristics of humility, and a strong quest for learning." Most of us will not learn from a teacher who comes across as knowing it all. We turn that person off. We tend to be much more open to learning if the teacher comes across as a learner, someone who is aware he still has a great deal to learn and who is working at that. But, the learner as well as the teacher needs to be humble. It is not possible to teach somebody something if he firmly believes he knows everything. The learner must have a quest for knowledge and understanding which comes from an attitude of humility. Therefore, *it is much easier to teach someone who comes to us asking a question.* That is another reason why this manual is set up to provide you with a way of helping a friend who comes to you *wanting* help.

STRENGTHENING THE FEELING CHANNEL

A person who is weak in the feeling channel of his life-style is sometimes characterized by his lack of awareness of his own feelings. Just as some persons find it difficult to monitor their pulse rate by feeling their wrist at just the right place, so some find it difficult to get a reading on their emotional state. The person is thus placed at a great disadvantage. He may be showing his anger without even feeling it. The impact of this bent message will further confuse him. You can help your friend strengthen this important channel (feeling) of his life-style by teaching him to monitor his "emotional pulse." What are some ways to do this?

Use Questions That Teach, Not Corner, Your Friend

Questions that may cause a friend to feel cornered include "Why did you feel that way?" and "Why did you do that?" Notice that both of these questions focus on the past. Questions that focus on the past typically are not very helpful. Also questions that begin with the word "why" are usually not helpful. Most behaviors are multiply-caused, that is, there are many causes for any single thing that we do. Therefore, most people cannot sort out all of these causes; and as a matter of fact, when they try to, they often miss some of the most significant causes.

Questions that tend to teach are open-ended questions such as "What are you doing about that?" "Is it helping?" and "How would you like to change?" These questions focus on present behavior for the most part. They are also goal-oriented rather than past-oriented. These kinds of questions will help get your friend to think about what he is *doing.* This is usually beneficial in bringing about change. Questions that help build an awareness of feelings include: "What emotion are you feeling right now?" "Describe what you are feeling in your stomach (or chest)." "Where do you feel tension?" "Even though you're laughing right now, you seem angry to me. Are you *feeling* any anger?"

Teach Your Friend to Feel His/Her Body Changes

Just as we have to touch our body if we are going to take our pulse rate, so we need to get in touch with our body if we are to be fully aware of our emotional changes. The secret to building awareness of our emotions is learning how to monitor the changes within our body. This takes some hard work. Most of us are not very aware of outer space, and are even less aware of "inner space."

Some changes to look for that indicate stress (anger, hurt, grief, disgust) starting from the head down include:

Is the forehead tightening or wrinkling?

Are the muscles tensing around the eyes?

Is the shape of the lower face changing so that the jaw is set and the teeth are clenched?

Are the throat muscles tightening?

Is there an acceleration in the pulse rate?

Are the fists doubling up, or even slightly closing?

Do you feel any tension across the upper and lower back?

Is breathing becoming more rapid?

Is the stomach feeling tense, quivering, or "dis-eased"?

Do the leg muscles feel taut?

By looking at these indicators of negative emotions, we can see two trends—there is a *speeding up* of the rhythm of our body (circulation and breathing) and a *tightening up* of the muscles. The body is making preparations to fight or take flight.

Pinpoint the Negative Emotion

Once you teach your friend to monitor what is happening in his/her body in order to build awareness of negative emotions, the next step is to provide help in distinguishing the exact emotion. Two emotions that are very difficult to differentiate are anger and hurt. Some suggestions are given below which may help you work with your friend more effectively in these two areas.

To illustrate how these two emotions get mixed up, let's suppose that Roy, who is employed as an auto mechanic, goes to work and finds one of his fellow mechanics has been promoted to shop foreman. The manager of this particular car dealership had told Roy two weeks ago that he was planning to name a new shop foreman and that Roy had an inside track on the job. Since that time Roy has had no further communication from the manager, so when he gets the news about the new foreman, Roy is upset—hurt. He is hurt because he did not get the job

THE INTERACTION OF HURT, ANGER, AND REVENGEFULNESS[1]

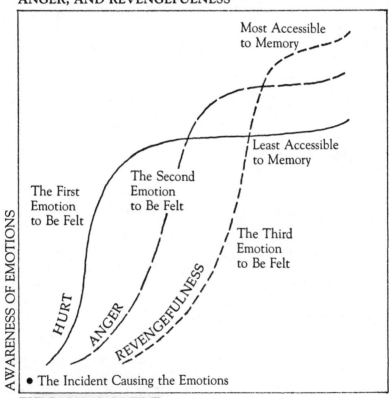

and because the manager did not talk with him to explain why the implicit promise was broken.

Notice on the drawing, "The Interaction of Hurt, Anger, and Revengefulness," that seconds after the event which arouses the hurt feeling, another feeling skyrockets into awareness—Anger. This overlays the hurt feeling so that Roy is no longer aware of his hurt; he is angry and is quite aware of his new emotion. A bit later he may begin to want to "get back at" the manager. This new emotion—revengefulness—can trigger some negative action if Roy does not keep it under control.

Another point of the drawing is that later when Roy thinks about the event that hurt him, he moves back into his memory and encounters the *last* emotion first. Therefore, instead of going to the manager and explaining his hurt and disappointment that the manager had gotten his hopes up and then dashed them without any further communication, Roy is more likely to respond in an angry way, or perhaps he may sulk. Sharing one's hurt feelings keeps one open and vulnerable. Sharing angry or revengeful feelings (when the original feeling was hurt) keeps one closed and may close off any possibility of dialogue. On the other hand, if Roy communicates his anger effectively by pinpointing *exactly* what it was that made him mad, there is still the possibility of getting some communication going. If he reacts angrily without discussing the real issue, then there is little chance of resolving the issue. The point is that we communicate most clearly when we talk with another person about the *first* emotion we felt in the interaction between us.

I work in a college, and sometimes I see girls and guys who respond to each other angrily or in a revengeful way when the original separating emotion between them was hurt. When they choose to hurt back instead of communicating the fact that they were hurt, they further widen the psychological distance between them.

If your friend is caught in this predicament, you may be able to help him/her get back to the original emotion and *feel* the hurt. This will take some doing, because it is hard to get beneath the anger. Use the approach discussed in chapter twenty-nine, "Listening and Resonating," for getting back to the hurt. Often when people move back beyond anger to their hurt, they sigh and relax and the tension leaves, just like the air going out of a balloon. Then they are usually able to go to the other person and discuss this hurt.

Teach Your Friend to Monitor His/Her Actions

In order to take our emotional pulse it is helpful not only to monitor what is happening in our bodies, but also the actions we are taking. For example, if we become aware that we are yelling, this tells us that we do not believe we are being heard. Probably we are feeling frustrated, perhaps angry. If this happens, it is usually effective to stop yelling and say something like, "I don't know if this is the way it really is, but I have the feeling you aren't listening to me right now."

If we become aware we are backing up, even very slightly, in a discussion with another person, it usually means we want to get out of the situation. We may be afraid or tired, or for some other reason want to terminate the conversation. It is helpful at this point to try to discover what is happening that is causing us to retreat, and to talk about that.

It is important to monitor the way we are talking. If we discover we are talking in a cutting way, this means that we want to hurt the other person. At this point, integrity would require that we apologize to the other person and discuss what is between us. This requires a considerable amount of both humility and courage.

As we learn to monitor our own actions and reactions, we may discover *positive* emotions within us also. The actor Bill Bixby found this to be the case when he played the father in the TV series, "The Courtship of Eddie's Father." Eddie was played by Brandon Cruz. Bill Bixby tells the following story about a peak event in his life that occurred with Brandon during the filming of the series.

I was having a terrible time with myself. Then one day that eight-year-old boy put his arms around me and kissed me on camera, and it wasn't fake. He really liked me. And I fell in love with him. In the rushes, there was a look on my face—it showed. And for perhaps the first time in my life I really liked the guy on the screen. I mean, I liked Bill Bixby. [2]

As Bill Bixby looked at the film, he felt the impact of this small boy's spontaneous expression of love. He became aware of his own response *which had already taken place.* I reread this story often because it is a good reminder to me of the power of the *awareness* of our emotions. It also is a reminder of the power of a freely given expression of love.

Teach Your Friend to Monitor the Other Person's Reactions

This can be done with the same guidelines mentioned above for monitoring our own actions. If the other person raises his/her voice, then we need to say something like, "I'm noticing you are now talking quite loudly; do you feel I'm not listening to you?" If the other person backs away from us, we need to ask ourselves if we are coming across as attacking. We can learn a great deal about our own emotions by becoming aware of what the other person is doing in reaction to us.

The above guidelines for teaching your friend to take his/her emotional pulse are based on the view that you have a close relationship with your friend and that your friend is seeking help. This provides the openness, trust, and motivation to allow these guidelines to work.

REFERENCES

1. This drawing is from my book, *Family Problems and Predicaments: How to Respond* (Wheaton, Illinois: Tyndale House, 1977), p. 103. Used by permission of the publishers. I am indebted to Dr. G. B. Dunning for the concept of anger overlaying hurt.
2. From "Here's Howe," by Pete Howe, in the *Sunday World-Herald Magazine of the Midlands,* February 13, 1977, *The Omaha World-Herald,* Omaha, Nebraska, p. 20.

16 Helping Your Friend Express Emotions

Task assignments are widely used. Dentists give instructions on the use of dental floss and then assign their patients to use it. A tennis pro gives his students lessons on serving and then makes suggestions about practice during the week. A minister may give a number of exhortations about changes in behavior which his hearers are urged to incorporate in their daily lives the next week. A teacher gives homework. Ah, there's the rub! There's something about the word "homework" which comes out as dull and something to be endured, in a word—busywork. But homework doesn't *have* to be busywork, and good homework never is.

WHAT ARE TASK AGREEMENTS?

The concept of task agreement rather than task assignments is used in this manual. A task agreement is an activity usually suggested by you that your friend decides to do in order to meet his/her goal. Notice the word "agreement." It is not like homework that the student does because he is overpowered. There has to be a desire and a commitment on the part of your friend to do the task. Some task agreements include monitoring one's actions, or other's reactions to us, physically touching those emotionally close to us, reading a book, talking in a lower voice, responding in no more than two sentences apiece, doing a word study on the subject of "forgiveness" in the Bible, smiling, writing a letter, or any of hundreds of other activities tailor-made to fit your friend's goal.

WHY TASK AGREEMENTS?

Many professional counselors now regularly use task agreements because they have found such "homework" brings about behavior change that talking alone can't do. There are several reasons why task agreements are so powerful:

1. *Tasks keep one's mind on the goal.* A friend comes to you for help in her predicament of loneliness. By careful observation and perhaps by suggesting she fill out the "Checklist for Discovering Strong and Weak Living Channels," she learns that she is weak in the feeling area, and specifically she is not *expressing* warmth. The two of you agree that for the next week she will take as her task complimenting one person each day. Now, as she does this she is reminded of the importance of expressing warmth. The task becomes a daily reminder and will help her move toward her goal.

2. *Task agreements require a commitment.* It is one thing (and an important thing) to talk about how miserable it feels to be lonely. It is another thing to commit oneself to a task designed to relieve the loneliness. The lonely person makes this commitment to you—a friend. There is something very powerful about making an agreement with another person. This is true whether the commitment is made in writing or whether there is an oral agreement reached. In a sense they both provide a strength and

push from outside oneself to get the job done. One of the most helpful services you can give your friend is to be the person he/she makes an agreement with.

3. *Tasks lend concreteness to the goal.* The goal of expressing warmth is more abstract than concrete. As your friend works on specific tasks, such as complimenting others, the goal becomes more real, more manageable, and more *attainable.* A task allows a person to actually *begin with one thing* rather than worry about many things. This bolsters one's self-confidence.

4. *The attainment of any skill is based upon practice.* Many of us get into predicaments because we are not skilled enough in some area. Expressing warmth is a skill. Those who do it well have worked at it. One of the many means of expressing warmth is to give compliments. Mark Twain once said he could live two months on a good compliment. In the example given in 1, above, your friend agreed that she would compliment one person each day for a week. She will learn many things by doing this. She will become better able to separate flattery (an untruthful statement) from compliments (the truth). She will begin to learn how to respond to people who do not know how to accept compliments. She will become more aware of people as she studies them for their strengths.

TASKS THAT HELP IN EXPRESSING EMOTIONS

Some tasks have already been mentioned that help in this area, such as giving compliments, smiling, and touching. I'll explain a bit more about these last two, and then suggest some other tasks.

1. *Smiling*—A college student about twenty-one years old, whom I'll call Bob, came to talk. As we conversed together I asked him what he wanted out of life that he didn't already have. He said he wanted to be happy. I replied that this was a goal I couldn't help him with since most people who have happiness as their primary goal in life are quite miserable. He said he felt miserable and that's why he wanted to be happy. We talked about the elusive nature of happiness for awhile,[1] and then I asked him if he had any other goals in life. He said he was lonely and he wanted some friends. This seemed to be a concrete, manageable goal, so we started talking about it. Here's our conversation as I recall it (the P stands for Paul and B for Bob).

P I've noticed you hardly ever smile.

B You wouldn't smile either if you felt like I did.

P Do you think a smile is for us or for other people?

B I don't know, but I think it's hypocritical to smile if you feel lousy. [Bob was a new Christian and was working hard to get hypocrisy out of his life.]

P I respect you for not wanting to be phony. Another way of looking at it is that we can help other people's scenery a lot if we smile once in awhile.

B Maybe. I haven't looked at it that way.

P Do you think most people want to make friends with someone who is somber and unsmiling?

B I suppose not. But it seems so artificial.

P Learning to serve a tennis ball in a different way may seem mechanical and artificial. But that doesn't mean it isn't real. Smiling won't violate your integrity if you can take the point of view that it's a way of welcoming another person into your presence.

B Well, I'd be willing to try it. How do I go about it?

P What I'm going to suggest to you won't make much sense to you, because if it did, you'd have been doing it already. For the next week smile at the mirror in your room five times a day so you get the hang of it and it begins to feel more comfortable to you. Is that something you'd be willing to do?

B Yeah. I'll feel funny doing it, though.

P Well, you've been going by your feelings for quite awhile, and it hasn't been working for you. Perhaps you're about ready to do what you need to do rather than what you feel like doing. [I had known Bob previously and we had built an involvement, so I could confront him when this was needed.]

B   Well, that's true.

P   Will you stop by in three or four days and let me know how you're doing?

B   OK, I'll see you then.

Bob stopped by and said he was doing what he said he would do and that it wasn't as bad as he thought it would be. He came in a number of times after that just to chat. I noticed that smiling seemed to be more natural for him. Several months later I saw him in the Student Union with a group of other students smiling and laughing. What had begun as an agreement to perform a task ended up becoming a part of his life-style. I'm sure there were many other factors in Bob's life that helped him begin to express warmth effectively. But I'm also sure the task agreement helped, too.

Concerning the use of the mirror—I recommend it to those who really need remedial work in an area. For example, I have used it with some persons who needed help in learning to say "No." I use it myself occasionally when I become aware I am accepting too many obligations and am spreading myself too thin. I get in front of the mirror in the bedroom and look into it and say "No." I practice saying that one word until it sounds convincing. It needs to be said without an edge on the voice. If an explanation needs to be given, at least one should feel no obligation to explain the explanation. I know standing before a mirror occasionally and saying, "No" (even though it *seems* like a dumb thing to do) helps me, and that it has helped others.

2. *Touching*—we live in a world of persons who are out of touch with each other. In order to get in touch with people, we need to avoid the two extremes, one of which says, "Never touch," and the other which believes in instant closeness. Perhaps a more reasonable point of view is that we earn the right to touch, after the initial customary handshake. Now with your friend whom you are trying to help express warmth, you don't have to worry that she will turn people off by touching too much. You need to help her begin to reach out to those persons in her life she is already fairly close to.

If she is a visual learner (we'll be studying later some special ways to help visual learners), you may suggest she do a study in the four Gospels of each time Jesus touched a person. He went through his ministry touching people's bodies—and lives. Other biblical passages also legitimize touching. Christians are instructed to "Greet one another with a holy kiss."[2] When the Apostle Paul left the elders at Ephesus, "... they all wept and embraced Paul and kissed him."[3]

People should never be expected to agree to a task which violates their conscience. This is why I spend time with them in discussion to make sure the task they are agreeing to do does not seem wrong to them. It may not make much sense to them, but that's all right; in fact, that is more often the case than not. It's like using dental floss, a task mentioned above that dentists assign to reduce dental plaque. We first agree to use it, not because it makes sense to us, but because someone we trusted recommended it. When we use it, we find that the dental floss really does get material out from between our teeth that brushing cannot reach. *Then* it makes sense to us. That is the way it usually is. The insight *follows* the action.

3. *Saying feelings*—Many people have said to me, as they probably have to you, "I can't tell people my deep feelings." My usual reply is, "I understand that you believe it is impossible to share your deepest feelings with others; could it be, though, that you *could,* if you chose to? Perhaps it's not so much that you *can't,* but rather that you *won't.*" This makes sense to most people and they begin to operate from a position of strength rather than helplessness.

Most of us realize the importance of telling those close to us that we love them, but probably most of us don't *do* this or don't do it frequently enough. A recent article in the newspaper told of a nurse who worked with the dying. She related that many of the dying urged those who visited them, "Each day tell at least one person you love that you love them."

Telling persons that we love them, or that we appreciate them, or that we like them is different from complimenting them. The latter confirms their competency, achievement, or appearance. But telling persons we love them or that we like them affirms *them.* Each of us needs to receive this affirmation regularly to nourish our growth as a person.

With your friend who has difficulty expressing warmth, it is best to agree on a task that is not too ambitious. Perhaps it will seem possible for your friend to tell one person a week for a month that she respects, likes, cares for, appreciates, or loves him/her (whatever her deepest feeling is for that person). You may need to model this sharing by telling her what she means to you.

I attended a Defensive Driving Course yesterday (for college instructors who sometimes drive state cars). At one point in a lecture, the instructor said, "People drive like they live." For example, if a person is typically discourteous, he will be a discourteous driver. If he is typically considerate, he will be a considerate driver. This same point of view is probably true for helpers. We don't help any better than we live. If we don't share our deep feelings with those close to us, we can't expect that our recommendation that another person do that would have much weight.

Persons also often need practice in expressing the emotion of *anger*. If we are angry with a person and we tell him we are angry with him, this usually drains the anger away. Even if it is still there, we at least are talking about the most important thing between us at the moment, and we can deal with it.

We usually upset other persons by *showing* them our anger, which is often unnecessary. We are less likely to upset them by *telling* them exactly what they did or said that made us mad. When we have reason to believe even this may upset the other person, we may need to precede that statement with something like, "I've got something nagging at me right now, and because I care about you, I want you to know it, even though it's hard for me to share it with you."

Suppose you have a friend who gets angry but won't tell the person he's upset at that he's angry. He just holds it in and is grumpy and grouchy for several days. The people close to him are upset with his sulking, and he comes to you for help. After you have talked with him, using the approach shown in chapter twenty-nine, "Listening and Resonating," he may ask for specific help in changing the way he's reacting when he gets angry. A task that he may find useful is to pinpoint whether his next upset is caused by anger or hurt. His second task would be to tell the other person whichever emotion he experienced first. It will be important not to press your friend to agree to these tasks. It has to be his decision. He will make the decision whenever he becomes sufficiently uncomfortable with the displeasure of his friends at his sulking.

What if He Doesn't Carry Out the Task?

Your friend has agreed with you to do a certain task during the next week. He comes back one week later and says, "I couldn't bring myself to do it." What do you do then? William Glasser in his book, *Reality Therapy,* [4] has spoken effectively to this point. He says it is important neither to excuse nor to condemn the person. It usually doesn't help you to say, "Why didn't you do it?" Helpful questions might include, "Was it clear to you what you needed to do?" "Is it still a task you would like to work at?" "Where could you find the courage to do it next time?" Remember if you excuse *or* scold your friend in any way for his failure, you are to that extent taking some of his responsibility away from him.

What if He Does?

If your friend carries out the task he agreed to do, it is generally not helpful to praise him for it. It is his success and carries with it its own rewards. Some statements such as the following may help: "You did what you planned to do. How do you feel now about taking that step?" "Is it something you'd like to do regularly—to make a part of your life-style?" "How could you go about incorporating this into your life-style?"

REFERENCES

1. A helpful study on this topic is the book by Calvin Miller, *That Elusive Thing Called Joy* (Grand Rapids, Mich.: Zondervan Corporation, 1975).
2. Romans 16:16a
3. Acts 20:37
4. William Glasser, *Reality Therapy* (New York: Harper Colophon Books, 1965).

Part

C THINKING—
*Helping
Your Friend
Consider
Consequences*

17 How to Slow Down the Impulsive Person

The person who is weak in the thinking channel is typically an impulsive person. As you will notice from the drawing, the impulsive person goes directly from feeling to doing without moving through the thinking and choosing channels. If it looks good, he buys it. If it tastes good, he eats it. If it feels good, he does it. He is a creature of his feelings, and to the extent that he is controlled only by his feelings he goes through life "out of control."

Using the framework of the four ancient temperaments—sanguine, melancholic, choleric, and phlegmatic—the impulsive person fits rather well the typical

THE BYPASS

FEELING

THINKING

CHOOSING

DOING

description of the sanguine. O. Hallesby has shown in his very helpful book, *Temperament and the Christian Faith,* that the sanguine has many strengths.[1] The sanguine, like a child, lives in the present. He therefore can enjoy life and can interact in a warm, effective way with others. But there are weaknesses as well. He usually leaves unfinished many tasks that he has begun. He has good intentions, but he often forgets these intentions and his problems. Because he is a child of the moment, he is not easily able to visualize outcomes of his actions. He is open to his senses, but to some extent they control him.

As a butterfly flutters from one flower to another, so his impressionable mind flutters from one sensation to another. He enjoys them all as long as they last, but when they are driven away by new impressions, he is through with them.[2]

How can you go about slowing down the impulsive person? If you are standing near a large slippery slide and you see a little child going down the slide at such a high rate of speed that you are sure there is some danger involved, the only way you can slow him down is to get very much involved with him, for example, catching him as he goes by. In a sense the impulsive person is on a slippery slide of his own, one that is polished with his own feelings and on which, in many cases, he is headed for a very hard landing place. Some suggestions are given below for ways to begin to slow down the impulsive person. This is necessary if you are to help him. Again, we are assuming that the impulsive person is open to help, and, because of some rather hard landings, he has come to you asking for help.

REALIZE THAT A LIFE-STYLE IS HARD TO CHANGE

This first step has to do with you as the helper. It is characteristic of the impulsive person that he tends to be impatient and to lack persistence. These are traits you will need to avoid as you work with your impulsive friend. You may observe your friend going on a crash diet to lose five pounds a week for the next couple of months and then gain the weight back just as rapidly, or buying expensive things on impulse, or making a flash decision about very important matters. This style of life is deeply ingrained in the impulsive person and will require your patience and perseverance if you are to make a difference. Most people learn by imitation. Your impulsive friend will treat your life-style as a model if he/she is involved with you and respects you. Because of the power of "modeling," an underlying theme of this manual is that we help our friends as much by the kind of persons we are as by the direct aid we give.

SHOW YOUR APPRECIATION FOR STRENGTHS

As mentioned above, the impulsive, sanguine, warm person has many strengths. It is in observing these strengths that the *helper* is helped. This is why the helping process is never a one-way task. It's like a swinging door—it works both ways. As helpers we need to hold ourselves open to receiving help.

It is therefore important that you observe the life-style of your impulsive friend closely. Then begin to incorporate in your own life some of the strengths you see that would be helpful for you. The logical next step is to let your friend know that you appreciate these strengths which he has, for example, the ability to live for today and to enjoy today. Let him know that you are working at strengthening your own life-style by drawing from some of his strengths. This affirms your friend as a person, and also makes it easier for him to receive help from you.

A middle-aged man was weakening his relationship with his wife by impulsively withdrawing and becoming silent whenever his wife disagreed with him or even made suggestions to him about things he needed to do or change. As we talked together, I looked for strengths and found that he was typically a gentle person. I learned from his gentleness and told him of this strength and the help he had been to me. Then we talked about the effects of his gentle approach to his wife, compared to her reactions to his "silent treatment." In this way he became aware of one of his strengths and was able to build on it to improve his relationship with his wife.

When I was talking recently with a young man and his wife, he asked me, "How do you keep from being dumped on? You listen to so much garbage each week." I thought about that for awhile and then told him I didn't have a "dumped-on" feeling because I learned something from every person I worked with. Then I told him the things I had learned from him and his wife. They were both surprised they had helped me. They had been much more aware of their weaknesses than their strengths.

EXPLAIN THE WAY YOU HELP

Your friend will likely come to you for help, as most impulsive persons do, when he has gotten himself into some predicament because of his shortsightedness. You need to do what you can to help your friend out of that immediate predicament. Then you need to clarify the way you can be most helpful. One way is by pointing out to your friend that you have observed that he sometimes makes decisions without thinking where these decisions will land him, much in the same way one might jump off the platform of a slippery slide onto the slide without looking at the bottom of the slide to see whether it has a hard or soft landing. Let your friend know that you feel you can be of help to him if he will talk with you about the decisions he is planning to make. He will still have the responsibility for those decisions, because you won't tell him what to do. However, just talking about the decision may help him to get a better understanding of the outcomes and consequences that he is committed to by making the decision.

ASK FOR A COMMITMENT TO CHANGE

When your impulsive friend comes to you and asks for help, and you help in whatever way you can to assist him in the immediate predicament, then there is another important step. You need to ask him if this way of living is working for him, that is, making impulsive decisions and finding the landings are hard. If he says that he wants to change his life-style and wants to think through the outcomes prior to taking action, then you will need to point out that it will take very hard work to change. Sometimes a statement like, "This may be the hardest work you have ever done," is helpful in letting impulsive persons count the cost. Otherwise, it is possible for them to embark on this venture in the same lighthearted impulsive fashion in which they begin other ventures. So questions like, "Are you *sure* you want to work at this?" may serve to secure an oral contract that will increase perseverance. And if your friend replies, "No, I'm not sure," then don't push for a commitment. He has to be *ready* to change before he can successfully bring about this move away from impulsiveness.

DO NOT ACCEPT IRRESPONSIBLE STATEMENTS AND ACTIONS

The impulsive person tends to blame circumstances for his unwelcome predicaments. He sometimes sees bad outcomes as just "happening." Sometimes he may blame them on fate. Sometimes he may blame them on God. If from your point of view the consequences are very natural, based on his actions, it is important to provide him with this information. This needs to be done, not in a blaming way or with an edge on your voice. Rather you need to point out in a matter of fact, natural way that it seems clear enough to you why the action which he took got him into the predicament that he is in now. And you need to line these out in a chronological, cause-effect way. Remember that the impulsive person often fails to connect cause and effect, so you need to review consequences with him from time to time.

PROVIDE ENCOURAGEMENT

The impulsive person is easily discouraged. He can go all the way from full speed ahead to a grinding halt in a few moments' time. Therefore, at times he will need help in slowing down his out-of-control, careening life-style; at other times he will need help starting up again when he has crashed head-on with a predicament or crisis. Remember that encouragement means your friend gains *courage* from being with you. He's then willing to go at it again and take risks when necessary to reach his goal. He will draw courage from your presence and from your affirming him as a person.

REFERENCES

1. O. Hallesby, *Temperament and the Christian Faith* (Minneapolis, Minn.: Augsburg Publishing House, 1962).
2. *Ibid.*, p. 23.

18 Straightening Out Crooked Thinking

The impulsive person is weak in the thinking channel. But this does not mean he is unintelligent. Rather it means he is often bypassing this channel in his daily living. How can you help your friend change his thinking and strengthen and use this channel? One method that has proven to be workable is to react to what the impulsive person says. If what your friend says appears to be based on faulty thinking, then you need to challenge the statement.

Again it needs to be said that this manual is based on the involvement that you already have with your friend. You would not be able to confront your friend in such a way if you did not have an existing involvement. But since you do have an involvement it is usually safe to assume that this involvement can sustain such a confrontation as this, and that in fact the straight feedback may increase the involvement.

Albert Ellis, founder of Rational Emotive Therapy, has been a leader in using counseling efforts to straighten out crooked thinking.[1] William Glasser's Reality Therapy approach also uses this method as one aspect of treatment.[2]

I Don't Know What Got into Me

Sometimes the impulsive person makes a statement that disclaims responsibility for an act. Such a statement is, "I don't know what got into me." This statement is similar to "The devil made me do it." The implication is "I did not tell myself to do it, therefore I am not responsible." You may wish to reply to statements that are disclaimers of responsibility in a way similar to this, "Right now you are sorry you did what you did because of the mess you got yourself into, but it seems to me that it wasn't some strange force that made you do it, you simply *chose* to do it." You need to say this in a matter of fact rather than an accusing way, if it is to be accepted. The main thing to be aware of here is that you do not accept the point of view of the impulsive person that he was *driven* to do the act without having time to think or freedom to choose.

Blaming Doesn't Help

The impulsive person often tends to blame others and to blame himself. Again, this activity is usually a genuine reflection of his point of view. He has difficulty tracing cause and effect, so he tends to confuse cause and blame. If an alcoholic friend of yours says to you, "I wouldn't drink if my wife didn't nag me so much," you may reply that he drinks because *he chooses to,* or because he is addicted, and there is probably little or no cause and effect relationship between his wife's nagging and his drinking.

Why Did I Do That?

The impulsive person wants to know, in the most genuine way, why he acts impulsively. The answer is that he failed to consider the outcome of his action. An answer like this is usually truthful and it avoids the past orientation of a why question. Trying to figure out what *motivated* the impulsive person to do what he did is usually a waste of time. This is because all behavior is multiply-caused and one can never be sure that all of the causes are clear. Holding the impulsive person responsible for the choices he makes at first may seem harsh, but as a matter of fact it helps the impulsive person to begin to find he has control of his life. He chooses to do the things he does.

Truth-in-Labeling

It is important to label a behavior or a behavior pattern accurately. To refer to a behavior as "impulsive" may help your friend see this tendency in a new light. Such terms as "shoplifting" need to be labeled "stealing," and "having an affair" needs to be called "adultery." A good guideline is simply to label the behavior as accurately and as simply as possible, without pulling any punches.

There are those who oppose the word "adultery," because it takes a moral position. But, as a matter of fact, the word "affair" also presupposes a moral stance. The moral position suggested by this description of sex outside marriage is that it is not related to morality. This is, of course, a moral judgment.

Mention a Pattern

If your friend mentions an incident in which he arrived late for an appointment and makes an excuse for it, then it is important for you to challenge that statement if you have observed that lateness is habitual with your friend. A response such as the following might be helpful, "I've noticed that lateness is a pattern with you. Is this a pattern that you want to change?" Comments and questions such as these help the impulsive person to "see" the picture. And the impulsive person needs help in doing this.

Impulsiveness may be observed with some children in their reading. The impulsive child may read "hunger" as "hungry" or "books" as "book," because he concentrated only on the first part of the word. In his rush to get through the reading task, he failed to take in the "big picture." (The caution needs to be given here that not all children who consistently miss the endings of words are impulsive. Some have difficulty controlling the fine muscles of the eyes so the right-sweep of the eyes is faulty. Others may have laterality difficulties.) Such a child needs help in slowing down. He usually can't do it by himself. The same is true of fast-moving adults.

Talk About Making It Right

If your impulsive friend comes to you for help and talks about getting into a situation in which his actions were harmful to others close to him, you need to challenge him concerning his obligations. One reason that Alcoholics Anonymous has been so useful is that one of its principles is *restitution.* One of the other major approaches dealing with restitution is O. Hobart Mowrer's Integrity Therapy. An Integrity Therapy approach may be something like this example mentioned by Dr. Mowrer, "All right now! You've dumped your garbage. What are you going to *do* about it? How are you going to clean it up?"[3] This is a pretty straightforward way of saying that restitution is necessary.

Making it right benefits not only the person wronged but also the impulsive person. The impulsive person feels guilty, of course, after he has hurt a person close to him. Then if no restitution is made he usually feels the ill will of that person. He may receive the quiet treatment, or get yelled at, or in some other way feel some bad effects from the transaction. As a result his guilt is taken care of and he no longer feels badly about the situation, so he is ready to go back and do a similar impulsive act. When he *makes it right* with the other person, then he bypasses this entire game.

A Common Trait

It's worthwhile reminding ourselves that the person whose life-style is characterized by impulsiveness is not a different kind of person than others. He just has more of the trait that each of us has to battle every day. In working to overcome impulsiveness in my own life, I've found it helps to say aloud the following poem (only part of the poem is given here).

Slow Me Down

Slow me down, Lord, I'm going too fast;
I can't see my brother when he's walking past.
I miss a lot of good things day by day,
I don't know a blessing when it comes my way...
Slow me down, Lord, slow me down to a walk.[4]

REFERENCES

1. Following are three sources that explain the rational-emotive therapy approach: a) Albert Ellis, *Reason and Emotion in Psychotherapy* (New York: Lyle Stuart, 1962); Albert Ellis, *Growth Through Reason: Verbatim Cases in Rational-Emotive Therapy* (Palo Alto: Science and Behavior Books, 1971); and Albert Ellis and R. A. Harper, *A Guide to Rational Living* (Englewood Cliffs, N.J.: Prentice Hall; and Hollywood, Calif.: Wilshire Books, 1971). Dr. Ellis in his writings is very much against the concepts of sin and guilt. He also opposes the use of "should," "ought," and "must." He prefers phrases such as "it is better to." But given the dogmatic statements with which many rational-emotive therapists put down religion, and with their encouragement of sexual relationships outside marriage, rational-emotive therapy turns out to be about as neutral as a bumper sticker.

2. William Glasser's teachings about Reality Therapy may be studied in the following books: *Reality Therapy* (New York: Harper Colophon Books, Harper and Row, 1965); *Schools Without Failure* (New York: Harper and Row, Publishers, 1969); *The Identity Society* (New York: Harper and Row, 1971). Most of the major therapies cover only one or at the most two of the living channels. For example, Client-Centered Therapy, as formulated by Carl Rogers, focuses primarily on the feeling channel. So does Gestalt Therapy as conceptualized by Dr. Fritz Perls. Transactional Analysis, propounded by Eric Berne, focuses, since it is an analytical therapy, on the thinking channel. Behavioral Therapy focuses on the doing channel. Reality Therapy, by contrast, focuses on three of the channels: thinking, choosing, and doing. This may be why it is the therapy approach that has earned the broadest acceptance in the public and private schools of our country.

3. O. Hobart Mowrer, "Integrity Groups: Principles and Procedures," *The Counseling Psychologist*, Vol. 3, No. 2, 1972, p. 20.
   Mowrer's paperback book, *The New Group Therapy* (Princeton: D. Van Nostrand Company, Inc., 1964), is helpful in providing guidelines for

Integrity Therapy, although he does not call his method by this name in the book. My own view of Mowrer is that he is a much better psychologist than a theologian. Although he does not particularly claim competence in the latter area, he discusses theology a great deal in his writings. As I understand him, he believes that Christians are too "Christocentric" in their point of view, thus leaving out people of other religions or no religion. But in his efforts to make the redemptive aspect of Christianity fit all these points of view, he misunderstands the central Christian doctrine of redemption through the substitutionary death and resurrection of Christ, a doctrine which Jesus himself taught.

But just as we go to a biblical commentary for the facts which it gives, not for the conclusions to which it comes, so we can go to Ellis and Mowrer for the important psychological understandings which they have. I like the old rhyme,

Read all the books upon the shelf,

But do all your thinking for yourself.

This, by the way, is a point of view that I urge you to take as you study *this* manual.

4. From the poem, "Slow Me Down," Anonymous.

19 Teaching Your Friend How to Plan

My weakest channel in my growing-up days was in the area of thinking. My first year in college I worked as a houseboy in a sorority, and for that effort I received my meals and $10 a month. I applied the $10 on the rent for a room where I was living. With the little money I had saved I could just barely get by. One day I was downtown and saw a ballpoint pen that I liked. Ballpoint pens cost more then and this was a very good one. In fact, it cost $12.50. I impulsively bought that pen and then spent the rest of the month wondering, "Why did I do that?"

I was the youngest in our family and it is my observation that the youngest member of a family is a bit more likely to be impulsive and to fail to plan ahead. The youngest member of the family, more than the other children, expects people to do things for him because he grows up surrounded by older, bigger, and more able people. At any rate, it seemed to me I had to work harder than most to reach the point where I was taking the initiative and planning ahead.

TWO WAYS OF THINKING AHEAD

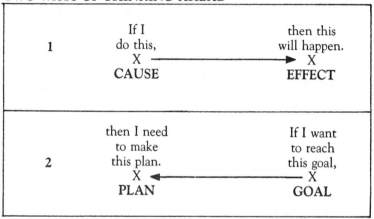

The person who is strong in the thinking channel is able to do two things well. He can go from cause to effect and visualize what the *outcomes* of his actions will be. He can also think backwards from a goal to a *plan* for reaching that goal. These two efforts require thinking in both directions—forwards and backwards. The person who is weak in the thinking channel is weak in both of these. We have worked in the last two chapters on helping a friend slow down and think through the results of his behavior. In working with the impulsive person, it is also helpful to encourage that person to state a goal and then to think back toward the present in establishing a plan. The following guidelines have been beneficial in doing this.

Tell Me Your Dream

The impulsive person needs a strong enough goal in the future to motivate him to plan carefully to reach that goal. One of the questions I ask persons who come to me for help is some form of the question, "What do you want out of life?" Another way of putting it is "What kind of life do you want?" or "Would you be willing to share your dream with me?" I did this just last week with a graduate student who replied, "Yes, I'll share my dream, and it's something I've only shared with two or three other people." Then he went on to share the kind of life he wanted ten years from now. You may have to phrase the question in several different ways, but the chances are you'll get an answer, because most people want a chance to share their dream.

What Is Your Plan?

William Glasser has written in a helpful way concerning the value of asking for a plan. He tells of his counseling sessions with a young man who wanted to recount his failures of the past in great detail.

> Instead I took the initiative. I asked him to tell me his plan (a favorite Reality Therapy question). Asking him for his plan tells him that he should have a plan, or at least start thinking of one, putting him in a position where, instead of unburdening his troubles, he should begin some constructive thinking about what he is doing right now and about his future. He reacted typically by asking, "What plan, what do you have in mind?" I said, "Well, here you are at college. You must have a plan, or a goal, some place you are heading for, some idea of how to get there."[1]

A plan is the bridge that connects the dream to the reality. Now there is something romantic-sounding and attractive about a dream. And the achievement of that dream is very attractive. But a plan? A

THE BRIDGE

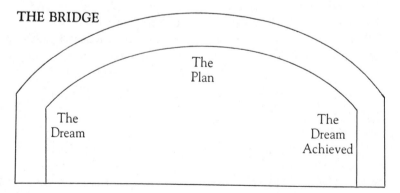

The
Plan

The
Dream

The
Dream
Achieved

plan sounds less attractive, somewhat tedious, hum-drum, and not particularly interesting. But a plan is what makes it all possible. And it need not be boring. There is nearly always adventure between a dream and the achieving of that dream. The purpose of a plan is to make the adventure successful.

Setting Up a Plan

To set up an effective plan, your friend will need your help to visualize his dream as specifically as possible. He will need to "image" the hoped-for outcome as fully and sharply as possible, perhaps using some of the methods discussed in chapter thirty-six, "Imagine That! The Use of Images." For example, let's suppose you have a friend who, although he has many fine characteristics, is quite impulsive. He is twenty-three years old, married and has one child, loves cars, and is deeply in debt. Both he and his wife have steady jobs, but periodically he buys a car on impulse, or buys sports accessories for his car. He comes to you for help because his marriage is getting shaky. His wife has told him to "grow up" and to use his money for rent and groceries.

During the conversation you ask him what it is he wants out of life—what his dream is. He may reply that he hasn't thought about this, or he may say, "I'd really like to have this neat Corvette I saw the other day!" You realize you have a tough one on your hands. You may have to shock him to do some serious thinking with a reply like, "I can't help you if your goal in life is just to get a different kind of machine. What kind of *life* do you want? Are you satisfied with your relationship with your wife and child?" If he still talks about cars, you may need to tell him that it sounds like he is not ready to make a change yet. If he does talk about wanting to get along better with his wife or have her get along better with him, try to get him to specify what this would mean. Suppose he says, "Well, for one thing, it would mean she would stop nagging me about money all the time." Now you have something specific to go on, and you can reply, "What is your plan for changing the way you do things so that you eventually will have enough money to meet the needs of your family?" The plan may include the idea that each partner in the marriage be given veto power over any expenditure $25 and higher. It may include putting a small amount in savings each month. Or agreeing to visit with a financial counselor. Loan officers in banks and credit unions are excellent sources for professional financial advice. You will need to help your friend establish a time line, by asking questions such as: "When would you like to be out of debt?" or "How long do you think it will take you to have enough money each month to meet your household needs?" Another question worth asking is, "How far on the way to your dream do you want to be one year from now?" Or, for a very impulsive person who can't think that far ahead, "... six months (or one month) from now?" Thinking through the answer to this question enables your friend to move backwards toward the present and begin to think more concretely in terms of the initiative he is going to need to take.

Can You Do It?

Questions like the following can help provide determination: "This plan is going to take a lot of work. Are things bad enough that you're willing to put out the necessary time and energy to improve them in this way?" "Is this plan realistic—is it going to be possible for you to carry it out?" At this point some will say they don't want to do it or they don't think they can. It is important not to urge them because they will not succeed if they don't think they can make it.

Another question that may prove beneficial is "What do you need to be doing now in order to proceed toward your goal?" The identification of this first step is extremely important. It should be clear and specific enough so that your friend knows when it is done. Finishing the first step is a strong reinforcer. Another question is "From whom do you need help?" This tells your friend he need not be alone in his plan and venture. As a friend you are in a good position to make other helping persons and agencies available.

REFERENCES

1. William Glasser, *Reality Therapy* (New York: Harper Colophon Books, Harper and Row, 1965), p. 37.

Part

D

CHOOSING—
Helping
Your Friend
Respond
Decisively

20 Approaching the Indecisive Person

You have a friend who comes to you for help. Your friend has some special problem or is in a predicament or crisis and wants your assistance in getting out of it. You can be fairly sure this predicament is not an isolated situation but is only an outgrowth of your friend's life-style. As was pointed out earlier, this is not always the case, because sometimes circumstances do occur or things happen over which we have no control. Probably most predicaments, however, are of our own making.

An important guideline used in this manual is that we must be *with* a person before we can do anything *for* that person. Being with your friend means that you listen desperately to what your friend is saying. You make no attempt to give any pat answers or easy solutions or advice. Being with your friend requires that you listen in such a way and respond in an accurate enough manner that your friend knows that he is being deeply understood. After you have worked through this first stage of being with your friend, and hearing him out, usually he will begin to want to move toward some kind of action.

Based on what you know about your friend, you may have already concluded that he or she is weak in the choosing channel. You may have shared the "Checklist for Discovering Strong and Weak Living Channels."

PINPOINTING THE SOURCE OF INDECISION

Once you have made the initial determination that your friend is weak in the choosing channel, you need to decide which of the three areas—meaning, values, or moral standards—is the weakest. This will enable you to help your friend fulfill his or her greatest needs. It is important to realize that these areas of the choosing channel overlap each other. The checklist will enable you to make a good guess about the weak area of the choosing channel. Items 1, 2, 4, 6, 11, and 12 of the checklist have to do with the whole area of meaning. Items 3 and 8, if not checked, indicate that there may not be a well-developed set of moral standards. Items 5 and 10 relate to values.

During the time you are establishing the specific area of the choosing channel that your friend needs help in, you will be assisting in helping him or her get out of the *immediate* predicament. A helpful guideline here is that your friend usually will find the way out of the immediate predicament by finding the *courage* to make the decision that needs to be made. It will be important for you to talk with your friend in terms of the concept of *life-style* and how the way we are living may involve us in predicaments. To avoid future predicaments we need to consider *changing* the way we live.

When your friend has made some progress in getting out of his or her immediate predicament, you are ready to begin helping with life-style change. It is important not to wait until the person has gotten completely out of the predicament, or else the motivation to change life-style may be decreased. Based on the specific area of change needed, you can find guidelines in one of the three chapters that follow, which deal with the search for meaning, clarifying and ordering values, and developing a set of moral standards.

CHARACTERISTICS OF THE INDECISIVE PERSON

There are several characteristics of indecisive persons that require one to relate with them in a special way. Traits that go with indecision include worry, dependence, and wavering (second-guessing oneself).

Worry

It isn't worth trying to figure out whether indecision causes one to worry, or whether worry causes one to be indecisive. Probably there is a circular effect. At any rate, the indecisive person is usually worried, sometimes edgy, and on occasion, panicky.

So what does this mean for the person who is trying to help? Well, for one thing it means that it doesn't work to say to the indecisive person, "Don't worry about it," because that just gives him one more thing to worry about. In fact, this particular admonition is not an effective one to give anybody. It's like ordering someone to stop crying.

We need to have peace and confidence in our own life. The worried person draws calm, not from our advice, but from us—from our *presence.* Can you think now of a time when you were worried, and the calming effect that the presence of a strong, peaceful person had on you? You can provide that presence for a person who comes to you for help.

Dependence

The indecisive person is usually excessively dependent on others for decision-making. He likes (and also sometimes resents) others' help in making choices. Looking back, I can see this characteristic in my own life. When I was about twenty or twenty-one, I frequently went to see Rev. Henry Weinberg, a retired seventy-five-year-old minister.

I thought it was "just to talk." Really, it was to get him to help me
with decisions I needed to make. Finally, one time after Henry (he
preferred "Henry" to "Rev. Weinberg") had sensed that I wanted
him to take the responsibility for my decisions, he said, "Paul, I'm
glad to talk with you, but you have to make your own decisions. I have
enough responsibility just making the decisions I have to make." That
straightforward statement, said in a gentle way, put some steel into
me. I found it more possible to make decisions after that.

So what I learned about helping from Henry was to open myself
to talk with others about the decision they needed to make, but not
to take away that important responsibility of *making* the choice. This
requires considerable strength and insight, because some persons push
hard and subtly. The ones who push the hardest are the ones who are
the most frightened of making a decision all by themselves.

The dependent person is often manipulative and may arouse the
ire of friends who want to help. Some see such manipulation as a
game and spend a considerable amount of time trying to give the
manipulator some insights about the games he is playing. I've never
found this approach very helpful. Most of the people I've observed
who analyze games get caught up in the game of analyzing and are less
helpful because of that than they might otherwise be. A more effective
approach is to give a straightforward "No" to a dependent person
who is trying to manipulate you into taking responsibility for his life.

Wavering (Second-Guessing Oneself)

The indecisive person fits the description of the doubter, given
in James 1:6-8:

> But let him ask in faith, with no doubting, for he who doubts is
> like a wave of the sea that is driven and tossed by the wind. For
> that person must not suppose that a double-minded man, unstable in
> all his ways, will receive anything from the Lord.

The ambivalent person leans one direction, then a new piece of
information arrives and he leans the other. The reason he is
leaning all the time is that he doesn't step out, he doesn't commit
himself in either direction; so since he doesn't move, he just leans.

The wavering person is thus characterized by a lack of
commitment. Are there special ways of working with persons who
lack this characteristic? First, you may expect his call for help to be

uncertain. He may come to you asking for help in some predicament, and may even want help in strengthening his choosing channel. The next day or next week he may have changed his mind. Knowing this in advance will help you accept him in his changeableness. Also it may keep you from taking it personally if he seems at first to want your help and then rejects it. You will understand that this changed attitude is more likely a function of his second-guessing himself than of anything you have done.

The most difficult aspect of working with this person is to get him to decide exactly what he wants to change and to follow through on his plan for change. Decisions and stick-to-it-iveness come hard to the second-guesser..So what does this mean to you? It means that your friend needs to encounter in you a person who does not waver back and forth and who is strong enough to lean on—for support, not decisions. Have you ever leaned on a post which was not firmly embedded in the ground? The harder you lean, the less support it gives. We need to provide a steadying influence.

You can also ask questions if your friend begins working on a plan and then changes his mind, such as: "You chose to do this and now you've changed your mind. What new evidences caused you to make a different decision?" "Do you think this reversing of your decision could be an example of the indecisiveness you are wanting to change?" It is important that the tone of such questions be matter-of-fact rather than persuasive. He needs to learn to make his decisions on solid information rather than because people are pushing him.

21 Encouraging the Search for Meaning

A person who lacks meaning in life does not have a basis for making important decisions. The decision to continue living is based on courage. One person called me at night and said, "I have a bottle of sleeping pills in my hand and I'm thinking of committing suicide. I almost had the courage to do it awhile ago and then I chickened out." After I thought a bit, I reminded the caller that it did not require courage to take the bottle of sleeping pills; it took courage to make the decision *not* to take the pills—to keep on living even when life seemed to have no meaning. At this point we began to build an involvement and he was willing to start a deeper search for meaning.

The same element—discouragement—that offers a clue that meaning is lacking in a person's life, also provides a starting point in helping your friend. What do you do with a discouraged person? You encourage him. A person who is discouraged lacks courage. To encourage someone is to provide him with courage. How is this done?

HOW TO ENCOURAGE

Rudolf Dreikurs has written in a most helpful way concerning encouragement.[1] He had said that although the ability to encourage is a prerequisite to any constructive influence with another person, most people have very poor skills in this area.

> We all know how to discourage; we find it easy to criticize and look down on others. But when faced with the need to encourage, we are clumsy and often do the opposite. We do not know where to start.[2]

Dreikurs has also pointed out that we must observe how the person reacts to our "encouragement." Although what he says relates primarily to children, the same principle applies to working with youth and adults.

> The same words spoken to two different children may encourage one and dishearten the other. For instance, telling the child how well he has done may lead one to increased self-confidence and stimulate further effort, while another may think this was just an accident and never in the future will he be able to do as well again. Therefore, encouragement requires constant observation of the effect. How to encourage cannot be learned in a mechanical way. It is more than a single action; it expresses the whole interrelationship between the persons.[3]

It is helpful to take a look at what encouragement is *not.* Encouragement is not urging. Sometimes, we may use the word *encourage* when we mean *urge,* as in the sentence, "I encouraged him to make the decision." Urging is rarely helpful. The reason for this is that it almost always creates resistance. As noted earlier, if you have had anybody come up behind you and push you with his hands against your back, you have noticed that your usual reaction is to dig your heels in and stay put. Psychological pushing usually accomplishes the same result.

Encouragement is not reassurance. Reassurance is an attempt to make someone feel better by telling him "Things are OK," or "Things will turn out OK." Reassurance is generally not helpful and can actually be harmful. If we tell somebody that things are OK when they are not OK, this only tends to confuse the other person. If we try to predict the future and tell that person things will turn out OK and, in fact, they turn out badly, this may tend to disillusion the other person and decrease the involvement between the two of us.

Let's suppose a high school friend has just confided in you what she would like to tell her parents in order to have a better relationship with them. A reply using the urging method might be "I think you should talk to them. Why don't you do it tonight?" A reply using the reassurance technique might be: "I'm sure if you would talk to them, they wouldn't get mad at you." An encouraging reply might be: "I can see you having the courage to sit down and talk with your parents just as you did with me."

Encouragement does not minimize the risk involved in an action. An encouraging remark might be "I can see that would be a risky thing to do. Could you find the courage to give it a try?" It is helpful in giving encouragement to point out the double risk that is inherent in most situations. For example, if you are talking to a good friend and he tells you that he has worked at the same place for some time without a raise, but he is afraid to talk to his boss, it may be helpful to reply in a way similar to this: "It sounds as though you're afraid to run the risk of losing your job if you ask your boss for a raise; on the other hand, if you don't, is it possible that you run the risk of continuing to build up resentment and putting yourself down for not taking action?"

The point that Dreikurs made is a good one. We must know our friend well enough to know what kind of remark would be encouraging and what kind would be discouraging. Remember that any two people may react exactly opposite. The essential thing is to find the approach that will enable our friend to face the risks squarely.

MY OWN SEARCH FOR MEANING

I don't know for sure how it is for others in their quest for meaning, but I know in my own search there were three factors involved. First there was a need for *identity*. I needed to know who I was. Then there was a need for a *relationship*. I needed a sense of belonging. The third thing I was looking for was a *cause*. I needed to belong not only to a person but to a cause. In the midst of my own search, a newly found friend shared with me the meaning that coming to know Jesus Christ had for him. I then began to study the Bible and particularly the life of Christ. I began to understand why Jesus had come to earth and had lived and died. The resurrection took on a brand new meaning to me. In short, I made a personal decision for Christ and committed my life to him. I began to identify myself as a member of the family of God. I saw myself as having been created in the image of God and redeemed by Jesus. And while I perceived creation and redemption as being an experience I held in common with others, yet I realized that God was no rubber stamp creator, and that I was as unique as my fingerprints. My identity thus became increasingly clear to me. The second part of my search, the quest for a relationship, was fulfilled by my entering into this relationship with God and into a fellowship of persons I began to see as my brothers and sisters. As Dr. Robert Manley, a Nebraska historian, has pointed out, the most important community is not a geographical community but is a community of those with similar values and beliefs. The third aspect of my search for meaning was a cause. I found this cause to be sharing the message and the love of Jesus Christ.

This then is the story of my own life journey when I was in the middle of my own search for meaning. I share it because it has determined the beliefs behind my own counseling style. I think a manual on helping has to be deeply personal. The helping relationship involves two people, each of whom has to be uniquely himself or herself.

HOW ABOUT YOUR SEARCH FOR MEANING?

If you have been deeply involved in your own search for meaning, then you are in a position to assist another person with his or her search for meaning. However, if you have been so busy with day-to-day living that you have not entered into a deep search for what life is all about, for your own identity, for a significant relationship and a cause, then it is doubtful if you can help another person with such a search. We cannot give what we do not have. If someone comes to us for help in the search for meaning, and we have not been involved deeply in this search of ourselves then we should do what we need to do in any helping area in which we lack confidence or skills. In such a case we need to refer the person to someone else who can help.

Questions Involving Daily Meaning

I have sometimes found it helpful to others in their own quest for meaning to ask them questions regarding their activities that have meaning for them right now. These would include such questions as the following:
1. What have you done today that has had the most meaning for you?
2. What relationship has the most meaning for you?
3. What meaning does your job have for you?
4. What do you do when you don't have to do anything?

Questions Involving Personal Goals

There are a number of questions that may be asked with profit concerning goals. These need to be asked in a matter-of-fact way, with goodwill, and with no intent to corner the person. Rather, the intent should be to teach. Questions may include ones similar to the following:
1. From your point of view, what seems important enough to live for?
2. What do you expect will be most important in your life five years from now?
3. If you had what you really wanted in life, what would you have?
4. What future goal, if you could achieve it, would result in your life being filled with meaning?
5. What is your dream?
These last two steps, which involve questions about meaning, employ the method of Socrates. His mission in life was helping people in the marketplace to examine their lives. Sometimes he even helped people who didn't ask for it. He discusses his approach in

his "Apology," as recorded by Plato.[4] He tells the jury what they can expect from him in the future if they permit him to go free.

> I shall go on saying, in my usual way, "My very good friend, you are an Athenian and belong to a city which is the greatest and most famous in the world for its wisdom and strength. Are you not ashamed that you give your attention to acquiring as much money as possible, and similarly with reputation and honor, and give no attention or thought to truth and understanding and the perfection of your soul?" And if any of you disputes this and professes to care about these things, I shall not at once let him go or leave him; no, I shall question him and examine him and test him; and if it appears that in spite of his profession he has made no real progress towards goodness, I shall reprove him for neglecting what is of supreme importance, and giving his attention to trivialities.[5]

It can be seen by Socrates' words, that his questions had as much to do with moral standards and with values as with a search for meaning. As was pointed out earlier, these areas in the choosing channel overlap. Now Socrates' approach differs in at least two respects from ours. In the first place, he often talked with strangers in the marketplace. Our approach is built on a relationship with a friend. In the second place, you can see from his questions that he tended to bring people up rather sharply. This approach is necessary sometimes. We need to say very directly, and sometimes in a way that gets the person's attention, whatever it is we have to say. However, in a friendly relationship, a more friendly approach is usually better accepted.

Where There Is a Sense of Failure

Many people feel as though they are failures and that therefore life lacks meaning. It is rarely helpful to try to convince a friend that he is not a failure when he feels as though he is. It is more effective to make a statement such as the following, "I can understand from your point of view that you see yourself as a failure," and then take the following two steps:

1. Ask a question such as, "All right, so you see yourself as a failure; if you became a successful person, would life be full of meaning for you?" Then introduce Victor Frankl's diagram showing the

relationship between failure and success, and despair and meaning. Frankl saw the line running from failure to success as being in a different plane altogether than the line running from despair to meaning. Therefore, just because one would see himself as farther right on the line (that is, would identify himself as a successful person), this would not necessarily mean that he would be any higher on the vertical line (that is, regard his life as being more filled with meaning). A simple diagram like this that you can draw on a napkin when you are having coffee, for example, often provides your friend with an image that he can remember. This is particularly true if your friend is strong in the visual channel.

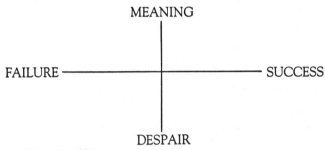

From Victor Frankl[6]

2. If your friend sees himself as a failure, and if you have a strong involvement with him, you may wish to ask the question, "What is your plan for becoming successful?" Often the answer comes out rather vague, because the person who has built a failure pattern typically lacks concreteness. You may use further questions to help your friend become more and more concrete. These questions may include, "Yes, but what will be your first step?" and "What is one activity you could do today or tomorrow that would move you toward becoming successful?"

Meaning—Invented or Discovered?

We discover the law of gravity. We invent an airplane wing with the correct slope to fly. We discover the electrical impulses that control the rhythmic heartbeat. We invent a pacemaker to provide these impulses when the central nervous system is unable for some reason to supply the necessary energy and signals.

Do we discover or invent meaning in our lives? Frankl refers to Jean-Paul Sartre, who believes that man designs what he should be or what he ought to become. Frankl disagrees. He says, "However, I think the meaning of our existence is not invented by ourselves, but rather detected."[7] My own experience tells me Frankl is right. I could not invent meaning for my life, but there came a time when, through the witness of a friend and through Bible study, I discovered or "detected" meaning. One of the most effective ways you can assist your friend is to encourage him in his quest as he seeks to discover meaning in life.

REFERENCES

1. Rudolf Dreikurs, *Psychology in the Classroom* (New York: Harper & Row, Publishers, Second Edition, 1968).
2. *Ibid.*, p. 64.
3. *Ibid.*, p. 65.
4. Plato, *The Last Days of Socrates* (Baltimore: Penguin Books, 1969).
5. *Ibid.*, p. 61.
6. Victor E. Frankl, *Psychotherapy and Existentialism: Selected Papers on Logotherapy* (New York: Simon and Schuster, 1967), p. 27.
7. Victor E. Frankl, *Man's Search for Meaning* (New York: A Clarion Book, Simon and Schuster, 1959), p. 101.

22 Aiding in the Discovery and Owning of Values

Your friend may have worked through the issues of identity, relationship, and a cause, and consequently have found meaning in life. However, he may still have excessive difficulty in making decisions if he is not aware of his *value system* or if he has not clarified and owned his values. I'm speaking here not of the core value in life which gives life meaning but of all the other values in life which are a part of everyday living.

A young minister recalled his days as a college athlete, and spoke honestly of how he valued the recognition he gained from his achievements in several different sports. He was having difficulty deciding whether to continue in the ministry or change his vocation to coaching, in which he might again gain recognition for his achievement. His integrity enabled him to own a value (the need for recognition) which otherwise might have continued to be his blind spot. A "blind spot" value is one which influences our behavior without our being aware of it.

Milton Rokeach has spent most of his adult life studying human values. He has given thousands of value surveys to people in different cultures and has analyzed and reported his results.[1] He gets at the meaning of the term with the following succinct sentence, "To say that a person has a value is to say that cognitively he knows the correct way to behave or the correct end-state to strive for."[2] Therefore, Rokeach divides values into desirable modes of conduct (instrumental values) and desirable end-states of existence (terminal values). Instrumental values are similar to personality characteristics such as "courageous," "independent," "loving," and "responsible." Terminal values include "a comfortable life," "happiness," "salvation," and "wisdom." It can be seen immediately that both instrumental values and terminal values play a large role in determining our life-style.

The approach we are taking in this manual is that most of us get into predicaments and crises, not because of some experiences in our preschool years, but rather because of the way we are living right now. And specifically because of a weak living channel—feeling, thinking, choosing, or doing. In this chapter we are focusing on how to strengthen a friend's choosing channel by helping that person in the area of values. If one has not discovered his values, he cannot make good decisions, because he is being pushed around by forces which are hidden to him. Also if most of his values are of equal importance to him there is no way he can make a value-based decision. If a man with a family is offered a promotion every two or three years, each involving a move to a different city, decisions become very important to him—and his family. It may be that some of his moves will enhance the family, and some will have a negative effect on the family. In the latter case he is faced with two values and he must choose one as the higher priority—work or family. Now obviously there are other questions involved here, such as how are decisions made in the family? Does the wife have an important part in the decision? But central to the decision is the value system of the person(s) involved in the choice.

How can you help an indecisive friend discover and own his or her values? This process can be an interesting adventure.

WAYS TO HELP A FRIEND DISCOVER AND OWN VALUES

During the years many different aids to discovering and owning values have come to my attention. I've tried many of them with myself and others, and have settled on three which have been most useful to me personally, and which I've been able to use in assisting a client or friend.

"Twenty Things I Love to Do"—A Way to Discover Values

The procedure for using the exercise, "Twenty Things I Love to Do," and the coding marks involved are given in Appendix A. I have modified the exercise somewhat from that described by Sidney Simon.

You will need to work through this exercise yourself before you use it to help a friend. The purpose of the exercise is to evoke—bring to an awareness level—our values. So you may discover (as I did) some values you didn't know you had. Your own experience with the exercise will help you to recommend it to a friend with confidence, and to discuss it in a meaningful way after your friend has worked through it.

"The Rokeach Value Survey"[3]—A Way to Own Values

Milton Rokeach, who is mentioned at the beginning of this chapter, developed his Value Survey after many years of work. This survey is copyrighted and may be purchased from Halgren Tests, 873 Persimmon Ave., Sunnyvale, California 94087. The price per copy at the time of this writing is 40¢. This price is subject to change, of course. I think it's a bargain. It consists of two lists of eighteen values each—one a list of Terminal Values and the other a list of Instrumental Values. The values themselves are on tabs which are to be pulled off and arranged in rank order according to your

156 *How to Help a Friend*

preference. There is no writing involved and the tabs are
self-sticking. I found that the rank-ordering process helped me to own
my values and to begin to see my values as a system. Again, it will be
necessary for you to obtain and work through this exercise if you plan
to recommend it to a friend. Having worked through it, you will be
in a position to have a good discussion with your friend. If you want
to know how your ranking compares with certain
populations—men, women, rich, poor, etc.—get Rokeach's book,
mentioned above, from your library or through interlibrary loan.

Dialogue—Putting It All Together

The third method that has proven helpful to me in discovering and
owning values has been dialogue. This consists of talking with a friend
about such value-based questions as "What do you want out of life?"
"What did you do today that has the most value to you?" "Are you
satisfied with the way you spent your time today?" "What did you
do this week to help you reach a lifetime goal?" "How important is
money to you?" "What trait in yourself do you value the most?"
"What personality characteristic is common among your friends?"
The specific method of dialogue makes a difference. One method is
that A says something about her values, then B says something about
his values. Another method is that A says something about her
values, then B responds in such a way that the focus remains on A.
He may ask her a question which sharpens her perspective, for
example. This latter method of focusing on one person for a period
of time has worked best for me.
The purpose of these two value exercises and the value dialogue is
to help your friend strengthen his/her choosing channel. This approach
to strengthening life-style should make it possible for your friend to
begin to move away from indecisiveness.

REFERENCES

1. Milton Rokeach, *The Nature of Human Values* (New York: The Free Press,
   1973). This large book can serve as an excellent reference to study values. Dr.
   Rokeach reports in the book the ways in which values differ: those of women
   from men, rich from poor, and black from white. He also reports how values differ
   among age groups and among cultures. He notes, for example, that whereas

college students in the United States value national security least in a list of
eighteen values, Israeli students value it highest.

2. *Ibid.*, p. 7.
3. Milton Rokeach, "The Rokeach Value Survey," 1967, Halgren Tests, 873
Persimmon Ave., Sunnyvale, California 94087.

23 Fostering the Development of Moral Standards

She didn't expect me to answer the question; she knew the decision had to be her own. But she asked it anyway: "Should I leave my husband or not?" By leaving she meant getting a divorce, because he had already left her. As a salesman, he traveled several days a week and had gradually stayed away for longer and longer periods of time. Finally, he actually took up residence in another city and came "home" only occasionally on weekends. He told her he didn't love her anymore, and she had been hurt so deeply that she didn't know whether she loved him or not. As she discussed her options in terms of making a decision, it became apparent that her deepest predicament was a moral one. Was it right to get a divorce? Was it right, under the circumstances, not to?

WELL-DEVELOPED MORAL STANDARDS

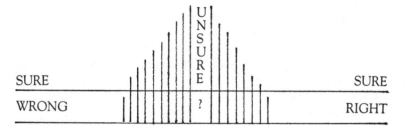

Most of us can decide what's right and wrong fairly easily in the majority of situations. In some situations, however, we may be unsure whether a given action (or lack of it) is right or not. In these cases the decision becomes very difficult. For example, is it just unthoughtful, or is it actually morally wrong not to write or otherwise maintain contact with one's aging parent?

AN UNDEVELOPED SET OF MORAL STANDARDS

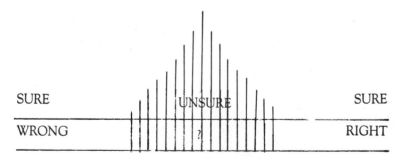

Notice the drawing concerning a strong and weak set of moral standards. If one has a strong moral base, the "unsure" area is relatively small. If one has a weak, underdeveloped moral base, the "unsure" area is quite large, and the clearly wrong and clearly right areas of behavior are significantly reduced in size. This person, then, has a weak choosing channel because of a lack of a strong set of moral standards. His indecisiveness can be helped only if he strengthens this area.

Moral indecision is the cause of many predicaments because there is a great deal of confusion in the area of moral standards. We grow up generally believing what we are told or what we read. But we are taught many confusing things by the mass media. For example, last week there was a TV show in which a divorced mother could not make up her mind whether to become sexually involved with her boyfriend. When her neighbor asked her the question, "How do you know you won't like flying until you fly?" she decided to make sex a part of the relationship. What started out to be a moral decision wound up being a decision made on the basis of fun, that is, "What would I *like* to do?"

Suppose you see a number of evidences that indicate that your friend has not developed a strong set of moral standards. If he/she comes to you and says, "What should I do?" in a specific situation, how will you answer? You probably will not make the decision because this would take the responsibility away from your friend, but how *will* you help?

A PLACE TO START

Many persons either have not had or have not taken the opportunity to discuss their ethical system with a good friend. Christian ethics is partially based on the Ten Commandments. But, as C. S. Lewis has pointed out, what is new about Christianity is not a set of right-wrong standards, but rather forgiveness through Christ for breaking the standards of a moral code already known to us. Lewis has explained this position in the following way:

A Christian who understands his own religion laughs when unbelievers expect to trouble him by the assertion that Jesus uttered no command which had not been anticipated by the Rabbis—few, indeed, which cannot be paralleled in classical, ancient Egyptian, Nevite, Babylonian, or Chinese texts. We have long recognized that truth with rejoicing. Our faith is not pinned on a crank.[1]

There is a sense then in which the Ten Commandments are neither specifically Jewish nor Christian. They are for all persons.

For example, in looking for support for the idea of the sanctity of life, we are not limited to the sixth commandment, "You must not murder." To return to Lewis:

> I could point to the confession of the righteous soul in the Egyptian *Book of the Dead*—"I have not slain men." I could find in the Babylonian Hymn that he who meditates oppression will find his house overturned.[2]

The Ten Commandments provide an ethical code which is both clear and concise. And, like most things that are obvious, they have regularly been overlooked. Many adults have not read the Ten Commandments in a contemporary translation. The Ten Commandments, of course, were not given to be memorized and forgotten by children (similar to the fate of the capitals of North and South Dakota) but to be followed by adults. The Commandments are given below as they appear in Exodus 20 of *The Living Bible*, except that explanatory verses are omitted:

1. You may worship no other god than me.
2. You shall not make yourselves any idols: any images resembling animals, birds, or fish. You must never bow to an image or worship it in any way; ...
3. You shall not use the name of Jehovah your God irreverently, nor use it to swear to a falsehood....
4. Remember to observe the Sabbath as a holy day.
5. Honor your father and mother, that you may have a long good life in the land the Lord your God will give you.
6. You must not murder.
7. You must not commit adultery.
8. You must not steal.
9. You must not lie.
10. You must not be envious of your neighbor's house, or want to sleep with his wife, or want to own his slaves, oxen, donkeys, or anything else he has.[3]

A discussion of the validity of the Ten Commandments as a beginning base for moral standards can serve as a way to expand the thinking of your friend. Many persons have not had a chance to talk to another person deeply about the way they make moral decisions. Often as persons talk they begin to build a stronger set of moral standards by saying out loud what it is they believe. This also provides some measure of commitment to live by a moral standard that they have voiced.

Continuing the Quest—The Law of Love

Although the Ten Commandments is a good place to start the quest for a personal framework of moral standards, it is not a good place to end. One can become very legalistic if he uses the Ten Commandments as his only moral base. The law of love both includes and goes beyond the Commandments:

Pay all your debts except the debt of love for others—never finish paying that! For if you love them, you will be obeying all of God's laws, fulfilling all his requirements. If you love your neighbor as much as you love yourself you will not want to harm or cheat him, or kill him or steal from him. And you won't sin with his wife or want what is his, or do anything else the Ten Commandments say is wrong. All ten are wrapped up in this one, to love your neighbor as you love yourself. Love does no wrong to anyone. That's why it fully satisfies all of God's requirements. It is the only law you need.[4]

One of the characteristics of love that makes it nonlegalistic is its lack of explicitness. This characteristic also makes it difficult to apply at times. It is at these times that it is helpful to discuss with a friend how to love in a given situation. For example, a friend comes to you for help. He has another friend whom he likes but who monopolizes many of their conversations. How can your friend apply the law of love in this situation? Being able to talk about it with you may help.

Sin

It is one thing to be unsure whether our behavior is right or wrong. It is another to violate our conscience. Sin, of course, covers more than just violating our conscience. Most people would agree that the sociopath is sinning (especially if he committed an act of violence toward them) even though he may feel no compunction about his acts. But if we could control just our sin that we are aware of, this would be quite an accomplishment.

If your friend comes to you feeling badly about some moral decisions he has made, some questions that may expand his thinking include, "Are you living by what you believe?" "Are you violating your own conscience by any of the things you are doing?" "Do you see what you have done as right or wrong?" The importance of asking these kinds of questions stems from the fact that many of us violate our conscience and then wonder why we feel so bad. There is no way to live bad and feel good.

In chapter thirty-four, you will be learning how to use bibliotherapy methods (giving to a person books and other written materials which deal with the predicament he/she is in). You may find it helpful to your friend to recommend Karl Menninger's book *Whatever Became of Sin?* and to discuss it after you have both read it.[5] Menninger points out in a thought-provoking way that there are a number of activities that are moral but not legal and a number of others that are legal but not moral. He also provides stimulating discussions of such sins as pride, gluttony, ingratitude, waste, sloth, greed, in addition to lying, cheating, stealing, and others. Talking with a close friend and identifying our own involvement in these and other sins helps to sharpen and internalize a set of moral standards.

Take a look again, please, at the drawings on the first page of this chapter. The main idea of the sketches was that as we develop a strong set of personal moral standards, the "unsure" area decreases, that is, we can clearly identify more and more activities as right or wrong for us. However, we may find a spiral movement going on in our thinking and choosing. As we carefully consider our actions, we may find some that we felt sure were clearly right earlier, fall under judgment as we become aware of, for example, some of our behaviors that involve pride or ingratitude. Therefore, we find ourselves constantly working at developing and redeveloping a strong set of moral standards.

When a friend comes to us for help, he/she is more likely to accept us if we come into the helping situation as a fellow learner. Humility is perhaps the first requirement for trying to help a friend in the moral area. As we find the humility (and courage) to face and admit the hypocrisy in ourselves, we will more likely be able to help our friend.

REFERENCES

1. C. S. Lewis, *Christian Reflections* (Grand Rapids, Mich.: William B. Eerdmans Publishing Company, 1967), p. 47.

2. *Ibid.*, p. 51.
3. *The Living Bible* (Wheaton, Ill.: Tyndale House Publishers, 1971).
4. *Ibid.*, Romans 13:8-10.
5. Karl Menninger, *Whatever Became of Sin?* (New York: Hawthorn Books, Inc., 1973).

Part

E

DOING—
*Helping
Your Friend
Take
Action*

24 The First Steps

A person who is weak in the doing channel is nonproductive. If friends with this particular life-style weakness come to you for help, it probably will be for assistance in getting out of a predicament they find themselves in because of their nonaction. As you work to help your friend get out of his immediate predicament, you will also want to assist him in strengthening his life-style.

You can tell when you have worked with a friend who is weak in the doing channel, because it will take some of *your* strength. The weak person draws strength from the strong. Therefore, you need to be sure that you have inner strength as you begin working with a friend with this particular weakness in life-style. Chapter forty-two, "Finding Strength in an Action Support Group," deals with "helping the helper" meet this particular need.

Now, what are some specific ways that you can be helpful to a friend with this life-style need?

Get in Contact

Persons who are weak in the action channel usually feel down. They look around and see all the work they need to be doing but they don't do it. They know they need to get to work, and others around them are telling them in one way or another the same thing. Now, a person who feels down usually looks down. This isn't helping him. There isn't much about most floors that will get people looking up and feeling good again. Therefore, to get your friend to feel "up," you need to establish eye contact and get him or her to look up.

You may want to get in contact by getting in touch with your friend physically. Putting a hand on the shoulder or in some other way establishing contact also helps a person who is feeling down to look up. Strength flows to another person through touch and through eye contact. It is most important then to establish contact in these ways.

Be Willing to Invest Time

I remember hearing one person talking about going to help a friend who had been on drugs and was depressed. He said, "I went over and talked with him for three days." Now you may not be able to or need to make this kind of time investment, but a person who is not functioning well needs a chance to talk at length and to have somebody talk back in a straight, warm, strong way. Therefore, you can expect to spend hours and hours listening and talking.

Get Your Friend Moving Physically

With certain diseases or impairments, it is necessary to get the person moving to avoid paralysis. The same principle is true here.

The longer a person sits, the harder it is to get up. This is where you as a friend can make a big difference. In many situations a helper who is a friend has a definite advantage over the professional counselor. This is one of those situations. You are already involved with your friend and you are in a good position to make use of your relationship to get your friend involved in activities. It will be helpful for you to call, drive by, pick your friend up, go for a walk or a ride while you talk, or in some other way involve your friend in movement.

Work for Honesty

It is important to respond in a straight way to your friend. For example, if she says regarding some activity, "Oh, I can't do that," it may be helpful for you to respond, "You probably could if you chose it. Do you mean that you can't do it, or you won't do it?" The use of the word "can't" is an indication that one is powerless and therefore is not responsible. As a friend, if you have built a good involvement with your friend, you may not want to accept this disclaiming of responsibility. The use of the word "can't" tends to weaken a person. You are doing your friend a favor and you will tend to strengthen your friend if you point out that it is really a choice, not an impossibility that she is facing.

Teach Your Friend to Focus

The immobilized person usually thinks of all the things that need to be done, and then does not do any of them because the task is too great. You can help your friend by teaching him or her to focus on one task that needs to be done, and you may need to offer to help accomplish the task. You can do this through a question. Let's say your friend says, "I need to shop for the week's groceries, vacuum the living room, and work in the garden." You can ask, "Which one needs doing the most?" The important word in this question is "needs." Most persons who are down think in terms of what they *want* to do. Their honest answer to their own question is "Nothing. I don't want to do any of those things." Therefore, it is crucial to ask the right question so you begin to teach them to differentiate between what they want to do and what they need to do.

Irma, a mother of two young children, had not been getting up until the middle of the morning. She had felt depressed and unable to face the day, so her husband prepared breakfast for the children and got them off to school before he went to work. After some time of this, she felt even worse because she was gradually becoming less involved with her family. When she was asked the question, "What is one thing you need to do most that you are not already doing?" she decided it was to get up and begin the day with her family. She made a commitment to do this for one week, whether she *felt* like it or not. So, by exercising a great deal of determination, she pushed herself away from the bed each morning and began her work. During that week she was able to increase her involvement with her children and her husband. This caused her to feel better and thereby confirmed her "getting-up" decision. She thus began her move away from her state of immobilization by focusing on one activity.

Be Positive

If you can tell by looking at your friend that he is feeling down, then it is just as well that you don't ask how he is. This only obligates him to tell how badly he's feeling, or to say, "Oh, just fine," and then feel worse because he wasn't honest with you. It is better to mention some good feelings. I'm not suggesting you be a Pollyanna and find something good in everything bad (although that might be better than the reverse). But I am suggesting that the person who radiates hope is good medicine for a discouraged friend. Several proverbs support the value of this kind of approach:

Anxious hearts are very heavy but a word of encouragement does wonders!

Pleasant sights and good reports give happiness and health.

Some people like to make cutting remarks, but the words of the wise soothe and heal.

Gentle words cause life and health; griping brings discouragement.

Kind words are like honey—enjoyable and healthful.[1]

This approach with your friend must not be an *act.* It has to be real with you or it won't work. If it is real, your friend will sense this and will draw strength and hope from you. This will help him "come to life" and start doing some of the things he needs to do.

REFERENCES

1. Proverbs 12:25; Proverbs 15:30; Proverbs 12:18; Proverbs 15:4; Proverbs 16:24.

25 Stopping Energy Leaks

Each of us has only so much energy. If we are not using it to get things done that need to be done, the chances are that the energy is draining away in nonproductive activities. If your friend is weak in the action channel of his life-style, he may need help in plugging energy leaks. There are several ways in which the nonproductive person may waste energy.

FEELING MISERABLE

It takes a great deal of energy to feel miserable. And generally the person weak in the doing channel spends a considerable amount of time feeling sorry for himself or for herself. However, it does not seem to be helpful to say to persons who are feeling miserable that they should stop feeling sorry for themselves. What they need at this point is some encouragement. They think too much (not necessarily too highly) of themselves. The reason they spend a great deal of time thinking about themselves is that they feel trapped. A friend can best help by being pleasant, friendly, and businesslike, as opposed to being condemning.

Let's suppose you have used the guidelines given in chapter twenty-nine on "Listening and Resonating" and you have been successful in discovering how your friend really feels—miserable! What do you do if he wants to continue telling how terrible he feels? One way to respond would be to say something like the following: "I think I understand how you *feel*—you feel sad and very discouraged (or miserable, touchy, grouchy, lonely, or whatever your best judgment is); are you ready yet to make a plan to get the things done you need to so that you can begin to feel better?" Glasser has discussed in a helpful way, as noted earlier, the value of asking the person we are working with for a plan.

If one shares his miserable feelings over a longer period of time than just acquainting a friend with how he feels, he begins to judge himself as inferior and this produces additional feelings of misery. Therefore, you will do your friend a favor by using the strength of your involvement to get him moving in making a plan.

REDUCE "HEAD" TIME

Many people who are weak in the doing channel spend a great deal of time in their own heads; that is, they fantasize. Fantasy involves the use of vivid imagination. It is an imagined event or condition involving two aspects. One is some hoped-for or feared outcome. The second is the clear image of that outcome in one's thoughts or imagination. The person who is weak in the doing channel may spend several hours each day in an *image* world. One of the best short stories on fantasy is James Thurber's "The Secret Life of Walter Mitty."[1] Walter Mitty's favorite fantasy was the heroic quest. He was a fearless pilot, a crack pistol shot, or a famous surgeon in fantasy, but in real life was a quiet, submissive man who sometimes drove down the wrong lane of a parking lot. In fact, he was likely to be engaged in a heroic fantasy and an absent-minded activity at the same time.

Focusing on the present moment is a means of strengthening the doing channel. We need to help our friend concentrate on the here-and-now. The *depressed* person is often thinking about the past there-and-then. He may be thinking, "That was an awful, unforgivable thing I did," or "That was stupid of me." The *anxious* person is caught up in the future there-and-then. He may be thinking, "Some dreadful thing is going to happen to me," or "I don't want to face him tomorrow." The daydreaming, or *fantasizing* person is often thinking about the there-and-now. The time is present, but the place distant and unreal.

If we observe people closely, we can get some clues to helping them (and us) concentrate. Why do some students study better while listening to a radio? Perhaps because the sound pulls them into the here-and-now. The music may actually be somewhat distracting, but not as much so as a mind caught in the past or the future, or "out there" in fantasy.

Why are some persons able to talk better while they are knitting, or building, or using their hands in some other way? Often it may be because the craft they are involved in brings their minds into the present. They have to concentrate on what they are doing *right now* if they are to be successful in their activity. Since they are involved in the here-and-now in their craft, they can also carry on a conversation in the here-and-now. Many alcoholic rehabilitation units use a crafts experience as a part of the rehabilitation because alcoholics who are caught in the past by their depression and guilt are pulled into the present by having to concentrate on needle art, building, or painting.

These clues tell us we may be able to help our daydreaming friend by getting him involved in an arts or crafts experience. It may take some doing to find an activity that will interest him enough to get involved, but the outcome is usually worth it. Such an activity is healing because it permits, even requires, the person to spend more and more of his time concentrating on the present. In addition, it provides a creative outlet which we all need. Finally, it provides end-products which may be shared with others and meet the need to give.

JUDGING OTHERS

A number of persons I have observed who are weak in the doing channel are those who spend a considerable amount of head time judging others. Usually they are not aware of this. They see others judging them, but they see themselves as accepting of others. However, when they look very closely at their own thought life, most of them realize that they are quite judgmental of friends, acquaintances, and relatives.

A friend of mine whom I'll call John is one of the most effective helpers I know. He is a person who is charged with energy. Recently he shared with me an action that he took ten years ago, when he was thirty, that plugged a large energy leak and enabled him to find more strength to help others. He had grown up judging his father and mother. His mother was emotionally disturbed and his father was bitter. John's childhood had been very unhappy, and he blamed his parents for this.

One day a good friend of his said to him, "When are you going to forgive your parents?" He replied, after thinking about it for awhile, "I don't know, because if I forgive them, I'll have to become responsible." At that moment he realized he had been expending his energy all those years judging his parents for his predicament instead of doing the things he needed to do to make a better life for himself and others around him. That day he forgave his parents and experienced new energy flowing through his life.

It isn't difficult to tell when a friend is judging others (it's quite difficult to know when *we* are doing it). Usually there are disparaging remarks, competitive statements, and conversation which compares people. What should you do when you realize your friend is failing to get things done because he is spending a significant portion of his time judging others?

Sometimes a helpful approach is to ask such persons if they feel judged by others. They almost always do. They are extrasensitive to others' statements about them. And they often judge others without knowing it, *because* they feel they are being judged. If your involvement is sufficiently strong that you can say things to your friend that are hard to say, you will be able to point out at a later time that your friend is judging another person by a given response—something that he has admitted has hurt him in the past.

If this seems too strong, you can ask your friend if the response *seems to him* to be a judgmental one. Then you may get a discussion going about the amount of time your friend spends judging others. However, don't be surprised if it takes awhile for your friend to become aware that he is being judgmental of others. Actually, we all have within us a little man in a black robe with a gavel in his hand who periodically pounds the gavel and pronounces someone guilty. We only differ in the amount of time we spend participating in this activity. A study of Matthew 7 (and other New Testament passages on the need to accept and love others rather than judge them), can be helpful to us in reducing the amount of time we spend "on the bench."

EXCESSIVE RESTING

Persons who are "down" and not productive spend a lot of "down time," that is, time in bed. They often are awake during the night worrying about the future or feeling depressed about the past or present. They rest often, even catch some short naps during the day. Therefore, they may complain of insomnia even though they spend a great deal of time in bed. It is important to work with your friends if they come to you for help in this predicament, to help get them on a sleep schedule so that they stay awake during the day even if they don't sleep at night. Now, of course, it is important for persons driving a car or operating other machinery to get their rest. But the point here is that if they are resting for long periods or sleeping during the day they will not ordinarily be able to sleep all night long.

A matter-of-fact approach is a helpful one with the "long-resting nonsleeper." If the problem is a severe one, you may want to make a referral to a physician. In most cases, if the person really wants help you can provide it in the following way. Suggest to him that he keep track for a week of the time he spends resting and sleeping. He can use a chart such as the accompanying one that shows the amount of time one spends resting (in bed or in a reclining chair without sleeping) and sleeping. One caution here—preparing a chart and recording on it is usually somewhat boring and the insomniac must be alert or he may go to sleep at the task!

CHART FOR RECORDING RESTING AND SLEEPING TIME*

		SUN	MON	TUE	WED	THU	FRI	SAT
MORNING	REST	1	2					
	SLEEP	2	1					
AFTERNOON	REST	1	0					
	SLEEP	0	0					
EVENING	REST	1	2					
	SLEEP	1	1½					
NIGHT	REST	5	4					
	SLEEP	2½	3½					
TOTAL	REST	8	8					
	SLEEP	5½	6					

You will need to define morning, afternoon, evening, and night according to your friend's day. For example, if he needs to get up at 7:00 A.M., morning would be from 7:00 A.M. to 12:00 noon—five hours. His afternoon might end at the time he begins his evening meal, and his evening would end when he usually goes to bed.

Notice on the "Chart for Recording Resting and Sleeping Time" that two days have been filled in for a person we'll call Paul. Paul was complaining of insomnia because he was getting only two to four hours of sleep per night. His pattern of sleeping and resting begins to emerge after only two days of charting. He tends to sleep in and rest in the mornings. He functions well in the afternoons. Then after dinner he reclines in a platform rocker in front of the TV and alternately rests and sleeps. So when night comes he doesn't feel sleepy until sometime during the morning hours. Usually just keeping a chart like this is enough to let a person know what he needs to do. By reducing or eliminating his rest and sleep during the day, he can expect to begin sleeping more at night. You should let him know that it may take several days or a week or two for his body clock to get settled in to the new rhythm.

Sometimes one may still have trouble getting to sleep at nights, even after he has gone on a new schedule. Often his head is whirring with images. Persons who watch TV may run the images through again when they go to bed. If one tends to do this, he may choose to read instead of watch TV because the images from written material tend to be less sharp than those from TV.

As you work with your friend, expect that you will be able to help him with his quest to sleep better at night. You have his need for sleep working on your side. Also, your confidence will provide a positive influence.

REFERENCES

1. James Thurber, "The Secret Life of Walter Mitty," Copyright 1939, *The New Yorker Magazine,* Inc., appears in *A Cavalcade of American Writing,* Gunnar Horn (Ed.), (Boston: Allyn and Bacon, Inc., 1961), pp. 244-250.

26 Suggesting Tasks to Get Your Friend Moving Again

When your friend comes to you for help and is weak in the doing channel of his life-style, it is usually helpful to use task agreements. As you may remember from chapter sixteen, "Helping Your Friend Express Emotions," task agreements are used as homework to help persons build skills in a given area of their life-style. They are not task *assignments,* such as a teacher would give a student who might have no choice concerning the homework. The tasks, although often suggested by you, are agreed to by your friend because he sees them as useful in reaching his goal.

FROM FANTASY TO ACTION

Many persons who spend excessive amounts of head time ask how they can control their thought life. They often feel at the mercy of any thought that races across their mind. I've found it helpful to reply to these persons who ask this very real, genuine question, that one way that does *not* work is to try to stop thinking about a specific topic. Usually the more we try to stop thinking about something, the more we think about it. This is like a child who comes home and uses a four-letter word which he heard on the playground that day, and finds that his parents are very upset. One of them says to him, "You are *never* to use that word again. I want you to forget it." This usually has the effect of flashing the word in neon lights across the child's mind in such a way that he cannot possibly forget the word.

There are two tasks that are especially facilitative in converting fantasy time to worthwhile activity, in addition to the ideas suggested in the last chapter.

A Learning Project

A number of persons who were spending several hours of relatively useless head time each day have been helped by a learning project. This is how it works: you talk with your friend who wants to reduce his fantasy time, about some area of learning he has always wanted to get into, but has never had the time for. Many cannot respond to this immediately, but after they have had some time for the idea to incubate, they come up with their "dream," something they have always wanted to learn. It may be intellectual—for example, learning a foreign language; it may be a skill, such as learning to use puppets, or constructing kitchen cabinets, or learning to play the guitar; it may involve a new area of awareness or appreciation—for example, gaining an appreciation for art by reading and by visiting art exhibits and museums. Achieving a dream is very reinforcing, and as your friend works toward the realization of his learning goal, he will spend less and less time in fantasy. When real life becomes more fun than fantasy has been, then he will drop his fantasy.

The Use of Images

A clue to working with people who spend a great deal of time
in fantasy is that they almost always have special strengths in the
area of imagination. They are able to evoke sharp images in their
mind. Therefore, the unreal fantasy and daydream images need to be
replaced with images by which one visualizes the outcome of a plan or
"sees" a desired goal. I asked a successful school administrator what
his secret was in accomplishing goals. He replied that it was very
important for him to *visualize* his objective. Once he could see it in
his mind, he was able to work effectively toward its
accomplishment. Further information on "imaging" is given in
chapter thirty-six, "Imagine That! The Use of Images." The main
idea here is that the person involved is already using images; he just
needs to substitute new images in his mind, and then work toward the
visualized outcome.

OVERCOMING FEAR

Fear is a paralyzing emotion for many persons who are weak in
this area of their life-style. Task agreements are helpful in the
area of fear. It is sometimes useful to ask someone who dreads to do
something that he needs to do, "What is the worst thing that would
happen to you if you were to do that?" Usually, as he thinks about this
question, he realizes that although there would be some risk, the
outcome would not be a dreadful one. Then it is important to work
together with your friend on a task agreement or two that will
require him to move directly into the face of his fear.

Tim's biggest fear was that he would be misunderstood. When he
talked to his friends, he nearly always explained what he meant—and
then explained his explanations! In this way he tried to be sure
others understood what he was trying to say. But his explanations
were so long and circuitous that his friends felt confused. Tim's
behavior was actually bringing about what he most feared—he was
being misunderstood by his friends.

He could see his communication style wasn't working for him, so he
agreed to the task of practicing short responses, usually two sentences,
or no more than fifteen seconds. He practiced this in one or more

conversations each day. It was surprising to him that his friends now began to understand him better than when he had used long explanations. Still, it took him weeks to begin to regularly use shorter responses. Old habits are hard to break and new ones difficult to form.

Tasks for the Withdrawn Person

The withdrawn person is weak in doing social tasks, often because he is afraid. I remember asking a first-grader to define "brave," and he said, "It's when you're scared to death, but you do it anyway." We need to share with a fearful friend that it is OK to be afraid, but it is ineffective to let our fear stand in the way of our doing what we need to do.

Often one of the first steps a withdrawn person needs to take is to smile more. There are many reasons why withdrawn persons don't smile much—they don't feel like it, they are afraid a smile may encourage a conversation, and they are not ready for that, etc. But the reasons aren't important. If they knew why they didn't smile much, that insight by itself wouldn't get them smiling again. They need to begin smiling, just as a way to treat others better; then they will *feel* more like smiling.

I have used several tasks in this area of behavior. First, if the person is really pretty glum I suggest the use of a mirror, as mentioned earlier. The task is to smile five times in the mirror each day. In this way he begins to get the hang of using his mouth muscles to smile, and he is beginning to treat *himself* better at the same time. The second task is to consciously smile at one person a day. If it feels awkward, that doesn't mean it's phony (unless he is smiling at someone he doesn't like). Smiling is a skill that has to be relearned for some people, and it takes awhile, just like any skill, for it to become automatic.

Another task for the withdrawn person is to move toward one person in a way that says, "I want to spend time with you." For example, a task that a factory worker agreed to was to go over and sit by a person at coffee break or lunch. For another person it might mean calling a friend. Along with this, the withdrawn person learns to take the initiative in beginning a conversation. This requires a great deal of courage because it means moving straight into his biggest fear. But as persons do this, they usually feel very good and quite reinforced for taking the initiative.

A Task for a Friend Afraid to Encounter a Special Person

Often your friend may not be withdrawn socially at all, but is still afraid to talk about a particular situation with a mate, employer, or other very close or important person. Your friend may function well in other areas of life but be paralyzed with fear at one point, in one relationship. It involves saying the "unsayable," getting to the core of the relationship, talking about what both persons are thinking about, but neither has the courage to say. If a friend comes to you for help saying, "I need to get straight with my wife [husband, father, daughter, boss, etc.], but I don't know how," you may translate the "But I don't know how," to "But I'm afraid to." If you have a good involvement with your friend, a question you can ask is, "What is it you are most afraid to say to your wife?" I usually follow this question closely with, "You don't need to tell me what it is; just identify it for yourself." Another question that sometimes helps is, "What would be the worst thing that could happen if you said it?" Saying the worst possible, most feared outcome *out loud* helps a person to gain courage, and to come to the realization that the feared outcome may be highly unlikely. The task agreement is reached when your friend makes the commitment to talk to the other person about the central issue that needs to be discussed. Let your friend know you'll be thinking of him and you'll be waiting to hear *how he did.* Using the sentence, "I'll be waiting to hear how you did," is more effective than, "I'll be waiting to hear what happened," because the former places the responsibility on your friend, while the latter leaves it up to chance.

Section Five

Finding Your Friend's Learning Style and Working with It to Help Him

Part

A

THE WAYS WE LEARN—
Hearing,
Seeing,
Touching/Moving

27 Each Person Has a Special Way of Learning

This manual uses a three-part approach to helping a friend. The first thing the helper does is determine the level of need: problem, predicament, crisis, panic, or shock. If the level of need is urgent, the helper meets the need immediately, if possible. If the need is not urgent, the helper attempts to discover his friend's *living channel* that needs strengthening—feeling, thinking, choosing, or doing. Finally, he tries to discover his friend's strong *learning channel* so he can intervene most effectively.

By learning style, I mean one's method of bringing in new information most efficiently and making sense of it. Right now you are using a visual method as you read this line of print. If this information were on a cassette, you would be using your hearing channel. Some persons learn more efficiently by seeing, some by hearing, and some by touch or movement.

As mentioned above, we can make our helping more effective if we can find out how our friend learns best. For example, a young woman came for help because her marriage was not as fulfilling as she expected and wanted it to be. Through observation and some methods to be discussed later, I decided that Beth was a visual learner (this was her strong learning channel). She liked to read and to summarize her reading by writing notes. So at this point I knew it would be helpful to use written matter in addition to the regular talk-listen approach of a counseling session. Each time I saw her, I loaned her a book or article to read. She also loaned me two or three books of hers to read (visual learners like to loan books). I found these books helpful, and we were able to spend some useful time discussing the books we had both read. From these books, and from our discussion of them, she was able to apply several new ideas to help improve her relationship with her husband.

Notice the diagram on "Learning Channels." There are a number of learning channels, but three primary ones. The hearing and seeing channels are well known, but the touch/movement learning channel is less well known. This channel includes the sense of

LEARNING CHANNELS

CHANNEL	SOME WAYS IN WHICH INFORMATION IS RECEIVED THROUGH THIS CHANNEL	BASIC HELPER STRATEGIES
HEARING	Listening to words, Listening to other sounds	Talk, listen, use a cassette tape, play music
SEEING	Reading, Looking at others, Viewing TV	Show, use illustrated or printed material, use other visual aids
TOUCHING/ MOVING	Touching, Getting "feedback" from joints and muscles	Touch, use gestures, roleplays, task agreements

touch (tactile) and the sensory input that comes from the movement of joints, muscles, and limbs (kinesthetic). Examples of touch/movement learning would be sensing with one's fingers where to hold an egg when breaking it, or learning something about another person through a handshake.

Society in general has relied heavily on the hearing channel. This has been particularly true of authorities who use this channel to "straighten people out." Witness what happens to a boy who is caught shoplifting. In terms of his learning channels, the person who steals is typically a strong visual learner. He sees something, he wants it, and he takes it. Now the typical authority who works with a shoplifter begins immediately to work through the weak channel. The first thing that happens is a lecture, particularly if the shoplifter is fairly young. The lecture "goes in one ear and out the other" because the person who steals is usually not a "hearing" learner. A more effective approach is to prepare a visual flip chart, much like an insurance salesman uses, which shows a youth the various events that occur when a shoplifter is caught. The flip chart shows the shoplifter being confronted by the store manager, police, parents, judge, juvenile authorities, and others. This helps the impulsive youth to connect cause and effect in a way that is much clearer to him.

Traditional counseling, with its talk-listen approach, is based on the belief that people who come for help are auditory (hearing) learners. But what if a person's auditory channel is his weakest means of learning? The chances are that he may neither listen nor talk. If he is a strong touch/movement learner, then he may profit from such approaches as roleplays and task assignments. If he learns well through the visual channel, you may introduce bibliotherapy, a counseling approach that will be outlined later in this manual, which uses books and other printed materials.

28 A Method of Discovering Learning Style

In the helping venture, we cannot give what we do not have. Therefore, this manual is put together in such a way that you have the possibility of learning more about yourself. The two primary areas will be your learning style and your life-style.

There are a number of different aspects of learning style. We are working with just one aspect—the primary sensory channel (visual, auditory, or touch/movement) that we use to acquire new information and understandings. Your learning style, for example, will make a considerable amount of difference in the way you can profit most from this manual. If your primary learning channel is visual, then you should be able to acquire the understandings in this manual by reading and studying it carefully. On the other hand, if you are an auditory learner then it would be beneficial for you to get together with a few other persons to listen and talk your way through this manual using the small group discussion approach outlined in chapter forty-two, "Finding Strength in an Action Support Group." If you learn best through the touch/movement channel, then the small-group approach using roleplays may be most helpful.

All of us, unless we have a sensory impairment such as blindness or deafness, use all three of these channels—as well as others, such as the sense of smell. Most people can identify a channel that is strongest. However, there are some persons who seem to learn equally well through all three of the major channels. As you work with learning style it is important to keep in mind that we are not talking about the *only* way a person learns, but rather that person's *most efficient* learning channel.

Look at the "Checklist for Discovering Learning Channels" and note that there is a place to check the items that are most descriptive of you. You will find that this is a difficult task because, if you are like most persons, it is something you have not thought much about. Now, using a pencil (because you may wish to erase and mark a different item), place a check mark in front of each item that would usually be descriptive of you. If there is an item which you cannot decide on, even after you have reflected on it for some time, ask another person in your family or a close friend how he/she would mark it for you. For example, a close friend might be able to note whether you should check: "Expresses self best by talking," or "Expresses self best by writing" as a more accurate description of you.

After you have finished, look at the results. Remember that no single item by itself will tell you your learning style. Rather you need to look for a pattern. You may find that you have about the same number of check marks in each column. If you do, then you will probably draw the tentative conclusion that you learn about equally well with each channel. However, it is somewhat more likely that you will find as you look at the completed page that the number of marks in one column will "stand out" over the number of marks in the other two columns. If that is the case, then you may draw the tentative conclusion that you are probably strong in that

CHECKLIST FOR DISCOVERING LEARNING CHANNELS[1]

I. STRONG IN VISUAL CHANNEL

✓ 1. Likes to keep written records
✓ 2. Typically reads billboards while driving or riding
✓ 3. Puts model together correctly using written directions
___ 4. Follows written recipes easily when cooking
___ 5. Reviews for a test by writing a summary
✓ 6. Expresses self best by writing
___ 7. Writes on napkins in a restaurant
___ 8. Can put a bicycle together from a mail order house using only the written directions provided
✓ 9. Commits a Zip Code to memory by writing it
✓ 10. Uses visual images to remember names
✓ 11. A "bookworm"
✓ 12. Writes a note to compliment a friend
✓ 13. Plans the upcoming week by making a list
✓ 14. Prefers written directions from employer
___ 15. Prefers to get a map and find own way in a strange city
✓ 16. Prefers reading/ writing games like "Scrabble"

II. STRONG IN AUDITORY CHANNEL

___ 1. Prefers to have someone else read instructions when putting a model together
✓ 2. Reviews for a test by reading notes aloud or by talking with others
✓ 3. Expresses self best by talking
✓ 4. Talks aloud when working a math problem
___ 5. Prefers listening to a cassette over reading the same material
✓ 6. Commits Zip Code to memory by saying it
✓ 7. Uses rhyming words to remember names
___ 8. Calls on the telephone to compliment a friend
___ 9. Plans the upcoming week by talking it through with someone
✓ 10. Talks to self
___ 11. Prefers oral directions from employer
✓ 12. Likes to stop at a service station for directions in a strange city
✓ 13. Prefers talking/ listening games
✓ 14. Keeps up on news by listening to the radio
✓ 15. Able to concentrate deeply on what another person is saying
___ 16. Uses "free" time for talking with others

III. STRONG IN TOUCH/MOVEMENT CHANNEL

___ 1. Likes to build things
___ 2. Uses sense of touch to put a model together
✓ 3. Can distinguish items by touch when blindfolded
✓ 4. Learns touch system rapidly in typing
✓ 5. Gestures are a very important part of communication
✓ 6. Moves with music
___ 7. Doodles and draws on any available paper
✓ 8. An "out-of-doors" person
___ 9. Likes to express self through painting or dance
___ 10. Moves easily; well coordinated
✓ 11. Spends a large amount of time on crafts and handwork
___ 12. Likes to feel texture of drapes and furniture
✓ 13. Prefers movement games to games where one just sits (this may also be a function of age)
___ 14. Finds it fairly easy to "keep fit" physically
___ 15. One of the fastest in a group to learn a new physical skill
___ 16. Uses "free" time for physical activities

11   10   8

(Column with most checks—the strong channel)

particular channel. A very low number of marks in one of the columns
may indicate that that is your least used, or least efficient, or a "weak,"
learning channel. Make sure at this point that your conclusions are
only tentative ones. You should leave room for changing your mind
about your strong channel as you gather more information about
the way you learn.

OTHER WAYS TO FIND YOUR STRONG LEARNING CHANNEL

I began thinking about the concept of learning channels when I
worked as a school psychologist testing children. I found that it was
often much more helpful for the teacher to know *how* a child learned
than it was just to have a number representing an IQ. Then I worked
at discovering my own strong and weak learning channels. I found
that if I wanted to remember something for someone else for a
short amount of time (for example, memorize materials for a test
the next day), my visual channel was most efficient. By reviewing
the textbook lecture notes and then writing out a summary of this
information, I found that I could remember almost anything for about
twenty-four to forty-eight hours. However, if I wanted to learn
something for myself and remember it for a long time, then I would
get together with others, listen to them talk, and then frame an
answer in my own words. I found when I did that I could make a
concept my own and have it from that time on.

Then I began to look at my family and discover how Lillian and
each of our children learned. I did the same thing for the people in the
office where I work. This has helped me to know when to use a bulletin
board, when to write a note, when to pick up a phone, or when to talk
with someone. This approach to understanding people has now
become almost automatic with me.

My introduction to learning channels, then, was through
school psychology and the whole field of learning disabilities which
has emerged since 1965. For several years I have asked all my
undergraduate and graduate students to determine their own strong
and weak learning channels and to write a paragraph summarizing them
so that I would be able to do a more effective job of teaching, and so
that they would be aware of this very important aspect of
themselves. I found after I had been doing this for about a year that

there is another approach that is available for helping people discover their strong and weak learning channels. This is the approach pioneered by Dr. Joseph E. Hill and used at the Oakland Community College, Bloomfield Hills, Michigan. Dr. Hill has constructed a "Test for Cognitive Style Mapping Interest Inventory" which students take when they enroll at Oakland Community College.[2] The results of this test are used at the college to place students in learning situations that are appropriate for their strong learning channels. For example, if a student is a strong auditory learner he may be placed with a history teacher who lectures. On the other hand, if the student is a visual learner he may be placed in an individualized learning situation using a media approach. This is an oversimplified introduction to the use of the Cognitive Mapping Test, because the test results show how the student learns not only in the three major channels but in many combinations of these channels.

Another way of gaining more information about your own strong learning channel is just to begin to be aware more each day of the way you learn. How important is a shopping list to you? If you ride a city bus to work, do you spend more time looking at the poster advertisements or listening to the conversations around you? You will discover on your own many other ways of adding to what you know about this very important aspect of yourself.

HELPING YOUR FRIEND

If a friend comes to you for help, you will be able to provide that help in the most effective way if you know how your friend learns. People need to receive help in their own special way. Part of that special way has to do with their strong learning channel.

Let's suppose that you have a friend who has an alcoholic husband. If your friend has a strong visual channel then you may choose to leave some printed materials on Alcoholics Anonymous. On the other hand, if she is an auditory learner, you may wish to talk with her about the resources of Alcoholics Anonymous.

Let's suppose that you have another friend who has a weakness in the choosing area of his life-style. He is discouraged because he is looking for meaning in life and can't find it. You would like to share the meaning that you have found from the Bible. It may make a difference how you share this meaning. If your friend has a weak auditory channel and a strong visual channel it is usually much more effective to leave a Gospel portion or a New Testament with him rather than quote Scripture orally to him.

How can you go about finding your friend's strong learning channel? One way is to use the "Checklist for Discovering Learning Channels" that you used for yourself in this chapter. Remember that it is seldom helpful for you to learn things about your friend that he doesn't know. It's his life and he's the one who needs to acquire the information. This also will keep you from being in the position of knowing more about your friend than he knows and therefore trying to "psych him out."

If you give the checklist to your friend and mention that you have worked it through and found your strong learning channel and would be interested in knowing your friend's strong learning channel, the chances are he will complete it. As you talk about the results, this will build an even greater involvement between you.

If it isn't appropriate to use a checklist with your friend, or if you have used it and still are not sure which is your friend's strong learning channel, finding answers to some of the questions below may aid you in helping your friend discover his strong learning channel.

1) How much time does your friend spend reading, in comparison to the time spent in listening to the radio or to music? This often provides a clue to your friend's strong learning channel.

2) Does your friend talk with you about new things he has *read* or new things he has *heard?* The answer to this question will tell you how your friend typically acquires new information.

3) What does your friend do when he does not have to do anything? In that activity, which of the three learning channels is most involved—visual, auditory, or touch/movement?

4) How does your friend memorize names and numbers? This requires careful observational skills. People memorize in many different ways. There is a person in the city in which I live who has perfect pitch. Having perfect pitch has a number of advantages. For example, this particular person has memorized her Zip Code and telephone number by humming them. When I heard her do this, it was the first time I had ever heard a Zip Code or a telephone number hummed. She assigns middle C the value of 1, C sharp 2, D 3, and so forth in order to know which number gets which pitch.

Obviously she has a very strong auditory channel.

5) If money is not a problem, does your friend prefer to call a relative long distance or to send a card on a birthday? Usually the strong auditory learner prefers to call and the strong visual learner prefers to write. This is not always true because sometimes money and even procrastination do enter in. An interesting thing to note here is that it would be more meaningful to the person who is having the birthday if we would make the decision to telephone or write a card depending on *that person's* strong learning channel. If that person is a strong auditory learner, he will usually appreciate a telephone call more than a birthday card. The reverse would be true for a strong visual learner.

The information provided in this chapter should be enough to enable you to discover your friend's strong learning channel. Remember that your decision should be a tentative one rather than a firm one. Go ahead and begin to work with the person as if the learning channel you have seen as strong is actually the strong one, but be willing to change your mind if you find evidence that you need to.

REFERENCES

1. From Paul Welter, *Family Problems and Predicaments* (Wheaton, Ill.: Tyndale House Publishers, 1977), p. 217.
2. Dr. Joseph E. Hill, "Test for Cognitive Style Mapping Interest Inventory," (Bloomfield Hills, Michigan: Oakland Community College, 1973).

Part B

How to Help a Friend Who Learns Best Through HEARING

29 Listening and Resonating

Do we have one way of talking at work and another way of talking at home? If we do, our effectiveness in one or both settings is lessened, and we ourselves are somewhat splintered rather than whole.

There is no way we can help a friend become whole if we are fractured in an area as close to the core of our personhood as the way we talk. This is not to say that we have to be totally put together twenty-four hours a day. Rather it means that we can't turn a method on and off.

The method of communicating with another person that is taught here will work in most interpersonal situations in which a person is sharing a predicament or crisis. It may be a spouse, child, parent, or friend. It will not work well with a person with whom you are not involved. That is because this particular method requires you at times to be tough as well as tender. If you are not really involved with another human being and you need to give him some straight feedback, he may think or even say, "Who are you?" In other words, that person must first be assured that we care.

This relationship is called by some the therapeutic relationship, and by others, involvement. Nearly all counseling theories have a name for that connection between two people. It can simply be called caring. You must care more about the person than just seeing him as someone who needs help. If we begin a relationship just in order to help someone, the other person usually backs off from that relationship because his own integrity tells him that he is more than just an object to help.

Many of the counseling techniques which have been taught for the last twenty years are based on what I call listening and resonating. For our purposes, we'll call this the L & R method (Listening and Resonating). This shows clearly that there are two aspects in communicating with a person who is in a predicament or crisis. The first involves listening desperately to the other person, concentrating deeply, and working as hard to *understand* the other person as that person is working to make himself or herself clear. The second step involves resonating. We respond to the other person in such a way that we echo, or vibrate (resonate) with the deepest feelings the other person is expressing, and with the main idea of what he is saying. Learning these processes that make up the L & R method require a lifetime of work. We never get perfect at it; we are always working and improving in this method. The more we use it, the more effective we become. I do not mean by this that you cannot help another person until you have had years of practice. You will be able to help right from the beginning, with the amount of help you give being proportional to your skills in the two processes involved. There are now many excellent skill-building handbooks on the market to aid persons in this core area of counseling process. Two such handbooks which I would recommend are Robert Carkhuff's *The Art of Helping: An Introduction to life Skills;* [1] and George Gazda's *Human Relations Development: A Manual for Educators.* [2] Carkhuff's book is written in a nontechnical, easy-to-read style. Gazda's book, although more technical, has the advantage of being in workbook format, with many exercises to complete.

These handbooks, like most other manuals for counselors, emphasize building the "core conditions for helping," such as empathy, warmth, acceptance, genuineness, self-disclosure, and confrontation. I have used a similar approach as a beginning point in training helpers. This method involves three processes in the building of listening skills and three ways of responding to build resonating skills.

THE L & R METHOD

LISTENING
   Use eye contact
   Monitor nonverbal behavior for feelings
   Concentrate on words for meaning
RESONATING
   Express warmth
   Talk straight
   Be strong

Use Eye Contact

We will work with these skills one at a time. The first one is eye contact. Where do you focus your eyes when you listen to another person? The chances are that your effectiveness will be proportional to the amount of eye contact you have. There are two reasons for this. First, the other person assumes, correctly or incorrectly, that you are interested in what he has to say and therefore interested in him, to the degree to which you look at him when he is talking. Second, you pick up much more information from the other person if you do look at him most of the time.

If you have an opportunity to be video-taped when you are talking with another person, you will find this an extremely valuable tool in improving your helping skills. If you do not have access to this, then try to get a good friend to observe you when you talk to another person and tell you about your body position and about the degree of eye contact. A number of people find eye contact to be uncomfortable for them. But nearly all persons can increase the degree of comfort by simply spending more time maintaining eye contact even though at first it is uncomfortable.

There is one difficulty, mentioned earlier, in maintaining eye contact, which is little understood. It affected my eye contact in counseling situations for years until I finally understood what was going on through a study of the emerging field of learning disabilities. This barrier to eye contact is *overloading*. Overloading occurs in our own senses just as it sometimes does in an electrical circuit. We prevent overloading without being aware of what we are doing. For example, have you ever, in an attempt to really take in what someone was saying, averted or closed your eyes? We often momentarily close off one sensory channel in order to prevent overloading our brain with information to be interpreted. As my awareness grew regarding the concept of overloading, I discovered that when I looked away from a person who was talking to me, I was processing in my mind the implications of what he or she had said, and was framing a reply. This effort on my part was taking my mind out of gear as far as listening was concerned and was taking away the visual connection between us.

In correcting my predicament, I worked very hard to separate the listening and resonating aspects of the helping process. I make a very conscious effort not to respond, even in my thinking, to the person until he or she has *finished* talking. Then if I am overloaded, I sometimes look away momentarily to work on all the data that has come in and is coming in and is processing, so that I can put it together and respond. This approach has enabled me to maintain much better eye contact.

Monitor Nonverbal Behavior for Feelings

The research from careful studies done has been consistent in the finding that one's nonverbal behaviors are much better clues to our emotions than are our verbal statements. Through eye contact we are constantly receiving information from small movements around the eyes and from movements of the mouth and other facial movements. In addition, through our peripheral vision we are collecting information from other body movements, such as arm and hand movements, trunk movements, and leg and foot movements. It's always important to remember that the reason we monitor other persons' nonverbal behaviors is not to psych them out, but to understand them. Nobody wants to be psyched out, but everyone wants to be understood.

Concentrate on Words for Meaning

The biggest barrier to concentrating on what a person is saying is anxiety or panic on the part of the helper. This feeling of anxiety or panic often comes because we wonder if we will be able to say something helpful to the other person or if we will be tongue-tied. We can reduce this anxiety and panic by realizing that it is counterproductive. The more we focus on ourselves and our ability to respond, the less we reduce our capability of responding in a helpful way because we are tuning the other person out. I have found it helpful to think, "What if, when the person is finished talking, I can't think of any helpful way to respond?" The way I have worked through this predicament is to take the risk, and on those few occasions when I really don't have a response that would be helpful to the other person, I simply have said something such as: "I'm feeling very much with you right now, but I don't know how to respond to you," and "I'm understanding what you are saying, but I can't think of anything helpful to say to you right now in response."

A second barrier to concentration is anxiety about a predicament that we ourselves may be in. Sometimes when another person is talking, this triggers a response in us and our mind travels off in some direction seeking a solution for that predicament. If we find ourselves thinking about us rather than the person to whom we are talking, this is a clue that *we* need help. We need to get with someone and share where we are. It doesn't work very well to "try to concentrate" on the other person when our mind keeps flipping back to ourself.

Now in terms of resonating, there are some concepts and guidelines that I have found helpful in communicating in a warm, straight, and strong way.

Express Warmth

If it is a friend who is talking with you and sharing a predicament, you probably already have feelings of warmth toward this person. You may have expressed them. Expression is a step beyond feeling. When we show friendliness, touch the other person, or use eye contact, we are expressing our warmth. The expression of warmth is not something we give one time and that does it. We need again and again to express in one way or another our warmth for a friend, because this is nurturing. Neither a plant nor a person can store up warmth for a long period of time. Both require constant warmth for growth and life.

Talk Straight

Talking straight to another person does not mean talking angrily or with an edge on our voice. Rather, it means talking in a businesslike, honest way. Talking straight is not something that we do naturally, ordinarily, but rather it requires hundreds of hours of practice. Otherwise we may hedge, beat around the bush, pull our punches, react too sharply, or in some other way fail to help the other person.

Be Strong

Coming across in a strong way to a friend means that we do not yell or use other attention-getting devices. We are calm and speak with confidence. It helps us to come across in a strong way when we realize that we do not have to come up with a solution the minute the person stops talking. All we have to do is to communicate in some way that we are very much with that person.

We can only be there for another person to lean on if we are strong. As mentioned earlier, if you have had the experience of leaning on a post that is broken off or a railing that is weak you realize how important it is that we feel strength from whatever or whomever we look to for support. The only way to build skills in Listening and Resonating is to practice. You will find that practice with those persons close to you is the most helpful way to build skills. You may wish to begin working on these skills in your daily conversations.

REFERENCES

1. Robert R. Carkhuff, *The Art of Helping: An Introduction to Life Skills* (Amherst, Massachusetts: Human Resource Development Press, 1973).
2. George M. Gazda, *Human Relations Development: A Manual for Educators* (Boston: Allyn and Bacon, Second Edition, 1977).

30 The Brief Response

Al has many of the characteristics of an effective helper. He is able to express warmth. He can resonate with the deep feelings people have about their predicament. He can confront when necessary in a kindly way. Yet people do not usually seek him out when they need to talk. His excellent potential as a helper is relatively unused. The reason persons do not go to him when they need help is that he tends to respond in paragraphs rather than phrases or sentences. One person said after a session with Al, "I couldn't get a word in edgeways!" He chose not to go back to Al again. When we need help, we usually go to a person who will listen carefully and not dominate the talking time.

What percentage of the time do you talk when you are with a friend? 50%? 75%? 25%? You may be thinking that in some situations you talk very little and in other situations a great deal. This is true. However, most people seem to have a *pattern,* so that some typically talk more than half the time they are with a friend and some typically talk less.

What if you and three other friends are together? If each of the four persons talked an equal amount of time, then each would be talking about 25% of the time. Do you see yourself as talkative or quiet? What percentage of the time do you talk in a group of four?

What Difference Does Talking Time Make?

When we are in the process of helping a friend, it is usually important that our responses be fairly brief. If we use brief responses, we will be able to keep the focus on the person who is seeking help. Also we will maintain the flow of the conversation. If our responses are long, then *the focus is taken off the person we are trying to help,* and the helping process is slowed down. If as helpers we typically give very long responses, we may interrupt the flow of the conversation and of the helping process.

On the other hand, it is important to give some response to the person we are trying to help. Good listening is not just saying nothing. Good listening involves *responding* in such a way that the persons to whom we are talking know they have truly been heard.

Talking Times of Helpers

For the last five years I have gathered information on some counselors-in-training, relative to their pattern of responding. The counselors-in-training had small group discussions and were taperecorded, with permission. A typical small group analysis is shown in the accompanying chart.

Numbers are used instead of names in Column A of the chart. These six persons were involved in a group discussion which, for ease of analysis, was stopped at 16⅔ minutes—1,000 seconds. When the discussion was over, each member was asked to estimate independently the percentage of time each member of the group talked. Total percentage of talking time would be 100. If every member talked an equal amount of time, the percentage for each would be about 17% (100/6) since this was a six-person group. It would, of course, be highly unlikely that the members of any group would ever talk exactly the same amount. Notice in Column B that the other members' estimates of #3's percentage of time talked were 10, 5, 5, 3, and 12. The average of these estimates is given in Column C, 7%. When the actual tape was analyzed, Person #3 was found to have talked 7% (Column H), just as the overall group estimated. Person #3, thus, was found to have talked the least of all the members. He overestimated his talking time somewhat—10%.

Person #3 talked 5 times (Column E) during the 1,000 seconds with an average talking time per response of 13 seconds (Column F) for a total of 65 seconds (Column G, $5 \times 13 = 65$). The actual percentage of talking time is found by dividing 65 by 1,000, which equals 6.5%, or rounded off, 7% (Column H).

Person #6 talked the most—6 responses at an average of 73 seconds each, for a total of 438 seconds, or 44% (438/1,000 = 43.8%). The overall group underestimated somewhat (39%) #6's percentage of talking time, and #6 significantly underestimated his own percentage of talking time (23%).

I CAN'T GET

A $\substack{\text{WORD}}$ IN EDGEWAYS!

It often happens that the person talking least thinks he talks more, and the person talking most thinks he talks less. In 25 groups the person talking least in each group more often than not (16 of 25) overestimated his talking time. The range of overestimates were from 1-11%, with the median being 4%. In these same 25 groups the person who talked most, more often than not (19 of 25) underestimated his talking time. The median overestimate was 7%, and the range of overestimates were from 1% to 64%. These findings indicate that often the "quiet" person in a group actually believes he talks more than he does, and the most talkative person in a group usually believes he talks less than he does.

ESTIMATED AND ACTUAL TALKING TIMES OF A DISCUSSION GROUP DURING A 16 2/3 MINUTES (1000 SECONDS) DISCUSSION

	A	B	C	D	E	F	G	H
	Member	Other Estimates of % of Time Talked	Other Avg. Est. of % of Time Talked	Self Estimated of % of Time Talked	Actual Number of Responses	Actual Avg. Num. of Sec. per Response	Total Secs. Talked	Actual % of Time Talked
	#1	15, 15, 10, 18, 16	15%	15%	6	22	132	13%
	#2	15, 15, 5, 8, 7	10%	10%	17	7	119	12%
	#3	10, 5, 5, 3, 12	7%	10%	5	13	65	7%
	#4	10, 5, 15, 10, 20	12%	10%	10	14	140	14%
	#5	25, 25, 15, 20, 15	20%	20%	10	12	120	12%
	#6	35, 40, 25, 50, 45	39%	23%	6	73	438	44%

For purposes of counselor training, we have found Column F, Actual Average Number of Seconds Per Response, to be extremely important. With over 160 persons studied so far, the average response length has been 12 seconds. In 12 seconds one can perhaps say two sentences, or a total of about 25 words. A response no longer than 12 seconds is usually an effective length in a counseling or helping situation. It permits the focus to stay on the one being helped.

Although the average response length studied was 12 seconds, the *range* of response lengths was from 3 seconds to 90 seconds. A consistent response length of over 20-30 seconds presents a major problem in a group discussion and can be counterproductive in a helping situation. A long response takes the focus off the person who is needing help. The implicit message that comes across is "I want to talk *to* you rather than talk *with* you."

The long response often more nearly resembles a "talk" or a speech than part of a dialogue. One can say the Gettysburg Address in a little over 100 seconds. As noted earlier, Person #6 in the chart talked an average of 73 seconds per response. In 73 seconds one can say aloud the last three paragraphs you have just been reading, and have some time left over. Therefore, we can see that in a long response—say over 30 seconds—there is such a vast amount of material to be considered that the process of dialogue is broken.

Have you noticed in committees, work groups, coffee groups, or family groups that you can predict fairly closely the length of time each person will talk? When the "long talker" begins, there is often some physical moving among the other participants (perhaps to find a comfortable position, or to "bed down"). Also, there is often some tuning out of the lengthy talker.

Jesus as a Model for Dialogue

The dialogue between Jesus and the Samaritan woman, recorded in John 4, provides an excellent model for a helping exchange. Notice in the chart "THE DIALOGUE BETWEEN JESUS AND THE SAMARITAN WOMAN," that there were 7 exchanges. Jesus talked 7 times and the woman talked 6 times for a total of 13 separate responses. If their words are spoken at a conversational rate, they add up to the approximate number of seconds shown on the chart. The 7 responses of Jesus total about 70 seconds. The woman's 6 responses total about 42 seconds. The approximate average number of seconds per response of Jesus was 10, and the approximate average number of seconds per response of the woman was 7.

THE DIALOGUE BETWEEN
JESUS AND THE SAMARITAN WOMAN[1]

Exchange	Approximate Number of Seconds in Each Response	
	Jesus	Woman
1	2	6
2	10	13
3	13	5
4	3	2
5	10	9
6	30	7
7	2	
Total Seconds Talked	70	42
Average Number of Seconds Per Response	10	7

Each time Jesus talked he responded directly to the statement that the Samaritan woman had just made. This was not a series of monologues in which each person resumed talking where he/she had left off prior to the other person's response. It was a genuine dialogue with both persons listening carefully and responding concisely. The exciting aspect of this conversation is that Jesus revealed himself as Messiah to the Samaritan woman not through a speech but through a dialogue. The first request was "Give me a drink." The last response was "I who speak to you am he [the Messiah]."

We can build a relationship and bring insights to another person much more effectively through dialogue than through a speech.

Keeping our responses brief, as Jesus did, will enable us to stay with the other person by being sure we are tuned in to his interests and his way of thinking.

Finding Your Own Response Length

What is your typical response length? You can study your own response pattern by getting a friend to time you in informal conversation. At first you will be very aware of the timing and may change somewhat your patterns of responding. However, as you get interested in a group conversation you will pay less attention to the timing process and become more involved. Several timings should establish some kind of an average for you in terms of the actual number of responses that you make in a given amount of time and especially in the average number of seconds per response. If your *average* response length exceeds 15 seconds, you may wish to begin to consciously limit yourself to one or two sentences when responding. Disciplining yourself in this way will enable you to become a more effective helper and will cause people to tune in to you more closely when you talk.

REFERENCES

1. This chart is based on the dialogue between Jesus and the Samaritan woman, as recorded in John 4 in the *Revised Standard Version*.

31 Making the Tender-Tough Connection

When I began counselor training over twenty years ago, I was taught to make only empathic, "tender" responses. I realized this was a good place to start and that somehow this was helpful in building an involvement with another person. But I also knew intuitively from the very beginning that it was not enough. There were many questions that were unanswered for me, questions like, "Are helpers only to be soft?" "Are there two kinds of persons, the tender 'helper' type, and the hard 'leader' type?"

I looked at my own life and particularly at those turning points in my life when I had been influenced by conversations with others. And I

211

realized that those who had been helpful to me had not only responded in "tender" ways but also had been "tough," telling me things that were hard for me to hear and probably hard for them to say.

I began to look at some of the major counseling theories. Some of them emphasized tenderness.[1] Other counseling theories emphasized tough kinds of responses that would tend to bring out one's hidden anger or straighten his thinking.[2]

JESUS—BOTH TENDER AND TOUGH

It was not until I made a study of the life of Jesus that I realized how tenderness and toughness are connected. I observed in the life of Jesus how these two qualities stood out. Scores of conversations of Jesus are recorded in the Gospels. He talked to members of his family, friends, enemies, demons, children, religious leaders, and down-and-outers. I noticed that he was sometimes tender and tough with the same person. For example, with his mother, who lost Jesus in Jerusalem when he was twelve years old, Jesus responded in a tough way. And from the cross just before he died, he looked down at his mother and tenderly made arrangements for John to care for her in her old age. In the course of one conversation with Peter, he responded in a warm, affirming way and a very tough, confronting manner.

In short, I discovered from the life of Jesus that *the connection is love.* Love requires us to respond to the same person tenderly at one time and in a tough way at another. In a helping relationship, there is a place for a warm, tender response. There is also a place for the confronting, tough response. The helper must learn to give both. The kind of person you are will make a difference in the kind of response you find more difficult to give.

Some persons, even though they are by nature tender in the way they communicate, lack the willingness or courage to confront another person even when that person needs the confrontation. Other persons who are harder and tougher by nature have difficulty expressing the warmth and the tenderness they feel.

If you are to be of the most help to people who come to you, you will need to be able to respond in both these ways. Questions to ask yourself are, "Am I afraid to be tender?" "Is it difficult for me to express the warmth that I feel inside to another person?" "Do I sometimes lack the courage to confront another person when he needs it?" "What do I need to do to change this?"

The way we communicate is a function of the kind of person we are, or want to appear to be. If a person typically comes across as *only tender* or *only tough,* the chances are that that person is pretending. That is, if some persons come across soft and tender in all situations, they are wanting to appear in this light and they are denying the tougher part of their nature. Likewise, if persons feel safe only in coming across tough, they are denying the tender part of themselves. The way to change this situation is to change the way we communicate. We need to practice talking both ways in situations that require these ways. If there is a caring relationship between us and the other person, that relationship will survive under both tender and tough conditions.

CHECK YOURSELF

Check the adjectives below that you believe typically describe your style of communication.

____	1. Gentle	____	11. Trusting
____	2. Direct	____	12. Powerful
____	3. Hard	____	13. Unyielding
____	4. Honest	____	14. Bold
____	5. Confronting	____	15. Sensitive
____	6. Warm	____	16. Firm
____	7. Affirming	____	17. Mellow
____	8. Strong	____	18. Daring
____	9. Empathic	____	19. Considerate
____	10. Friendly	____	20. Forceful

Numbers 1, 6, 7, 9, 11, 15, 17, and 19 are those qualities which are typical of the person who uses tender communication. Numbers 3, 5, 8, 12, 13, 14, 16, 18, and 20 are those qualities typical of the person who uses tough communication. Numbers 2, 4, and 10 would be true of both styles. Your checks may help you determine whether you tend to use one or the other ways of communicating most of the time, or if you use both equally. The exercise in the next paragraph will help you to further discover your communication style.

On the line from one to ten below, place an X toward the tender end of the line or the tough end of the line on the approximate position in which you see yourself in terms of the way you communicate. If you always come across in a tender fashion, express warmth effectively, but never confront another person directly, and always seek to avoid "touchy" situations, then you would put an X on the "1." On the other hand, if you have the courage to always be direct and honest in confronting another person, but you are more comfortable in always disagreeing with a person to whom you are talking, and you find it easier to express harshness and anger rather than tender, warm feelings, you would put an X on the "10." Most persons, while not "1's" or "10's," do tend to fall toward one end or the other.

TENDER									TOUGH
1	2	3	4	5	6	7	8	9	10

COMMUNICATION

When your friend comes to you for help, he/she needs to talk to a person who is both tender and tough. Carl Sandburg said of Abraham Lincoln that he was a man of steel and velvet. These are qualities that effective helpers need, and they are qualities that come across in our voice. Some steps are given below for persons who want to grow in these areas.

For Improvement in Tenderness

After working through the checklist and noting your position on the continuum, if you wish to be more effective in communicating tenderness, you may wish to follow these suggestions.

1. Be friendly.
2. Accept your friend. Become aware of any judging you are doing, and remind yourself that judging others is not your task.
3. Slow down your voice rate if you tend to speak fast.
4. Affirm the other person. Tell him his strengths as you see them. Let him know you're glad to be with him.

5. Work hard to get with the emotion he is feeling.
6. Try smiling with your eyes as well as your mouth.
7. Think about his interests and his needs.

For Improvement in Toughness

If you need more steel, more firmness in your communication, you may want to try these suggestions.
1. Don't "pull your punches."
2. Don't "take the other person off the hook." Let him face his situation squarely.
3. Talk in terms of consequences of actions.
4. Don't make excuses for your friend.
5. Sit and stand tall.
6. Use direct eye contact.
7. Use short responses.
8. Confront your friend with any gap between what he is saying and what he is doing.
9. Be willing to discuss behaviors in terms of what is right and what is wrong.

WHOLENESS

The whole person communicates both warmth and strength. As a helper, it is crucial that you not only *possess* both, but that you also *express* both—by the kind of person you are and by the way you talk.

I have asked many college students who were planning to become teachers this question: "What was the outstanding characteristic of the teacher who taught you the most?" There have been many answers but two main themes—warmth and strength. These themes showed up in many responses: "He liked students"; "She didn't put up with any nonsense"; "When he said something, we knew he meant it"; "She never put anyone down."

At first it seemed that these themes were divergent, even opposite. Then it occurred to me that they were parts of a more inclusive characteristic—caring. If, as a helper, we possess either of these important characteristics to a high degree, we will be somewhat effective. If we possess both, we will be much more effective. The source of both is caring. Learning to make the tender-tough connection—Love—will allow these two very different qualities to fit naturally into our lives and to flow out to others.

HELPING CHARACTERISTICS

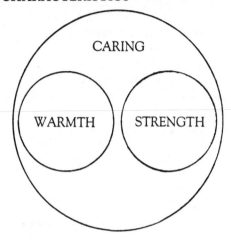

REFERENCES

1. One example is the approach advocated by Carl Rogers.
2. Fritz Perls and Albert Ellis.

32

The Fragile Connection— Using the Telephone for Helping

The telephone is used for many purposes—setting up a time to have coffee with a friend, complaining about faulty merchandise to a customer relations manager, proposing marriage, giving enough hope to a friend to prevent a suicide attempt, and saying "I love you" to a grandchild.

Americans spend a considerable amount of time calling friends. The United States has approximately 145 million telephones.[1] Of these telephones, a little less than three-fourths are residence phones and a little over one-fourth are business phones.[2] We have about sixty-five phones per hundred people. This compares to twenty-two phones per hundred in France, eighteen in Spain, six in the

U.S.S.R. and seventeen-one-hundredths phones per hundred people in Laos.[3]

The average telephone in the United States originates at least five completed calls per day. Based on the above figure of 145 million telephones, there are about 725 million calls per day in the U.S.A. Since all of these (except for "Time and Temperature" and similar calls) are to another person, there are an estimated 2 X 725, or nearly 1½ billion personal telephone contacts made daily in the U.S.[4]

Long distance calls in the Midwest are averaging 4.7 minutes at this writing, down from 6.3 minutes two years ago. At the present time, and for many years, Mother's Day has had the highest volume of long distance calls in a twenty-four hour period.[5]

The telephone is not only a busy instrument; it is an extremely important helping tool. Its significance in the helping process has increased in the last ten years. When drug use among youth in the United States started to increase in the early 1960s, this movement was followed in the latter 1960s and early 1970s by the formation of personal crisis lines around the United States. These lines, usually open for calls at night, serve to make a person available to a caller at a time of crisis. When persons are in a crisis state they often respond readily to immediate help. If immediate help is not available, they may move from a state of crisis to a state of panic.

Most of these personal crisis lines expanded to help people in many kinds of crises. The lines are usually staffed by volunteers with some training. Trained volunteers have now established themselves as being able to deal with many kinds of crises.

Trainers and volunteers soon found out that helping via the telephone was the same in some ways and different in other ways from helping face to face. The same helping process is involved whether one is on the phone or working with a person in the same room. The same attention to the person's level of need, and the same general method of helping holds in both cases. However, there are some differences. The most noticeable difference is that the person who is trying to help does not have access to visual clues about the person with whom he or she is talking. Another difference is that time is usually more at a premium on the telephone. A third difference is that the caller can end the conversation somewhat more abruptly than he can face to face. A telephone conversation is, in fact, a fragile connection.

SUGGESTIONS FROM A TELEPHONE COMPANY

The following suggestions for telephone use are from the booklet, "What Every Telephone User Should Know (Telephone Manners From A to Z)" prepared by the General Telephone System. You can request it or one like it from your local telephone business office.

The safe rule is: treat your telephone "visitor" as if he or she were present. Make your voice warm and pleasant. Get a "glad to hear from you" ring into it.

When you telephone, speak distinctly with your lips about a half inch from the mouthpiece. And talk normally. Some people ... and we don't necessarily mean you ... completely change their personalities when they pick up a receiver. Some roar like a bull moose paging its mate. Others whisper ... talk so quietly they keep what they're saying a deep dark secret from themselves and the other party. Still others affect a "telephone voice." Talk throatily or huskily or flat and mechanically. Or cute. Or stilted. All are intended to convey an impression. And they do. But is it the right one? When you telephone, be natural. Be sincere. Be distinct.[6]

The best starting guideline to effective telephone use is to show courtesy. An informal test, "What's Your Telephone Courtesy Quotient," can help you evaluate this aspect of your telephone use.

Voice Quality

The quality of your voice is even more important in telephone conversation than in face-to-face dialogue. Have you evaluated your own voice quality? One way to do this is to ask three or four good friends to talk with you on the telephone and make some judgments about your telephone voice. Have them rate you on the factors below:

Loudness—Is your voice so loud that it's hard on the ear, or so soft that others can't understand what you're saying?

Pitch—Is your voice too high, squeaky, or perhaps a low rumble?

Rate—Do you talk in a hurried fashion, or do you talk so slowly

WHAT'S YOUR T.C.Q.?*

(From the booklet, "What Every Telephone User Should Know," Published by the General Telephone System)

	ALWAYS Score 10	SOME-TIMES Score 5	NEVER Score 0
1. Is there a smile in your voice?			
2. Do you speak distinctly ... lips about a half inch from the mouthpiece? .			
3. Do you pronounce numerals and letters carefully?			
4. When you answer your telephone, do you identify yourself quickly? . .			
5. When it rings, do you answer your telephone immediately?			
6. When you answer someone else's telephone, do you leave clear, complete, written messages?			
7. When you're making a call, do you identify yourself promptly and state your business pleasantly?			
8. When you place a call, do you wait near your telephone until it is completed?			
9. Do you have the materials you need (pencil, paper, facts, records) handy, before you make your call? .			
10. Do you tell your secretary or telephone operator where you can be reached when you leave your desk?			
11. Do you avoid wrong numbers by: pronouncing distinctly ... dialing carefully ... looking up doubtful numbers?			
12. When finishing a call, do you hang up gently?			
13. Do you call people by their right names—and correct titles?			
14. When the party you're calling is out and you want him to call back ... do you leave YOUR name and telephone number?			

*Telephone Courtesy Quotient

that it is hard for the listener to concentrate on what you're saying?

Clarity—Is each word understandable without effort?

Pleasantness—Is your voice attractive, inviting, or abrasive?

Warmth—Does your voice have a friendly inflection (I like talking with you), or a cold inflection (I'm busy right now)?

Then sit down and get feedback from your friends. Open yourself to their criticism. The gift of criticism is perhaps the least appreciated but one of the most valuable of all gifts. Making changes in the way you talk will be very, very difficult. But with sufficient commitment, change is possible. Speaking more softly, or more clearly, or at a slower rate can do much to make one's telephone voice more attractive.

How Do You Rate on T.C.Q.?

If you scored 100 points or more:
Nice going! If you scored more than 120, give this booklet to someone else—you don't need it.

If you scored 70 to 100 points:
Better brush up on some of the fine points.

If you scored less than 70 points:
We suggest you read this book again.

Maintaining and Enhancing Involvement

You already are involved with a friend who calls you for help. You can enhance that involvement by responding in a warm, straight, and strong way. Using short response lengths will also heighten involvement by keeping the focus on the caller. Recognizing the feelings (getting the vibrations) of the caller, and reflecting or resonating with the deepest feelings present is crucial to the involvement and helping process. There are other skills that will be important to develop as you seek to help the person on the other end of the line.

Helping Your Friend Move from the "Panic Button" to the "Hold Button"

There is a fuller treatment in chapter ten concerning how to work with persons who are panicked. However, there are special additional skills involved in doing this over the telephone. Panicked persons are caught in the future. They are contemplating some fantasized event in the future that seems terribly dreadful to them. Until you move them from the panic button to the hold button they will probably not hear a word you say. That is, you cannot begin by trying to interact with them on the crisis or the predicament they are in. Rather, you must begin by getting their attention. In a face-to-face situation you can use touch and eye contact. These are unavailable to you on the telephone, of course, so you must resort to another method of "touching" them. One such approach is to use your friend's first name. People are conditioned over a period of many years to tune in when their name is used.

Often a panicked or excited person who calls may speak very rapidly. It will be important for you to respond with a slow rate of speech. Also, you may need to say something such as, "Jim, I want to hear every word you say. Please talk more slowly." His act of controlling his voice rate will help him feel more control of *himself*, and may reduce his panic.

Avoid complex fact-finding questions at first. Questions centering around "What happened?" deal with the past. You will need to help your friend move from his future dread to the present—to the here and now—before collecting data about the past. Therefore, your responses are most helpful in reducing panic when they focus on the here and now, such as, "It's good to hear your voice"; "I'm feeling with you right now"; or "I'll stay on the phone with you until you have decided what to do next." This assurance of your *presence* is the most effective factor in reducing your friend's panic and fear.

The Management of Silences

Suppose a friend who is in some kind of crisis situation calls you and then becomes silent. There are pauses of two or three seconds and perhaps longer. What should you do? Persons in our culture are typically not used to long pauses, or even short ones, for that matter, in either a face-to-face or a telephone situation. (It was determined in one study that the average length of time that a teacher waited for a student to answer a question before going to another student to get an answer was one second.) Often the person on the line just needs time to think. It's important to recognize this by saying something such as, "It's all right to take time to think. I just want you to know that I'm here ready to listen to you," or "It's hard for you to talk right now; you're feeling so deeply, and I understand that. Just wait and talk when you are ready."

Saying something like the above relieves the other person, because he is probably afraid he is making you uncomfortable with his long pauses. Also, he will probably be freed to talk if he doesn't feel he *has* to.

Before You Say Good-Bye

After the panic is reduced and your friend is able to dialogue rationally, it is crucial to check on three things.

Does He Need Someone to Be with Him?

Many times a person calls someone on the phone at night when there is no one close by to talk with face-to-face. Therefore, it is important to see if your friend needs someone with him or if he can make it through the night alone. If your friend is having a drug reaction, for example, it is crucial to have someone there with him. If he is threatening suicide, it is important to have someone with him unless you have sufficiently resolved the situation by phone. Probably the best question to ask is simply, "Do you need someone to be with you?"

What Will Be the Next Step?

It is not necessary, and usually not possible, to come up with a plan of action over the phone. It is, however, most helpful if your friend has firmly in mind the *next step* he will take after hanging up the phone. Get him to go over it with you. It may be that he will see a counselor tomorrow, or go to the emergency room of the hospital tonight, or get together with you for coffee tomorrow, or rest while you or someone else comes over tonight, or call the Veterans Administration this week for information, or call his parents tonight. Whatever it is, there needs to be a discussion of a next step that seems necessary and *possible* to your caller.

A Way to Follow Up

You will probably want to build readiness for some kind of follow-up. It may be with a statement like one of the following: "I'm interested in how it goes at the doctor's." "Would you give me a call after you get back from the office?" or "I'll be waiting to hear from you about how your telephone call goes tomorrow," or "I'll plan to drop by tomorrow evening for a few minutes. OK?" However you choose to follow through, it tells your friend you are interested in him, will remain interested in him, and will check to see how the next step goes. Often this commitment on your part will help him take the next step.

REFERENCES

1. Personal letter from J. K. Thompson, Director of Public Affairs, General Telephone Company of the Midwest, Grinnell, Iowa, July 6, 1976.
2. From the booklet, "The World's Telephones" (American Telephone and Telegraph Company, December 1974), p. 5.
3. *Ibid.*, pp. 6-9.
4. The figures in this paragraph are also from Mr. Thompson's letter of July 6, 1976.
5. Letter from Mr. Thompson mentioned above.
6. From the booklet, "What Every Telephone User Should Know (Telephone Manners from A to Z)," published by the General Telephone Company of the Midwest.

33 Using Recordings

A young woman asked me recently, "Why am I so frightened to be alone?" Underneath her analytical question, there was a deeper, more personal question: "Am I abnormal in this fear?" We were in my office, so I reached for a cassette player and played Dory Previn's recording of "Scared to Be Alone." After she listened to the song, she understood others had the same fear. This began to free her to look for ways to overcome or control the fear.

A couple came to talk about their relationship. Both had to rush to make the appointment. I felt hurried also, so we listened to a recording of "Have You Never Been Mellow?" sung by Olivia Newton-John.

This beautiful song tells about the need to slow down, to be mellow, and to let the other person be strong. The song provided a time for centering on the present moment and for focusing on each other.

I often play music for persons I am in a caring relationship with. Sometimes, as with the above couple, it is as much for me as for them. Nearly always it is helpful in getting a truth across or in bringing us into the present.

What are the taped or other recorded sources available to use in helping a friend? Although there are not as many such resources as there are printed resources, there are more and more recordings available. We will look first at recorded music, then at recorded messages.

Recorded Music

The most exciting helping venture in recorded music that I know of is Recordings for Recovery.[1] This nonprofit ministry was founded by Ralph L. Hoy, and has distributed 18,000 recordings to over 500,000 persons in twenty-five countries since 1957. They send tapes without charge to hospitals, prisons, and other institutions. Some of the world's top musical talent is represented on the tapes.

The tapes have been used successfully with some highly antagonistic young men back from Vietnam, with prisoners (they like Johnny Cash), and with an eleven-year-old girl who was in a coma for ten months after being struck by lightning. She loved music, and the special recordings helped her out of the coma. She sent a tape to Mr. Hoy with her first word, "Hi!"

The phenomenal circulation of music tapes by Recordings for Recovery demonstrates the healing power of music. There are, of course, other proofs of this healing power. These evidences may come from a long time ago, as when the despairing Saul asked David to play for him, or from the present, as in graduate Music Therapy programs at a number of universities.

Let's suppose you have a friend who is very depressed. You are doing what you can to be supportive. Also you are working to make a referral to a professional counselor. In the meantime, you may wish to try music as an aid. Some depressed persons have more difficulty getting out of bed in the morning than others do. It may be that music will help get them going. Music often assists persons who are "down" in the morning to get "up." It may range from Handel's *Messiah* to Bill Gaither's "Let's Just Praise the Lord." You will need to know your friend's musical tastes, of course. Some recorded music you can check out from your local library, some may come from your own collection, and some you may be able to obtain from Recordings for Recovery, by writing to the address in footnote 1.

You may have a friend who is very anxious. It is sometimes a healing experience to sit down with an anxious person and listen to music together. This time investment may mean a great deal to your friend, and you may find yourselves talking about the music after it has been played.

Music and love are universal languages, and often they can be spoken together—by a recording and by your presence. If you have not yet used music in helping a friend, this could be an exciting adventure.

Recorded Messages

During the last decade there has been a cassette explosion, that is, publishers have found that many people prefer to listen to taped information rather than obtain the same information by reading. In junior high school, a student can check out a cassette which *tells* about a career the student is interested in exploring. When he gets to college, he may take General Biology by independent study and receive part of his instruction by audio tape. Later he may keep up with what is happening in his profession by subscribing to a cassette tape service.

What are some sources from which you can get recorded materials for a friend who would rather listen than read? One such source is the eight cassette album on "The Christian Life and Your Emotions,"[2] by Dr. Neil C. Warren, Dean, Graduate School of Psychology, Fuller Seminary, Pasadena, California. It is designed for use by laypersons. The study begins with the negative emotions of fear, anger, despair, and guilt, and moves to the positive emotions of hope, joy and love. Each of these emotions is experienced by every human being.

The source and price for this cassette study are shown in the reference noted above. A source which utilizes several cassettes is necessarily much more expensive than the average book. Many persons therefore cannot afford a cassette study. An approach which I've taken to this situation is to request my church to order worthwhile cassette studies, either as supplementary curriculum material for the Sunday school, or for the church library. This usually also makes possible a wider circulation of the tapes.

There are many persons who need and want help in Bible study in order to improve the quality of their lives. Yet some don't learn effectively visually, and so they find a correspondence course, or a Bible commentary is not for them. Dr. Don Williams, a gifted Bible teacher who has spoken throughout the country in Renewal Conferences, has moved to fill this gap.[3] He has produced scores of cassette tapes under the general heading, "Teaching on Tape." Dr. Williams worked on the streets with youth during the 1960s in Hollywood and Los Angeles, and he knows how to communicate in a straight, effective way. He has studies of many of the individual books of the Bible, as well as of special topics, such as the inductive method of Bible study, atonement, conversion, and Christian character. A brochure noting the topics and costs of the tapes is available from the address given under the reference noted above.

Another source for cassettes which you may use to help a friend is *Faith/at/Work* magazine.[4] Each magazine has a section headed "Emergings," described in this way: "Emergings is like the bulletin board in your neighborhood laundromat: a place to exchange ideas and resources, new directions and experiments. The ideas expressed are not necessarily endorsed by *Faith/at/Work* or by Word, Inc."[5] Usually Emergings includes some cassette offerings along with a number of printed sources. Since these sources have not been screened by the magazine or others, you will need to use your judgment as to which are substantive and sound. Often it is helpful to write the source for more information if the point of view of the tape is unclear.

Talk About It

Loaning a cassette tape to a friend, or recommending one to him makes an important experience possible—talking with your friend about the tape. Some questions that may be worth asking include: What did you learn? Were there statements on the tape which were untrue? Was there one special idea which seems worthwhile to apply to your life?

Such a discussion in which you both share your points of view provides the opportunity to learn new ways of coping with life. Having the chance to talk about one's learning can be very worthwhile to auditory-vocal persons. Such persons learn not just by listening, but by talking. They discover a truth when they say it. They put together a new way of living, not just by hearing it, but by expressing it. Talking it out becomes a means of putting their lives together. You can be a part of this exciting experience by sharing a good tape with a friend and then discussing it.

REFERENCES

1. Recordings for Recovery, Box 288, Oakmont, PA 15139.
2. This album is available from THESIS Publishers, P.O. Box 11724, Pittsburgh, PA 15228, for $35. Price subject to change.
3. Dr. Don Williams's teaching tapes are available from Vericom, Inc., 1277 N. Wilton Pl., Hollywood, CA 90038.
4. The address of *Faith/at/Work* magazine is 11065 Little Patuxent Parkway, Columbia, MD 21044.
5. This quotation is from *Faith/at/Work,* December 1976, p. 1.

Part C

How to Help a Friend Who Learns Best Through SEEING

34 How to Use Books in a Helping Way— *by Anita Norman*

People ordinarily turn to books and to libraries when they have information problems. They consider the resources of libraries less frequently when they have emotional problems, but, in this respect, the imaginative literature of libraries is a resource of great power. Books can be channels of immeasurable good in the healing and helping process for people with special needs.

The idea is really an old one. Inscriptions over libraries in ancient Greece read "Medicine for the Soul."[1] Shakespeare wrote "Come, and take choice of all my library,/ And so beguile thy sorrow."[2] And Dr. Samuel Johnson is reported to have said, "A book should teach us to enjoy life, or to endure it."

Still others testify to the power of literature in their own lives. Malcolm X declared, "I have often reflected upon the new vistas that reading opened to me. I knew right there in prison that reading had changed forever the course of my life."[3]

In a biography of Eugene O'Neill, Arthur and Barbara Gebb document O'Neill's debt to the playwright August Strindberg. O'Neill felt that he might never have begun writing if he had not read Strindberg. In his acceptance of the Nobel Prize in 1936, O'Neill said, "It was reading his plays when I first started to write, back in the winter of 1913-14, that, above all else, first gave me the vision of what modern drama could be, and first inspired me with the urge to write for the theater myself."[4]

Karl Menninger retells the story of John Stuart Mill and his recovery from depression which he attributed to the reading of Marmontel's *Memoires.* [5]

Teachers, librarians, counselors, pastors, parents—almost everyone can similarly recall from their own experience examples of children or adults who have received psychological help from a book they have read. The formalized technique for making use of books in this manner is called bibliotherapy.

HELPING WITH BOOKS—BIBLIOTHERAPY

In the United States the practice of bibliotherapy goes back to the early 1800s when the earliest of the pioneers, Dr. Benjamin Rush, recommended the Bible as therapeutic reading for institutionalized patients.[6] Programs have existed since that time, but in no clearly defined pattern. William and Karl Menninger were leaders whose interest dates from the 1920s. William Menninger read a paper on bibliotherapy to the American Psychiatric Association in 1937.[7]

Ruth Tews, librarian at the Mayo Clinic, serves as an example of the American Library Association's early and continuing effort in providing national leadership and coordination for bibliotherapy.[8] Educators are ably represented by Caroline Shrodes, whose work has been important in establishing a theoretical basis.[9] *Reading Ladders for Human Development,* [10] now in its fifth edition, and *Facilitating Human Development Through Reading: The Use of Bibliotherapy in Teaching and Counseling*[11] are among the most useful books published. Additional titles are given in the Bibliotherapy Bibliography at the end of the chapter.

But What Is Bibliotherapy?

Partly because of the number of helping professions that are involved, and partly because of a pattern of informal and formal use and preventive and therapeutic aspects, authorities feel that bibliotherapy is yet to be acceptably defined. However, a definition in *Webster's Third International Dictionary* is appropriate for the purpose of this discussion: guidance in the solution of personal problems through directed reading.

As a librarian I have seen this kind of therapy at work. On one occasion at a public library in Austin, Texas, an Indian searched with obvious intensity for a particular book for his son, one that he himself had read as a child and that had been meaningful to him. It seemed that he needed the book because it contained an example of an individual's fortitude, courage, and triumph in the face of prejudice and ridicule.

The book he wanted for his son was a biography of Jim Thorpe, and the wisdom manifested by this parent is the wisdom of the art of bibliotherapy. You, too, can offer the right book to persons with special needs. It requires sensitivity, an understanding of how books help, and a knowledge of those books that can help.

Understanding Bibliotherapy

The explanation for how, for the way in which bibliotherapy works, is found in these words: universalization, identification, catharsis, and insight.[12] The reader realizes, first of all, that he is not the only one to face a particular problem. A sense of relief and a release from tension, anxiety, and guilt accompanies this. Then, as he identifies with a character, his attitudes and values are affected. Temporary relief from repressed feelings occurs in the process called catharsis. Insight is achieved as the reader perceives the motivation of the characters, and as he considers the problems and various solutions.

Knowledge of books is best acquired through reading the books themselves. Annotated lists can be consulted such as Zena Sutherland's *The Best in Children's Books*.[13] This guide not only provides reviews of exceptional quality, but includes a subject index and a developmental values index.

The reading of fiction should be, preeminently, a pleasure. Any involvement in that experience should be a sensitive one, not didactic, not destructive of the reader's pleasure. In making selections, it is reasonable to avoid material with a pessimistic or negative outlook or with despondent and depressed characterizations. Arleen Hynes, Librarian at St. Elizabeth Hospital in Washington, D.C., believes that "Literature that reveals beauty, humor, or a genuine reality to the reader is appropriate material."[14]

Patricia Jean Cianciolo, writing in the *Personnel and Guidance Journal* that "Children's Literature Can Affect Coping Behavior," stresses the importance of follow-up activities.[15] While the material itself must be of good literary quality, it is equally important to discuss the problems and evaluate solutions to those problems. Usually, it takes effort to turn bad fortune into something good, or sorrow into wisdom. Ecclesiastes tells us: "For the more my wisdom, the more my grief ..."[16] Bibliotherapy is guidance, a means for making books into sources of help for the troubled.

How to Suggest a Book to a Friend

1. *Think* about the book. Reread it, making note of the quotations that are meaningful to you. What is it that makes you sympathetic toward the characters or situations? Is the book intellectually satisfying to you? Does it provide insights into life?

2. *Select* the appropriate episode, character, idea, or sentence from among those about which you have been thinking. What is it that appeals to you that might also appeal to others: What is touching, humorous, or interesting about the book? Consider mentioning just one or two of these to your friend since you do not want to be overwhelming or lengthy in your approach.

3. *Suggest and offer* the book with the genuine and natural enthusiasm that you feel. The book has meant something to you. Speak of that meaning. You are offering to share that which you have found to be consoling and helpful for life-healing, "medicine for the soul."

SOME BOOKS FOR HELPING

Physical Handicaps

> Christopher, Matthew F. *Sink It, Rusty.* Boston: Little, Brown and Company, 1963. Grades 4-6.
>
> Because of the encouragement and understanding of an older boy, Rusty, despite his lameness, becomes an important member of his town's basketball team.

> Killilea, Marie. *Karen.* New York: Prentice-Hall, 1952. Grade 7—.
>
> One of the best known books about a handicapped child with cerebral palsy. The author is the mother of Karen and writes with poignancy about the first years of her daughter's life. She is indefatigable in her dedication toward making Karen's life as normal as possible.

Mental Handicaps

> Byars, Betsy. *The Summer of the Swans.* New York: Viking, 1970. Grades 5-9.
>
> A story so gracefully told, tender, and honest about a girl growing up, that its achievement in depicting a sister's love for her mentally retarded brother is apt to be slighted. When Charlie is lost in the woods, Sara is the one who finds him and finds her perspective again.

Divorce, Broken Homes

> Eyerly, Jeannette. *The World of Ellen March.* Philadelphia: J. B. Lippincott, 1964. Grades 7-9.
>
> An intelligent and sensible Ellen March has had to cope with moving, making friends, and new schools more times than most sixteen-year-olds, but adjusting to her parents' divorce is another matter. Ellen eventually realizes that life sometimes holds very hard and difficult circumstances which cannot be changed.

> Hunt, Irene. *Up a Road Slowly.* Chicago: Follett, 1966. Grades 7-9.

Distinguished by the fine quality of its writing, its sensitivity and compassion, this story is about a girl who is sent to live with an aunt after the death of her mother. When her father remarries and wants his daughter to return home, Julia discovers that she loves her aunt too much to leave her.

Sibling Relationships, The Middle Child

Kingman, Lee. *The Year of the Racoon.* Boston: Houghton Mifflin, 1966. Grades 6-9.

The narrator is a middle child who has neither the musical talent of his older brother nor the scholastic ability of his younger brother. He proves, however, the value of other abilities, and develops maturity during the year that also includes caring for a pet racoon. Affectionately told, the author's sympathy is evident in all of the characterizations, but especially in her treatment of the despair of the older brother.

Estes, Eleanor. *The Middle Moffat.* New York: Harcourt, Brace and Company, 1942. Grades 4-6.

The dignity and imperturbability of this middle child and her family have an appeal that has lasted for more than thirty years. Jane's matter-of-fact and cheerful insight emerges in episode after episode while humor and a happy ending add to the pleasure of the story.

Drugs

Wojciechowska, Maia. *Tuned Out.* New York: Harper and Row, 1968. Grade 9—.

Jim is bewildered and frightened when he learns his brother Kevin has "tuned out" with drugs his first year away at college. A bad trip forces the truth into the open and it is a shattering experience for each member of the family. Written with gentleness and understanding, this book for young people is recommended to parents.

Parents and Children

Potok, Chaim. *My Name Is Asher Lev.* New York: Knopf, 1972. Grade 10—.

The hurt that is felt by both parents and child when ideas and philosophies conflict is sensitively presented in this story of a young Jewish artist and his parents.

Self-Concept

Powell, John Joseph. *Why Am I Afraid to Tell You Who I Am?* Chicago: Argus Communications, 1969. Grade 10—.

Developing the idea that honesty and openness in dealing with emotions are crucial to a fulfilled and mature life, this book is representative of numerous excellent nonfiction titles of inestimable help in understanding the human condition. The title provides a sample of the style and perception of the author.

REFERENCES

1. Eleanor Francis Brown, *Bibliotherapy and Its Widening Applications* (Metuchen, New Jersey: Scarecrow, 1975), p. 13.
2. Shakespeare, *Titus Andronicus* IV. i. 34, 35.
3. Malcolm Little, *The Autobiography of Malcolm X* (New York: Grove, 1965), p. 180.
4. Arthur and Barbara Gebb, *O'Neill* (New York: Harper and Row, 1965), pp. 233, 234.
5. Karl Menninger, "Reading as Therapy," *ALA Bulletin,* 55 (April, 1961), 317.
6. Brown, p. 14.
7. William C. Menninger, "Bibliotherapy," *Bulletin of the Menninger Clinic,* 1 (November, 1937), 263-74.
8. Ruth M. Tews (ed.), *Library Trends,* October 1962.
9. Caroline Shrodes, "Bibliotherapy: An Application of Psychoanalytic Theory," *American Imago,* 17 (1960), 311-319.
10. Virginia M. Reid, *Reading Ladders for Human Relations* (5th ed.; Washington, D.C.: American Council on Education, 1972).
11. Joseph S. Zaccaria and Harold A. Moses, *Facilitating Human Development Through Reading: The Use of Bibliotherapy in Teaching and Counseling* (Champaign, Illinois: Stipes, 1968).
12. S. R. Slavson, *A Textbook in Analytic Group Psychotherapy* (New York: International Universities Press, 1964), pp. 142-158.
13. Zena Sutherland, *The Best in Children's Books: the University of Chicago Guide to Children's Literature 1966-1972* (Chicago: University of Chicago Press, 1973).
14. Arleen Hynes, "Bibliotherapy at St. Elizabeth's Hospital," *Health and Rehabilitative Library Services,* 1 (October, 1975), p. 18.
15. Patricia Jean Cianciolo, "Children's Literature Can Affect Coping Behavior," *Personnel and Guidance Journal,* 43 (May, 1965) p. 901.
16. Ecclesiastes 1:18a, *The Living Bible.*

BIBLIOTHERAPY BIBLIOGRAPHY

American Library Association. Association of Hospital and Institution Libraries. *Bibliotherapy: Methods and Materials.* Chicago: American Library Association, 1973.

Brown, Eleanor Francis. *Bibliotherapy and Its Widening Applications.* Metuchen, New Jersey: Scarecrow, 1975.

Gillespie, John and Lembo, Diana. *Introducing Books: A Guide for the Middle Grades.* New York: Bowker, 1970.

Monroe, Margaret E. *Reading Guidance and Bibliotherapy in Public, Hospital and Institution Libraries.* Madison: University of Wisconsin, 1971.

Palmer, Julia Reed. *Read for Your Life; Two Successful Efforts to Help People Read and an Annotated List of Books That Made Them Want to Read.* Metuchen, New Jersey: Scarecrow, 1973.

Porterfield, Austin E. *Mirror for Adjustment: Therapy in Home, School and Society Through Seeing Yourself and Others in Books.* Leo Potishman Foundation, Texas Christian University, 1967.

Reid, Virginia M. *Reading Ladders for Human Relations.* 5th ed. Washington, D.C.: American Council on Education, 1972.

Rubin, Rhea Joyce, ed. *Health and Rehabilitative Library Services* Vol. 1 No. 2, October 1975.

Schultheis, Miriam. *A Guidebook for Bibliotherapy.* Glenview, Illinois: Psychotechnics, Inc., 1972.

Schwoebel, Barbara. "Bibliotherapy; A Guide to Materials," *Catholic Library World,* 44 (May-June 1973), 586-592.

Somerville, Rose M., ed. *Intimate Relationships: Marriage, Family, and Lifestyles Through Literature.* Englewood Cliffs, New Jersey: Prentice Hall, 1975.

Sutherland, Zena. *The Best in Children's Books; the University of Chicago Guide to Children's Literature 1966-1972.* Chicago: University of Chicago Press, 1973.

Tews, Ruth M. "Progress in Bibliotherapy," in Melvin J. Voight, *Advances in Librarianship*, Vol. 1, p. 171-188, New York: Academic Press, 1970.

Zaccaria, Joseph S. and Moses, Harold A. *Facilitating Human Development Through Reading: The Use of Bibliotherapy in Teaching and Counseling.* Champaign, Illinois: Stipes, 1968.

35 Using Napkins and Note Pads

Persons with a strong visual channel often change their behavior more after seeing a simple sketch than after a long listen-talk session. After I finally discovered this fact, I began to keep a piece of paper nearby for helping relationships with "visual" persons. If we are in a restaurant, it's a napkin. If we're in my office, it's a note pad. Just last month a twenty-five-year-old man said to me, "Those little drawings you make have helped me understand where I am and what I need to do."

I'll share with you a few of the drawings I use and the kind of predicaments which the drawings speak to. Along with the drawing,

I'll include what I say about the drawing, although my explanation varies with each person and situation. There are hundreds of other sketches that could be created for as many different situations. You may want to build a repertoire of your own sketches. Try them with a friend, then keep those sketches that make the most sense to the other person. You can tell from your friend's expression and response when a sketch has added a new dimension to the listen-talk interaction.

WHAT GOOD DOES IT DO TO TALK?

If someone asks me this question, I may reply, "Sometimes it doesn't do any good. But other times it helps to explore one's thoughts and feelings. It prepares us for action, as this sketch shows.[1] Some people can move directly out of a serious predicament by taking immediate action, but most cannot. Most persons profit from sharing their predicament with a friend. The process usually helps them to understand themselves and their situation better, so they can put together a plan of action and begin to follow that plan."

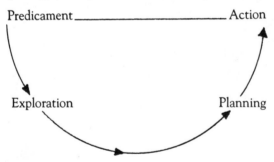

Why Do I Get Involved in These Messes?

Some people seem to have more than their share of predicaments. In many cases these persons have done nothing to bring them on—a series of circumstances seem to invade their lives. In other cases, persons become immersed in predicaments because they have acted impulsively. Therefore, when someone asks me, "Why do these things happen to me? Why do I get involved in all these messes?" I usually reply, "I don't know." Then if it is my observation that impulsive behavior may have been a factor in causing the predicaments, I may say something like the following:

"What I'm going to say to you now, you'll need to take with a grain of salt; it may be accurate or it may not be. You have to be the judge. From my point of view, you sometimes do something you *feel* like doing without giving it careful thought and then making a considered decision about it. It's like this drawing shows; you may be going from feeling to doing, and bypassing the thinking and choosing channels. When we short-circuit this process, we sometimes cause a blowup. How do you see yourself here? Does this seem to fit you and the way you do things, or not?" I've found it helpful to offer my sketch as a tentative explanation, and not to push the other person to see it this way. It is much more effective to listen to the person and respond to his point of view.

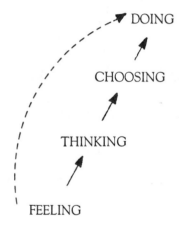

Is My Marriage Worth Working on?

This question is usually *not* asked. It is an underlying, unspoken question deep down below such statements as "I'm tired of trying to make it go all by myself," "I don't know what to do," or "I don't think I love him [her] anymore." After a time of listening and resonating with your friend's deepest emotions, it is often appropriate to deal with this unasked question. One way I do this is by saying something like this, while drawing the sketch shown here:

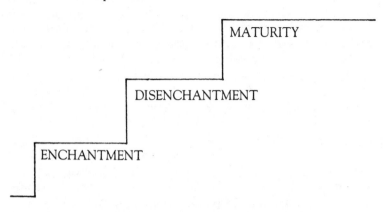

"One of the ways I look at where you are is that you are very much disenchanted with your marriage. There may have been a time when you were enchanted with your relationship, and this kept you from seeing things as they really are, as you do now. Another way of looking at your marriage is that you may be a step closer to maturity *now* than you were then. Some couples apparently can take the long step from enchantment to maturity and miss the disenchanted stage, but most seem to have to spend some time in the disenchantment stage just to get back to reality. Do you fit into this pattern anywhere? How do you see it?"

I also use the sketches taught to me by Dr. G. B. Dunning.[2] When I'm talking with a person who is angry and is taking revenge on a loved one, I often use the sketch shown here, while saying something like this: "I don't know if this is where you are, but try it on for size. Sometimes when someone says or does something that deeply hurts us, for instance at point H, we feel the hurt for a moment

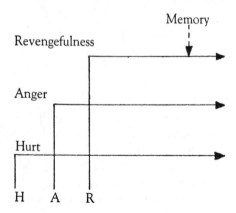

and it rises within us, but we may not say anything about it. Then a little later, at point A, we feel anger beginning to rise within us because the other person hurt us. If we do not report our anger to the other person, we may experience a feeling of revengefulness (R) coming up inside us, and at that time we begin to hurt the other person. Now when we *remember* the event, we encounter the last emotion first, because it is the one freshest in our memory. The hurt has been layered over by other emotions and we are out of touch with it. Therefore, whenever we think of the event we get angry and start hurting the other person again. One way to break this cycle is to think back beyond the revenge and anger to the event, get in touch with the hurt we felt at that time, and report the hurt to our mate by saying something like, 'When you said [or did] that, it really hurt me.' What do you think of this approach? I can feel the anger and the desire to hurt Jane which you have (if this is something I really do feel). Is there any hurt deep down inside *you?*"

Sometimes someone will say to me about his/her husband or wife, "We just don't communicate anymore; what can be done so that we start talking to each other again?" One possible reply is, "Some couples don't talk with each other because they don't do much together. If you work or play alongside each other, it is more natural and easy to talk with each other. Have you looked at your shared activities? You can see in these little sketches that some couples, like in A, have many things they do together. The overlapping area of the circles may include doing the dishes or shopping, skiing, taking a coffee break, teaching a Sunday school class, mowing the lawn, hiking, sharing hobbies, picnicking with the family, or doing hundreds of other activities. Other couples,

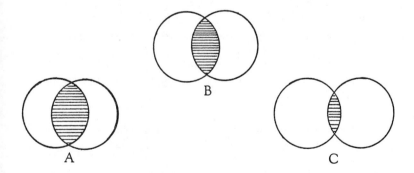

SHARED ACTIVITIES

such as B shows, have a few things they do together. Still other couples, as C shows, do almost nothing together. Where do you fit into these drawings? What activities do you and Al share?"

Many couples feel hopeless about their lack of communication with each other because they feel they don't know how to talk with each other. However, it often is not so much a matter of skill but of closeness. Communication is built on a sense of community, and having common, shared tasks can restore this sense of community. Then communication will often be renewed. The above overlapping circles help people *visualize* the need for shared tasks and activities.

SOME GUIDELINES IN SKETCHING

You will come up with drawings of your own if this approach makes sense to you as you respond to a friend's call for help. Following are a few guidelines that may prove helpful to you in this venture:

1) Keep your drawings simple. Two or three lines or circles can map out a profound truth. The more complex a drawing is, the more likely it is to obscure rather than reveal what you are trying to get across.

2) Study the great cartoonists to learn how they communicate with simple lines. *The New York World Telegram and Sun* has noted this special skill of communication which one cartoonist, the creator of "Peanuts," has demonstrated:

Charles Schulz is the only man we know who can make a round circle, a dash, a loop and two black spots express the following: an abiding love for Beethoven, a disillusionment with all women or an eight-day crusade of hate against a paper kite.

If Charlie Schulz jiggles the circle, spots, dash and loop one way a comic strip character named Charlie Brown will tear your heart out with man's inhumanity to man. If he wiggles them a little differently he will set you to laughing so hard your sides will ache.

The ability to make these little ink scratches into facial expressions is, of course, the mark of the great cartoonist—and Charlie Schulz has only recently been voted the greatest of them all by the National Cartoonists Society.[3]

The chances are we will not learn how to become a great cartoonist by investing some time studying comic and political cartoons, but we may learn how to communicate more effectively using lines, circles, and squiggles.

3) Offer the drawing, as well as what you say, to your friend with a tentative, "Could it be ..." approach. He is the only one who can make the decision about whether the concept is accurate and fits him or not.

4) Orient the drawing so it is the right side up from your friend's point of view. Place your pencil at different points on the drawing as you talk about the concept involved.

5) After a brief explanation of the concept behind the drawing, ask your friend how this fits his situation. An open-ended question like this may bring about some important thinking. Also, you will learn how accurate your view of the situation is. Such feedback will help you become more perceptive.

6) Be open to sharing your pencil and your napkin or note pad with your friend who may be wanting to sketch his situation the way *he* sees it. You will then have the opportunity to "listen with your eyes" as he expresses himself in this way.

REFERENCES

1. This idea is discussed more fully in the book by Robert R. Carkhuff and Bernard G. Berenson, *Beyond Counseling and Therapy* (New York: Holt, Rinehart and Winston, Inc., 1967, pp. 135-144). The authors discuss the "downward" phase of therapy during which the client moves to deeper levels of self-exploration. This is followed by the "upward" phase, which is a time of "emergent directionality," i.e., a time for planning and action.
2. G. B. Dunning is a counseling psychologist living in Greenwood, Nebraska. I am indebted to him for the concept of hurt overlaying anger as shown on page 244, and for the shared activities drawing on page 245.
3. From the cover of *The Wonderful World of Peanuts*, by Charles M. Schulz (New York: Fawcett World Library, 1954). This was quoted from *The New York World Telegram and Sun*.

36 Imagine That! The Use of Images
by Marvin G. Knittel

It was one of those warm fall afternoons when my older brother, sister, and I started that last half-mile across the pasture to our farm home on the back of our cow-pony. I was excited about having just completed another day in the first grade, totally unaware that what was to happen within the next twenty minutes would have a greater impact on my life than any other single event. As the pony came into the barnyard, he broke into a fast trot, turning sharply to the right, hurling the three of us to the ground. Three days later, the surgeon was explaining to my parents that it was necessary to amputate my left arm a few inches below the shoulder in order to stop the spread of gangrene.

Reflecting on the years that followed brings back vivid memories of how difficult it was to change the image that I had of myself as a person with two arms to that of a person with one. Reflections in a mirror, photographs, and logic were clear enough. There was but one arm. The image from the window of my own mind continued to reflect two arms. Accepting reality was not an easy matter. This new image was not acceptable to me, and at first I was convinced that it was not acceptable to anyone else. Gradually I began to learn a very important lesson. The more I began to acknowledge and accept myself as I was, the more it seemed other people accepted me for what I was. Slowly but surely, when I reformed an image of myself, the absence of one arm became part of that image; and the difference that I was so strongly rejecting became a difference that made no difference.

Thirty-six years later, I find myself recalling those times when, as a psychologist, I help other people find ways to deal with problems and events in their lives through their power of imagination. Take Mary, for example. It was only eight months after her mother had died when her father was found in the living room one evening, lying dead, with a revolver in his own hand. "I don't know what to do; everything seems so strange," she said, with an emptiness in her voice. Trying to capture the depth of her feelings, I said, "It feels as though you've just walked into a familiar room but someone has removed part of the furniture and rearranged the rest." "Yes," she said, "nothing is the same. It's like I keep searching for that comfortable chair that was mine, and I know should still be there, but I can't find it." What I had attempted to do was to sharpen the image of Mary's dilemma. It helped bring into focus some feelings that were fuzzy and vague, but nonetheless overwhelming. From that point on, we began to talk about how she could begin rearranging her life even though two very important parts were missing. Six months later when Mary turned sixteen, the "furniture" in her own life had been rearranged with complete acceptance of the fact that two worn but comfortable items were missing and could never be replaced.

Phyliss, also, was dealing with a loss. The only difference was that instead of losing her parents, she had lost her husband. She came to me after six months of being desperately lonely and having closed the door on almost all parts of her life with other people. "I feel so alone; and nothing seems to matter anymore," was almost her first tearful statement. The importance of capturing an image of her desperation was significant. I said, "You've been cast adrift alone on a raft with no sense of direction or any land in sight." "Exactly," she said, "I don't even care if I survive—in fact, there are a lot of times that I hope I don't." "Would it make a difference if you found the oars and could begin moving in one direction or the other?" I asked. Staring down at the floor and shaking her head, she said, "I don't think I would even know how to use them." At least by then Phyliss had formed a visual image of how she saw life at that point. The interesting result of my sessions with Phyliss was that she continued to build on that original image, step by step, assuming greater responsibility, learning how to "work the oars," "set a course," and "welcome the sight of an approaching ship and accept the help of those on board." The sharpness of the image of where she was and the development of an image of where she could go made a difference for Phyliss because she could unfold the panorama of her own life through the window of her own imagination.

Jesus used the power of images as he touched the lives of those around him. You will recall in Matthew 7:24-27, Jesus speaks of building a house on sand or on solid rock. The images of his words lingered and helped those who listened to understand and to remember the importance of building faith on a solid foundation. The image of a camel passing through the eye of a needle as mentioned in Mark 10:23-27, created an immediate and lasting image of the futility of man hoping for eternal salvation without a trust and belief that with God, all things are possible.

How can you, as a helper, use the power of imagination to help someone in time of trouble? There are many who need, and can use, a strong visual image to help themselves deal effectively with a problem or a predicament. At the risk of oversimplifying the helping process, I am going to outline a few steps that you may follow.

Step One: Capture an image of what your friend is feeling about the problem or predicament.

Your friend Fred comes to you and sooner or later gets around to saying something like, "I try, but nothing ever seems to work out right. I just make life miserable for myself and everyone I care about!" One of the first questions you must ask yourself is, "What is Fred telling me about the image he has of himself right now?" Is he saying, "I feel worthless," and no one seems to know? Is he a prisoner in his own dungeon, tapping a message on the wall, desperately hoping someone will hear? The important thing to deal with at this point is how Fred *feels* about his predicament, instead of trying to determine exactly what the predicament is.

Fred: "I try, but nothing ever seems to work out right. I seem to, etc...."
You: "You're feeling worthless and guilty."
Fred: "Maybe they would all be better off if I just left."
You: "You can't seem to face the disappointment you feel in yourself and that you're sure they feel in you."
Fred: "It just seems like I'm always down."
You: "Right now, you feel like you're a sponge that has been squeezed and squeezed until it is absolutely dry."
Fred: "That's right! Everything is drained out of me."
You: "And you haven't found any way to fill yourself back up again?"
Fred: "No, I just don't know how; it seems I will stay dry and empty."

Two things have happened. First, Fred has found someone who understands his predicament, and second, the image that he has of himself at this point in time has become sharper.

Sometimes this first step can be completed after an hour of talking with your friend, and sometimes it may take several hours, depending upon the trust that your friend has in you, as well as the depth and confusion of his feelings.

Sometimes your friend will begin by describing his predicament with an image. For example, I recall a young man began by saying, "I feel like I'm in a dark closet." Instead of helping him *build* an image to sharpen his perception of the predicament, I tried to interpret what message he was giving me with the image. "Are you saying that you feel lonely, frightened, and not sure anyone cares?" was my reply. "Yes, I don't think anyone cares if I live or die," he said.

So we see that two types of discussion may take place in Step One. First, your friend may say straight out how he or she feels, around which an image can be built to sharpen the understanding of the predicament. Or, second, your friend may describe his feeling by using an image, in which case you can respond by saying what feelings the image seems to be describing.

If this seems a little contradictory, keep in mind that your friend will tell you about himself or herself in whatever way is most comfortable and least threatening. By describing the predicament with an image, your friend avoids having to say straight out, "I'm lonely, miserable, and rejected." Such a straightforward approach may be much too difficult, so he or she may describe the predicament with an analogy or an image. You become an interpreter. Don't be afraid. Your friend needs you to help put things into perspective with straight language.

Step Two: Help your friend build a different image.

You will recall earlier in the chapter how difficult it was for me to form an image of myself with one arm. Any change in the way your friend sees himself or herself would be no less difficult. Perhaps you could say to your friend, "We know what kind of image you have of yourself now. What kind of image would you *like* to have of yourself?" Let's go back to Fred and imagine some things that might happen.

Fred: "Frankly, I would like to be treated with a little more respect."
You: "Would you like to be king and master?"
Fred: "No, that would be phony. I just want people to treat me like a human being—like what I said was worth listening to."
You: "Right now you feel invisible, but what you would like is to be included and noticed. Could it be that your life is like a mirror? That when you frown at it, it frowns back: When you growl at it, it growls back? Or, even when you smile at it, it smiles back?"
Fred: "Are you saying, 'I get back what I give'?"
You: "Do you think you could build an image like that for yourself?"
Fred: "Maybe. It wouldn't be easy."
You: "Maybe, together, we can work on it, piece by piece."

Help your friend take one small step at a time by identifying along with him or her specific things that could be done which fit a new image. For example, in the case of Fred, it is not likely that he will feel listened to until he learns how to listen. A simple thing Fred could be taught to do would be to paraphrase the comments of other people, demonstrating that he has heard what they have said, paving the way for others to more intently listen to what Fred has to say.

Step Three: Give your friend support.

The process of building a new image and letting go of the old is frequently a very lonely and, sometimes, painful process. The relationship that you form with your friend presents a bridge on which your friend can depend as he crosses from one image to another. The strength, warmth, and patience of that relationship represents the strength and stability of that bridge. The investment that you make in your friend may yield high returns; however, the possibility of a low return is always there. Your willingness to make substantial investments with no guarantee of an interest rate is what distinguishes you, as a person who can help, from others less willing.

Conclusion.

This chapter has attempted to give you some idea of how you may use the power of imagination and imagery to help your friend confront and visualize a dilemma, as well as find ways to capture a new and different image of him or herself. Describing our thoughts by creating visual images is not a new phenomenon; however, the deliberate use of such an approach, particularly with people who are very visually oriented, can be very beneficial in a helping relationship. Capturing an image that may linger serves as a very useful and important tool for some people as they search for new understandings and reach for new levels of development. Each of us has that tool at our disposal and we have frequently translated our experiences, thoughts, and feelings into images that help sharpen our understanding and translate "pictures" to other people.

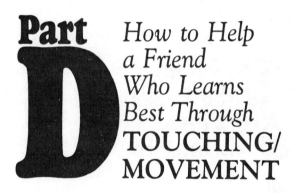

Part

D

*How to Help
a Friend
Who Learns
Best Through*
**TOUCHING/
MOVEMENT**

37 Helping the Person Who Learns By Doing

Do we learn to move or move to learn? As with the chicken and the egg, it is difficult to know which comes first. In this case, perhaps both processes go on at once. Certainly movement is a crucial factor in learning, as we can see by observing a baby. During the first few weeks of life, he has many involuntary limb movements. Sometime in the early months he may hit a rattle with a reflex movement. If he is sufficiently developed, he will turn his head toward the object that he feels and hears. Later, visual steering will take over and he will look at the rattle and *then* reach for it. He has both moved to learn and learned to move.

Moving in order to learn seems to be as valid a method for learning with adults as with babies. Obviously, it is essential in learning physical skills. One can only learn so much about a tennis serve, for example, by reading a book by an expert or listening to a tennis pro. Movement also helps us in learning *social skills*. As a rather ridiculous example, I point to my own work with a mirror. I have had a tendency to spread myself too thin because it has been hard for me to say no to those asking for my involvement. A method that has helped me is to practice saying no in front of a mirror (I use the one in our bedroom when no one else is around. It is not the sort of activity that is improved by an audience). I say it and watch myself in the mirror until I become comfortable and skilled in saying no without an explanation, without an edge on my voice, and without an apology.

Other persons tell me they have found the mirror practice beneficial. One melancholic-appearing young man who wanted to make friends practiced smiling at himself in the mirror five times a day for a week. Later he went out and began smiling at other people. He was so desperate for friends that he kept working at it until smiling came naturally—he didn't have to *work* at it anymore. He had felt warm and friendly deep inside all along, but he finally learned to express it. He had learned by doing.

As mentioned earlier, we do the same thing with dental floss. The reason we use it the first time is not because we know it's helpful in preventing tooth decay. We use it because our dentist or another person we trust suggests it or urges us to use it. Then when we use it and see for ourselves that it gets out particles between teeth that toothbrushes do not, we have learned the value of using dental floss.

The auditory learner is often a "people" learner. He listens to and talks with another person, and learns by doing this. The visual learner is often a "thing" learner. He reads a book or looks at a film and learns from that experience. The touch/movement learner usually is an "action" learner. He learns by doing. Now the above classification is an oversimplification, of course. We all learn in all three (and other) ways. But if we view the channels of learning as being of different sizes, it makes the most sense to approach our friend through the "biggest" channel, the one through which information can be processed most quickly and efficiently.

What percentage of people learn most efficiently by touch/movement? During the last six months I have administered the

Learning Styles Checklist (shown on page 191) to 213 college students. The results are shown in the chart, "Learning Channel Preferences of College Majors."

LEARNING CHANNEL PREFERENCES OF COLLEGE MAJORS*

VISUAL		AUDITORY		TOUCH/MOVEMENT		COMBINATION	
Elem. Educ.	8	Elem. Educ.	10	Phys. Educ.	16	Phys. Educ.	8
Bus. Educ.	7	Undecided	6	Ind. Educ.	11	Elem. Educ.	7
Phys. Educ.	6	Phys. Educ.	4	Elem. Educ.	10	Spec. Educ.	7
Math. Educ.	4	Bus. Educ.	3	Art	9	Biology	5
Journalism	3	Music	3	History	4	Bus. Educ.	3
Speech Path.	3	Home Ec.	3	Biology	3	English	2
English	2	Journalism	2	Music	2	Home Ec.	2
Art	2	Math. Educ.	2	Math. Educ.	2		
Biology	2	Psychology	2	Undecided	2		
				Home Ec.	2		
				Bus. Educ.	2		
				Pre-Nurs.	2		
Other Majors*	14		13		7		8
Totals	51		48		72		42

*Each of the students in this category represents only one major. For example, the 14 students shown in this category in the Visual column represent 14 different major departments.

Most of the 213 students were sophomores and juniors. The students were asked to fill out the checklist first, then to put those results with other information they could think of about how they learned. They were also asked to question those near them in an effort to get others' opinions about their learning. Based on the total of this information, they were to make a judgment about their preferred learning channel. It could be visual, auditory, touch/movement, or combination. The latter category was used if there was no clear superiority among the channels.

The numbers and the percentage of students reporting the various preferred channels are shown in the chart. More persons reported their preferred learning channel as touch/movement than any other single channel—almost 34%. The next highest was the visual channel with about 24%, followed by the auditory channel—about 23%, and combination, about 20%. It needs to be noted that these results are based on self-reports, not a set of intensive observations. However, the use of the checklist, the input of others' judgments, and some introspection on the part of each person gives some weight to the results.

Some of the results were expected. Most of the physical education majors (sixteen) were touch/movement learners. Nearly all the industrial education and art majors were touch/movement learners. Some of the results were unexpected. The four history majors were touch/movement learners rather than visual, as one might expect. The three speech pathology majors were visual rather than auditory as I had anticipated. Of course, the numbers involved in these last two majors (four and three) are too small to provide the basis for any firm deductions. Deductions we can make, however, are that a significant proportion of people are touch/movement learners, and that we need to use communication methods appropriate to them if we are to be effective helpers.

SOME GUIDELINES FOR HELPING THE TOUCH/MOVEMENT PERSON

An Activity Usually Helps the Touch/Movement Person to Talk

Apparently the disciples had some of their best talks with Jesus when they were walking, or mending their nets, or fishing. They were men of action, and movement was important to them. This fit into Jesus' method of teaching because he could point to a lily or a sparrow or a flock of sheep to illustrate a spiritual truth.

If a friend who is a touch/movement learner comes to you for help, you may want to go for a walk, or a ride, play a Scrabble game, build a bird cage, repair a car, or go shopping—whatever activity appeals to your friend (assuming, of course, there is not an urgency in his predicament).

One counselor who has reported some success in working with children who are reluctant to talk has an unusual approach. He plays checkers with the child. By the fifth or sixth game the child is often carrying on a conversation with the counselor. Later they begin talking about the child's predicament. There is something about the shared activity, the joint time investment, that makes talking natural.

A couple talked with me this week. One of them said, "The problem is we just don't communicate with each other anymore." When they began to talk about shared activities, they found she was spending nearly all her time with their three small children and her church, and he was spending nearly all his time with his work. They are fine persons who had no intention of falling out of love. But they were beginning to discover that communication has to be built on community. And community is built partly on shared activities. They decided to begin *doing* some things together. Although the wife is a strong auditory learner, the husband is a touch/movement learner, and he talks to the persons he *does things with.* This is one reason why he has a very close relationship with his fellow workers, and not a close relationship right now with his wife.

A number of women report that their husbands "never share their feelings." In most cases these men are action persons. The wife may find it helpful to begin, not by trying to get her husband to talk, but rather to share some activities together that are acceptable to both. This helps reestablish the relationship and makes talking more natural and possible.

Practice Social Skills with Your Friend

Touch/movement persons typically value action more than talking. Therefore, they often have not worked to improve their dialogue skills. If they are in a predicament because they are not communicating effectively, and if they come to you for help, you are in a good position to use action, their strong channel, to help them improve their listening-talking skills.

You may begin by noticing what your friend does with his body while you talk together. If he slouches, you can let him know this stance may carry with it an "I'm not interested" message to the other member of the dialogue. Ask if this is something he wants to change. If it is, you can suggest he begin by sitting tall or leaning forward as the two of you talk. If he requests, remind him when he slouches again. It is crucial that you find out, as mentioned above, whether he really wants to change. Otherwise, this activity is a waste of time and may cause him to resent you.

You can also teach your friend (again if he desires to make this change) to use eye contact effectively. It is a discount to the person talking when the other person looks around the room or down at the floor. Some listeners do this without being aware of it. And they may be receiving every word. But the person talking is not affirmed as he would be if the listener looks at him. You can teach eye contact by letting your friend know you appreciate it when he looks at you as you are talking, and by asking him if he is "with you" when he is looking away. He needs to build both his awareness and a habit of eye contact.

Sometimes it is helpful to practice actual dialogue. A friend asked me why people didn't listen to him when he talked. We had known each other for some time, so I knew his dialogue style, and I knew I could confront him. The reason people didn't listen to him was that he typically talked in 90-120 second segments. You could, for example, read most of this page aloud in that time. His friends were tuning him out because they felt left out of the conversation. He was, without intending to, giving a series of short speeches, instead of carrying on a dialogue. It happened that he had a very strong need to be understood, so he often explained his explanations. I chose to help him deal with his actual speech pattern rather than help him find out why he had this strong need to be understood. There were probably twenty-nine (or forty-three) reasons why he had this need. Once he discovered them all, he would still have to make the change in his communication style.

So once he had committed himself to changing the way he talked, we bypassed the analytic approach and moved instead to the present moment. I used my wristwatch, which has a sweep second hand, and while we talked over a half-hour period, I held my hand up when he had talked fifteen seconds. He stopped talking and I began. Often I cut him off in the middle of a sentence. Toward the end of the thirty-minute conversation, he was keeping most of his responses to ten to fifteen seconds. Of course, communication patterns are very deeply ingrained, so this was just the beginning of change for him. He committed himself to sharing with several other close friends his desire to change the way he talked. I considered this an important commitment, because he needed massive support and help to make this change.

Sometimes persons need help in saying, "I love you." In an informal setting with several persons present, a thirty-five-year-old man said he could never remember telling his mother he loved her. After he made a commitment to do this, a woman in the group took the role of his mother, and they began talking. In the first try they wound up in an argument before he could say what he wanted to. But this was helpful in his understanding of the power struggle that was going on between them. Another person took his role a second time through and demonstrated how it was possible to avoid the power struggle by talking about their *relationship* rather than about opinions and values on which they differed. At the next gathering of the group, he shared his experience with his mother that week. He said, "We were talking and I just blurted out, 'I love you, Mom.' " It had been a very warm, rewarding moment for both of them. And he said he didn't think he could have done it if he hadn't tried it once as a "dry run."

Use Task Agreements

A person who learns by doing needs practice not only with a friend once a week, but usually also profits by working on tasks throughout the week. One way to decide which tasks would be helpful is to look at your friend's *life-style* channels. If he is weak in the feeling channel, he can usually profit from tasks which emphasize the expression of warmth to others. For example, he can use the approach mentioned above involving smiling; he can work on listening, posture, and eye contact with others during the week; he can work at getting physically closer to others. If he is weak in the life-style channel of thinking, he can work to reduce his impulsiveness, by not making immediate decisions—by writing out expected consequences of his decisions. If he is weak in the choosing channel, he can read books which involve the search for meaning, he can rank order his values, and he can begin making little decisions "on the spot" rather than putting them off. All these methods are discussed more fully in Section Four of this book.

In summary, you can help the touch/movement learner, the action-oriented person, best by getting him to take action designed to change his life-style or communication style in a positive way. You need to have a close enough involvement with your friend that he is willing to commit himself to a course of action that may not make sense to him. If he trusts you enough to take action, then the learning will follow.

REFERENCES

1. Paul R. Welter, "Preferred Sensory Learning Modalities of College Students," *Platte Valley Review,* Spring 1977, Kearney State College, Kearney, Nebraska, pp. 36-46.

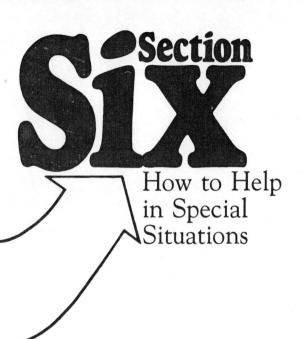

Section Six

How to Help
in Special
Situations

38

Divorce— Finding a Way to Help

This chapter is limited to one aspect of divorce—how does one help a friend who is going through the divorce process? Let's suppose we have done what we could as a friend to bring about reconciliation using, for example, some of the methods described in this book. Others have tried to help too, but the couple, or in some cases one of the two, has determined to separate and obtain a divorce. It is this situation that this chapter speaks to.

I agree with Britton Wood regarding marriage and divorce:

The issue is not whether people should or should not divorce. God's intention in marriage is consistent and the church should

267

continually uphold the ideal of one man and one woman as long as both persons live. The fact is, however, that people are divorced and will continue to divorce. What do we do as a church to minister to these broken lives?[1]

LOOKING BACK AT DIVORCE

One important thing a friend does is to look at the predicament through the eyes of the person involved in it. It helps us to gain this kind of empathy if we listen carefully to a person discuss how he/she felt during the separation and divorce process.

To begin this process, we interviewed four persons who have been divorced, and taperecorded their comments. When they learned some of their experiences would be used in a book to teach people how to help their friends, they were pleased to be involved in the interview, and to give permission for the taping and reproduction of their comments. They each wanted to help reduce the human suffering involved in divorces, even if only to a slight degree. Information about these four persons is shown below:

Male, 26, store security guard, married 1½ years, no children.
Female, 22, college student, married 3 years, daughter, age 3.
Male, 23, college student, married 1½ years, no children.
Female, 30, bank auditor, married 7 years, no children.

We asked each person several questions regarding his or her divorce. Some of the questions and responses are given below.

Separation

Question: "Who was most helpful to you during your separation leading to divorce?"

Responses:

Combination of family and friends with some direction from a psychiatrist, but not to the same degree.

My family helped a lot. My mom is divorced and so even though she tried to make it seem like it was all my husband's fault, which I didn't want to hear, she did help me emotionally ... I didn't turn to any professionals. I think I kept too much of it to myself and tried to handle it myself instead of turning to somebody outside. It didn't work real well.

The most helpful person to me during my divorce was the manager of the office where I worked. I was the assistant manager to him and we were good friends. He didn't say a whole lot. He was thirty-one and still single, so he couldn't say a whole lot because, you know, he didn't know anything to say. In the long run, that turned out to be the best thing, I think. He just listened. He would let me rant and rave and listen to me work things through. Occasionally, I would get upset, and once or twice I went in the back room. We were in a cockroach infested building in the heart of the downtown area, and I put my fist through the wall once, I was so upset and this sort of stuff. He didn't say anything about it. It didn't matter to him. The building was falling down anyway, I guess. But he didn't say a whole lot and I think that was probably the most helpful.

I contacted Dr. L [a psychologist] a little before Christmas and talked to him.... He gave me ideas which I could try. He presented them to me. He didn't give me just one idea, he gave me several. I think the more ideas you have in front of you the better choice you can make.... I didn't want to accept that she was going out with another guy, so I think through counseling I could accept it and see what was going on.

Divorce—Help Given

Question: "How were your friends helpful to you during your divorce?"

Responses:

Just in trying to make me realize what had happened and that I wasn't entirely to blame or it was not completely a failure on my part. Probably more than anything, they just listened ... and tried to help me restore confidence in myself.

Well, I could identify with her.... She felt the hurt. And that helps, just to have somebody else understand the way you feel makes a big difference.

I felt he was always there, whenever I needed to call I could. No matter when it was. Somebody who I could go to.... You need to be able to call them when you have a problem and then talk about it.

Divorce—Help Not Given

Question: "What help did you need but not receive?"

Responses:

I think if I could have communicated more with D. to know what he was thinking about and why he thought our marriage was not good, then I would have been able to accept it more.... That was part of our problem, that we didn't communicate as well as we should have.

At the time I wanted a man to show me that he cared about me as a person. Of course, I was afraid to get close enough to a man to let that happen, but that would have helped. I'm not close to my own father; maybe that would have helped. If he could have given me some support at the time.

It would have been better if people just had given me an ear instead of trying to dig out all the gruesome details of the divorce. "Did she throw things at you?" If people would have just shut up.... Or a lot of people would try to get me to talk about it, "Well talk about it, it'll be good for you." Talking about it is good for you when you're ready to talk about it, right? When you're just fresh a couple of days out of your divorce, you need time to *think* about it and reflect and see what was going on....

Becoming a Helper

Question: "How would you be able to help a friend now who is going through a divorce?"

Responses:

By listening to the person and by ... helping him reason things out for himself. You can't tell him what to do because you haven't been a part of that relationship, so it's hard for you on the outside to say what was wrong with it....

I'd try to make them see that they're still worth a lot as a person. I think that, well, I had a tendency to think I was just less of a person. I really did feel bad about that ... I feel our divorce probably wouldn't have happened if we both had realized that we had to try more. I think that we could have overcome ... as we grew up a little bit. And I'd tell this person going through the same situation not to be afraid to say, "Hey, let's try it ... let's not get a divorce yet, let's try a little harder ... I think maybe we can make it."

As far as me helping a friend, I think the best thing I could do would be to support him. Try and relate my experience to his in some way so he could see that you aren't going to shrivel up and die or anything, which is your first response to it.... However, whoever is helping cannot make the decision and should not try to make the decision for the person ... I guess that's what's important.

Like when you hit the down periods, the loneliness and the depression, "Oh, my God, what am I going to do?" type of things. If you know there is somebody you can call and talk to, not hear a lecture from, or hear, "Keep busy at work, that's going to take care of everything." 'Cause a lot of people, my parents too, say, "Oh, you just keep busy, then you don't have to worry about it." That's not true. There are too many hours when you can't keep busy. You lie in bed and you say, "Wow, what did I do wrong?" You don't want to be around a whole lot of people in the beginning. After you start to mellow out, it's not too bad.

Themes

There are several themes that emerge from the above verbatim material from persons who were looking back at their own divorce process and the anguish they went through. One theme had to do with the value of an effective *listener* ("He just listened. He would let me rant and rave and listen to me work things through"). Another theme was the need for *expressed caring* ("At the time I wanted a man to show me that he cared about me as a person"). Still another theme was the need for special caring from a *family member*

("I'm not close to my own father; maybe that would have helped."). *Empathy* was another theme ("She felt the hurt. And that helps, just to have somebody else understand the way you feel makes a big difference"). Another theme that emerged was the importance of the *availability* of a friend ("I felt he was always there, whenever I needed to call, I could. No matter when it was"). Another strong felt need was for *acceptance* ("If you know there is somebody you can call and talk to, not hear a lecture from ..."). Finally, a recurring theme was the expressed need for the *supportive presence* of a friend ("As far as me helping a friend, I think the best thing I could do would be to support him").

APPLYING THE METHOD

We have looked at divorce through the eyes of some of the persons who have felt the pain. They have spoken to us of very strongly felt needs which we as friends can help meet. How then can we best proceed? One way is by using the methods shown in this book. We need to be willing to invest generously our time and skills. We need to work harder at being *with* our friend, at being available, than at doing something *for* our friend. We need to listen desperately.

We will want to determine the level of need of our friend. Is he at the predicament level, or has the need deepened to a state of crisis, or even panic or shock? Chapters six—eleven provide guidelines for determining the level of need and meeting the need.

If we are fairly deeply involved with our friend, we probably know his/her learning style. This will permit us to use the most effective means of communication. For example, you may have a friend living some distance from you who is needing help in a divorce process. If your friend is a visual learner, you can have a very effective letter-writing ministry.

You probably also are aware of your friend's life-style, as viewed through the living channels of feeling, thinking, choosing, and doing. The approach suggested in this book has been to work to strengthen the weak channel. This will not only help your friend in the immediate predicament of divorce, but will also help him change his life-style in a positive direction.

ADDITIONAL CONSIDERATIONS

Expect Strong Emotions

There are a number of separation crises. Two of the deepest are death and divorce. John Bowlby has spent most of his adult life studying separation crises. Volume II of his series, *Attachment and Loss,* is entitled *Separation: Anxiety and Anger.* [2] In this book he makes the point that we can expect the twin emotions of anxiety and anger in separation crises. However, probably most of us are not prepared for the anger that is usually there in both bereavement and divorce. As helpers we need to expect anger to be present and then we are not surprised, or worse yet, angered or hurt ourselves.

We may also expect that our friend at times will feel sad, enraged, depressed, lonely, hurt, relieved, confused, guilty, and judged. If we are able to accept him as a friend as he expresses all these emotions, he will feel less alone. I was walking near a small group of people last night, and I heard one person say to another, "You shouldn't feel that way." That is a bit like saying "You shouldn't be suntanned," or "You shouldn't weigh 150 pounds." The feelings are just as real, at the moment, as the suntan or weight, and it is always confusing to ask a person to deny reality.

Help Your Friend Slow Down

Often a person who is considering a divorce, or going through the process of separation or divorce, is in a hurry to make decisions, e.g., Should I file for a divorce? Should I move to another town? In some cases the need for decisions is urgent. In other situations there is no real urgency for such major decisions. If the need is not there for an *immediate* decision, you will usually do your friend a favor by helping him temporarily suspend the drive to make a decision until the emotional level has subsided somewhat. At that time, decisions will likely be more carefully thought out.

Provide a Redemptive Community

Britton Wood, who was mentioned at the beginning of this chapter, is the single adult minister at Park Cities Baptist Church in Dallas,

Texas. He urges the church to reconsider its attitude toward divorced persons:

> We need to care in healthier ways for persons going through divorce. I find I can no longer be unresponsive when I learn that a friend is having marital problems or is in the process of divorce. I am not so much interested in the details of the divorce as I am interested in the person in the divorce. I can't change anything that has happened, but I can care and be a friend in the midst of the changes that are occurring.[3]

Another minister to single adults, Jim Smoke of the Garden Grove Community Church in Garden Grove, California, ministers to over 800 single adults (never married, formerly married, and widowed). He has noted that the formerly married face a great deal of rejection in most churches.

> In many churches divorce has long been the unforgivable sin.... They [those divorcing or divorced] are now among the permanently blemished. If they are allowed to stay around, the fear is that they could contaminate others. Little wonder their wounds, hurts, loneliness, guilt, frustration and fears go ignored.... Their sin is highly visible while the reasons the never coupled remain unmarried are only speculated. The divorced persons in some congregations would be in no worse state if we branded a big "D" on their foreheads.[4]

We all need at least one action support group. Such a group provides a warm, honest, sometimes confronting team of people to whom we can go back periodically to share our lives. If that group is redemptive, that is, centered around the person of Jesus Christ, it can meet spiritual as well as human needs. To introduce your friend to such a group sets up the potential of providing far more help than you can give just by yourself.

Love the Children

All children profit from the presence of other caring adults in addition to their own parents. Children in a single parent family are no different in this need; in fact, they may have an even greater need for expressed warmth from other adults. Your friendship for a child in a single parent family may meet a special need of the child—and of the parent.

REFERENCES

1. Britton Wood, "The Formerly Married—The Church's New Frontier," *Theology, News and Notes*, Fuller Theological Seminary, Pasadena, California, March 1976, p. 18.
2. John Bowlby, *Separation: Anxiety and Anger* (New York: Basic Books, Inc., 1973).
3. Britton Wood, "The Formerly Married—The Church's New Frontier," *Theology, News and Notes*, Fuller Theological Seminary, Pasadena, California, March 1976, p. 20.
4. Jim Smoke, "Single on Sunday," *Theology, News and Notes*, Fuller Theological Seminary, Pasadena, California, March 1976, p. 2.

39 Moving Anxious, Depressed, and Suicidal Persons Toward Professional Help

Dr. Gary Collins has made an important contribution to those seeking effective helping methods by his book, *How to Be a People Helper.* He makes the following point concerning referral:

One of the most significant ways in which we can help people is to refer them and sometimes take them to more professional sources of help. To do this is not an admission of failure; it is a mature recognition that none of us can help everybody.[1]

There are three crucial questions each helper needs to answer concerning referrals: 1) When should I refer? 2) To whom should I refer? 3) How do I make an effective referral?

WHEN SHOULD I REFER?

To answer *this* question we need to look at ourselves, at the relationship, and at the other person.

A Look at Ourselves

I consider making a referral if I find myself beginning to dislike the person I'm working with. That hasn't happened often, and I don't like the fact that it's happened at all, but it has. Sometimes I can work it out with the person and begin to change my attitude, but if I can't, I want to make a referral. A person immersed in a predicament needs a "helper" who likes and accepts him. This is one of the reasons I continually monitor my own feelings about the relationship. In terms of healing and growth, my feelings about the other person are usually more important than the conversation that is going on at any given moment.

I want to refer if I believe the other person needs helping skills I don't have. So I need to know my friend's needs very well, and I need to know my own capabilities and limitations. Am I able to work with someone who is very angry, or do I attack, or back off? Am I able to get a depressed person moving again? The point needs to be made that we will probably never feel *comfortable* working with any of the above situations. But we will grow in our ability and our confidence as we continue to read and study in methods of intervention, and as we reach out to persons in need.

A Look at the Relationship

In the helping relationship, if the other person and I get to the place where we are continually "circling" in our conversation and I cannot break the impasse, I work toward referral. Of course, there are times in most helping interactions when we circle for awhile until we find new courage or insights. But a prolonged impasse often indicates a "blind spot" of sufficient size to impair the helping relationship.

If I sense the other person is not comfortable with me, or is becoming uncomfortable with me, I usually ask him if he would feel more comfortable working with another person. It is important to ask this question rather than coming to that conclusion on our own without checking with the other person, because our perception may be incorrect. The other person, for example, may be comfortable with us but uncomfortable with bringing up the *topic* he knows he needs to talk about.

A Look at Our Friend

There are several questions that we can ask ourselves as we look at our friend and decide whether to refer to a professional for additional help. Notice that I said *additional* help. If you have been involved as a friend, you are a significant helper in the life of your friend. It is important that you not make a referral and then sever the relationship. Your friend might see this as abandonment. We make a referral to a professional counselor because the person we are helping needs additional, specialized help.

One question that can be asked as we contemplate referring is, "Are there evidences my friend may harm himself?" Edwin S. Shneidman, Director of the Laboratory for the Study of Life-Threatening Behavior, in the Department of Psychiatry at the University of California at Los Angeles, is one of the outstanding researchers and writers on suicide. He has studied suicide notes, has done many taped interviews using preventive methods with persons considering suicide, and has sat with dying persons. His writings constitute an extensive, caring portion of the literature on suicide.

Dr. Shneidman says that there are three components in a suicidal act: heightened inimicality (self-hate), growing perturbation (roughly translated, a "shook-up" feeling), and increased constriction of mental functioning (seeing only a very limited area of reality).[2] Dr. Shneidman has suggested viewing a person's self-hate and the extent to which he is "shook-up" on a scale of low to high. If either of these is high we should be concerned. But if *both* are high, we need to be very concerned.

THE DEGREE OF SELF-HATRED

(Low)   (High)

1	2	3	4	5	6	7	8	9

It is not that some people hate themselves and others do not. It is rather that in some the amount of self-hatred is so small as to pose no barrier to mental health, while in others the degree of self-hatred is quite high. A person who calls himself "stupid," and puts himself down in other ways, would be practicing a low degree of self-hatred. One who overeats or smokes would be engaging in a bit higher form of self-hatred (life-shortening behavior). One who drives a car recklessly at a very high rate of speed would be toward the upper end of the scale.

It is also possible to show on a scale the degree of mental upset. This has to do with what Dr. Shneidman refers to as the extent to which one is perturbed or "shook-up." The person may appear disturbed, anxious, generally upset, agitated, or violent. One would be at the far left of the continuum if he is tranquil and serene. If he is somewhat nervous, e.g., pacing the floor, wringing his hands, or talking very rapidly, he might be at two or three on the scale. If he is breathing very rapidly and is having dizzy spells, he might be at six or seven on the scale.

THE DEGREE OF MENTAL UPSET

(Low)							(High)	
1	2	3	4	5	6	7	8	9

The third component in a suicidal act is constriction, the "tunneling" of one's vision or awareness. A person called in the middle of the night to say, "Taking this bottle of pills is the only way out of the mess I'm in." In reality there are many ways out, but in this person's reality this was the only way out. Dr. Shneidman has noted that "The suicidal person abandons the sense of life's continuum and uses such words as 'only,' 'either/or,' 'always,' 'never,' and 'forever.' "[3] The suicidal person is in a state of panic. As noted in the earlier chapter on panic, the panicked person, whether a runaway or a suicide, sees only one way out. The mentally healthy person has a wide field of awareness and can see many alternatives. He is capable of meaningful dialogue. On the other hand, it is extremely difficult to carry on a conversation with a suicidal person. As shown in the drawing, his awareness is so constricted that he is not seeing the things we are seeing and talking about. It is as if he is viewing life through a keyhole and is seeing only his suffering, and perhaps a means of escape.

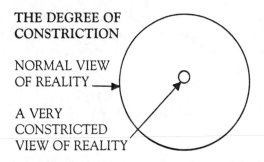

THE DEGREE OF CONSTRICTION

NORMAL VIEW OF REALITY

A VERY CONSTRICTED VIEW OF REALITY

Dr. Shneidman has pointed out that a fourth element, the idea of *cessation,* of ending it all, is what combines with the three above components to bring about the suicidal act. "Talk of being dead, of going away, of ending it all (especially in the presence of the three other factors) should alert one to a highly lethal suicidal state."[4] If our friend has shown one or more of the above characteristics—self-hatred, mental upset, and constriction—then we need to be especially aware of conversation which indicates a desire to escape, to end the pain. Sometimes the suicidal person is able to share the thought of cessation with a friend easier than with a professional counselor.

INTERVENTION METHODS

Before discussing the issues of "To whom should I refer?" and "How do I make an effective referral?" we need to consider what can be done to intervene in a positive way with a person who is so anxious or depressed that he is considering suicide.

The methods discussed in chapter ten, "Panic—The Wild Flight," should be useful. Ways to recognize a panicked person are shown in that chapter. Some approaches designed to move the person from the "panic button" to the "hold button" are also described.

There are additional considerations in working with a person who shows signs of being self-destructive. We will look at some of these so that even though you are working at a referral, you will be of help to your friend until you can secure the additional aid of a professional counselor. The first consideration is that nearly always the suicidal person is ambivalent (of two minds) about ending his own life. He wants to, and he doesn't want to. Shneidman has pointed out a persistent myth about suicide:

> *Fable:* Suicidal people are fully intent on dying. *Fact:* Most suicidal people are undecided about living or dying, and they "gamble with death," leaving it to others to save them. Almost no one commits suicide without letting others know how he is feeling.[5]

Suicide or "hot" lines are built on this idea of ambivalence. The fact that hundreds of people in any given month of the year all over the United States call a friend or a crisis line volunteer to discuss ending their own life shows their desire to live as much as their wish to die. And when you are talking with an anxious or depressed person who has displayed the components described above, it helps to know that you have ambivalence working for you.

In working with persons contemplating suicide, I have formulated the following guidelines. You need to take them "with a grain of salt," because most guidelines only work some of the time, and with some people.

1) Listen.

2) Don't give "pat answers" and easy advice.

3) Make every effort to understand the mind-set of your friend.

4) As much as possible, communicate through your friend's *strong learning channel*—visual, auditory, or touch/movement.

5) The chances are you are working with a person who is weak in the *thinking channel of his life-style,* that is, he is *impulsive.* You may find the suggestions in chapter seventeen helpful ("How to Slow Down the Impulsive Person").

6) Avoid arguments and power struggles. As a helper you need to aid your friend in becoming less perturbed, not more perturbed.

7) Let yourself feel some of the other person's sufferings, and acknowledge the reality of his sufferings. A fundamental cause of discouragement and depression is a feeling that no one cares—"Not one person really cares about me." By responding in an empathic way, you

may come across as saying, "*I* care." This is sometimes an effective way to reduce the amount of self-hatred.

8) Work to reduce the amount of mental upset. You may do this by listening intently, by talking calmly and slowly, by touching the other person when that is acceptable, and by relying on the strength of your presence. The weak person draws strength from the strong, and your confident, calming presence can help reduce the "frantic" feelings of your friend.

9) With persons who are in the early stages of contemplating suicide, I think it has been helpful at times when I've talked with them about the effects of a suicide upon surviving loved ones. *But* in situations when the suicide act is imminent, constriction (limited awareness) has reduced the effectiveness of this approach. The suicidal person does not "see" the logic of this point of view.

10) I work in two ways to relieve the constriction noted above, thus enlarging the person's awareness. The first method is by discussing present meaning. The fact that the suicidal person is ambivalent means there is some meaning present in his life right now. I want to discover what that is and discuss it. It may be a relationship that he has, or a task that he's involved in. I have used an approach such as the following, "It means a lot to me to be able to talk with you. I understand that you see little or no meaning in life right now. Could we talk about one thing that has meant something to you recently, no matter how small that meaning was?"

A second way I work to relieve the constriction is to ask a question like this: "What is one thing you haven't accomplished yet that you would still like to?" Another form of this same question is, "Many people have dreams of what they would like to do or be. Right now I'd guess your dream may be pretty dim and hard to see, but I'd guess that it's there somewhere. Would you share your dream with me?"

The idea behind this focus on the future is that the suicidal person needs to be pulled rather than pushed into his future. The chances are I can't urge him into continuing to live. Even if I do, he may kill himself when I'm not present. Usually we cannot "push" other persons into their future (get them to continue life) by providing them with a list of reasons for living. On the other hand, if I can help a friend discover or rediscover, *a reason of his own* for living (no matter how small), this will provide a powerful pull into the future—a reason to continue his life.

11) On two occasions I can remember using a confrontation or "mild shock" approach. This approach, if used, must be used in such a way that it does not put the other person down. The first example I'll mention from my own experience is one that I described earlier in chapter twenty-one, "Encouraging the Search for Meaning." I received a phone call late at night and the caller said, "I have a bottle of sleeping pills in my hand and I'm thinking of committing suicide.... I almost had the courage to do it awhile ago and then I chickened out" (The caller was someone I didn't know, and who had been given my phone number by another person). I replied, "No, it doesn't take courage to swallow a bottle of sleeping pills; it takes courage to go on living when you can't find any meaning in life." This response relieved the constriction a bit and helped move the caller from the panic to the hold button. The result was a fairly long phone conversation followed by an invitation to get together personally with the caller that night to plan the next step.

A second call, again from a person who had been given my phone number as a referral, came another night. This person had a gun, had been drinking, and was threatening self-destruction. One of his hands was bleeding because he had run his fist through a window. I listened without saying very much until the caller said, "When you've lived long enough to suffer a lot of grief like I have, you'll want to die, too." I said, "I know what grief is; I held my father's hand when he died." Then the caller's voice changed—it became much less tense. We were able to continue talking until he was less perturbed and able to make it through the night on his own.

Some who are reading this may be thinking, "But I haven't had anyone close to me die," or "I haven't had much suffering so far in my life; how do I react in an empathic way to another person who is suffering a great deal?" If this is your situation, you might respond by saying, "I don't think I've experienced suffering like you're experiencing now. But I know what it is to experience hurt, and I want you to know that as much as I can, I'm feeling with you now." The word *with* is powerful, because it takes away some of the loneliness.

TO WHOM SHOULD I REFER?

A referral is more likely to "take" if you know the helping person to whom you refer. It is worth making the effort to get to know professional counselors in your community. Many ministers are effective crisis counselors; others have not received training in crisis intervention. Mental health centers are serving many communities. Most of them have an open house or a similar event once a year. This affords an opportunity to become acquainted with their services and their personnel. Some school counselors have excellent crisis intervention skills. Many communities have psychologists or psychiatrists, or both, in private practice. You may have the opportunity through your church, social organization, or service club to get acquainted with some of these professional counselors.

If you do have the opportunity to get to know some professional counselors, be willing to find out what they believe, what their values are. In chapter two, I mentioned that the Christian is a person of two ages—the present age and the age to come. The Christian counselor is able to bring to bear human insights and helps from the behavioral sciences, and he/she can also use specifically Christian, redemptive insights and helps.

Counselors who do not operate from a specifically Christian point of view can still be very helpful, providing they respect the faith of the person they are counseling. It is often helpful if a Christian friend or minister can see the counselee during the period of time he is receiving counseling help, so the counseling can be integrated with the person's Christian life. There are a few counselors who are uncomfortable with a person who has a strong religious faith and who may even try to discount the client's faith. These counselors should be avoided. It is possible, of course, for a professional counselor to leave a client worse off than he found him, just as it is possible for a well-meaning friend to do more harm than good. When we enter into a helping relationship, we have the potential to either give or to take away.

If a friend needs emergency help at night when most agencies are closed, you may be able to use a telephone crisis line. These are listed under different names in different communities, e.g., Crisis Line, Personal Crisis Line, or Hot Line. The volunteer on the line can usually refer you to a backup person who can provide help right away.

In many communities, help is available through the Emergency 911 telephone number. In some situations you may need to use the resources of a hospital emergency room. In some instances you will need specific technical information. If a friend says to you, "I took eight of these green pills; is that enough to hurt me?" you will need to ask for the bottle they came in and then head for the phone. You can call a hospital, describe the situation, and ask for the physician on duty. Another source of technical information is a pharmacist.

There is nothing that takes the place of your own collection of information concerning counseling professionals in your community. I suggest you get together with some of your friends and discuss, and perhaps write down, a number of referral sources. In some communities there is already a booklet of mental health service resources. Your county or city Department of Social Services or your local Mental Health Center can usually tell you if such a directory has been compiled.

HOW DO I MAKE AN EFFECTIVE REFERRAL?

So that we can consider a concrete situation, let's suppose you are talking with a friend who is emotionally upset, who has shown signs of self-hatred, and whose awareness is constricted. You have been successful in helping your friend move away from the panic button for the moment. Following are some questions, one or two of which may be helpful in moving your friend toward professional help at this point. I'm assuming you've built a relationship that is fairly strong, so that you can be direct.

What is your plan for getting better?

Have you considered getting help from an experienced counselor?

What is the biggest barrier to your seeing a counselor?

You need to "educate" your friend concerning the function of a counselor by saying something like the following: "Going to a counselor is quite different from going to a physician. Most people are pretty passive when they go to a physician. They expect the physician to do something *for* them that will make them well. A counselor is a person who does something *with* you. You will have an active part in the getting well process. It will require hard work and courage on your part. In return for this investment you'll probably find some new ways to make life better and to get rid of some of your anguish."

It is important not to promise too much concerning a referral. Don't make it sound easy, because it isn't. It is also important to build a point of view that enables your friend to go to a counselor expecting to take an active role in the counseling process.

Go over with your friend the exact steps involved in a referral. Give him specific names, agencies, and telephone numbers. Ask him if he needs any other help from you in making plans to see a counselor. Don't push too hard. Newton's Third Law of Motion, "For every action there is an equal and opposite reaction," has a psychological counterpart. When we push someone, he resists. The harder the push, the greater the resistance. The referral needs to be more of an invitation than an urging.

If your friend does not want a referral, or does not want one yet, the next best alternative is to mobilize what caring forces you can. You may be able to enlist the aid of a mutual friend or two who will give supportive help. Relatives and fellow workers may be other resources. This enlisting of helpers has to be done carefully and you need to select them with care. A group of "helpers" descending on a distraught person may cause as many predicaments as they resolve.

Finally, remember that your *presence* is one of the most powerful forces for good in the life of your friend.

REFERENCES

1. Gary Collins, *How to Be a People Helper* (Santa Ana, California: Vision House Publishers, 1976), pp. 108, 109.
2. Edwin S. Shneidman, "A Psychologic Theory of Suicide," *Psychiatric Annals*, November 1976, Vol. 6, Num. 11, p. 53.
3. *Ibid.*, p. 57.
4. *Ibid.*, p. 60.
5. *Ibid.*, p. 39.

Section
Seven

Putting It
All Together

40

Practice Situation #1: Mark

You are now ready to look at a practice situation and plan how you would be able to give help in such a situation. Remember that the method calls for you to determine three things about your friend: 1) What is his level of need? 2) What is his weak living channel? and 3) What is his strong learning channel? You do not need all this information at the moment your friend comes for help. The first thing is to be sure that you listen and resonate. Now read through the situation with Mark below, and decide how you can go about being helpful to him. Use the space at the right of the pages to jot down clues about life-style, learning style, level of need, ideas for your approach, and other reactions you have.

Mark is one of your good friends at work. You have noticed for the last couple of days that he seems preoccupied. Today as you eat together in the company cafeteria, he says to you, "It's been hard for me to keep my mind on my work the last few days. I've got a problem at home with my oldest boy, Phil. You know he's fifteen years old. And he's getting so he doesn't think he has to mind me anymore. It seems like we aren't as close as we used to be. When he was in elementary school we used to spend a lot of time together. Now, it's different. You know how it is here. I have to work some evenings and weekends. But in a way, it's not so bad working so much because if I were home I don't know what I'd talk with him about. It's uncomfortable for us to be together. He seems to get along OK with his mother and with the other kids, but he and I clash all the time. I don't know what to do."

Mark has always been a person who is task-oriented. If there is a job to be done, he can get it done. He has always been willing to take on more tasks at work. Work has a great deal of meaning for him.

Actually he is more at ease with work than he is with people. You are his only good friend at work. He seems generally to hold himself somewhat aloof from others. He doesn't seem to think he is better than other people; rather he just seems to feel uncomfortable in close relationships. The kind of work he does requires excellent craftsmanship. He is well-coordinated, moves easily, and is good at games requiring physical skills.

Mark looks at you in an expectant sort of way after he has shared his "problem" with you. What would be the first thing you would say; how would you plan to proceed in the next few minutes; and what would be some of your long-range ideas for helping Mark?

After you have noted how you would respond, turn to Appendix B and compare your responses with "A Plan for Helping Mark."

41 Practice Situation #2: Carol

One of your neighbors is Carol, a young woman who now lives alone and is getting a divorce. Her husband left her because of his involvement with another woman, and he is now planning to marry the other woman. Carol worked hard to bring about a reconciliation. Her husband refused to go for counseling with her. She has come over for coffee with you this morning.

After you have talked for awhile, she

Notes

Notes

says, "Today we are going to work on a property settlement. I know in my head that it's all over, but I still love him. I have never felt so bad in my whole life as I do right now. There's not much for me to live for, but I know I have to go on living. I feel like quitting my job this afternoon when I go in to work, and moving out of town. I can't stand to see them together. What do you think I ought to do?"

You have learned how to appreciate the kind of person Carol is. She is warm and able to express her feelings easily and accurately. She enjoys talking and she listens well. It seems to help for her to talk through a situation she is in. You have also noticed some growth that she needs to make. She often fails to plan ahead, and when she does plan, she sometimes doesn't keep to her plan. She sometimes will act first, then not seem to be aware of the consequences of her actions until she encounters them later.

Based on what you know about Carol, and on what she has said to you in the above statement, jot down some notes in the right-hand column of these pages showing what would be your first response to her question, how you would proceed from there in the conversation, and some ideas you have for helping her today and during the next few weeks.

_____

After you have noted how you would respond, turn to Appendix C and compare your responses with "A Plan for Helping Carol."

Section
Eight
Back to You

42 Finding Strength in an Action Support Group

When we set about trying to help friends who are in predicaments or crises, we often go through the same stages that persons do in marriage: 1) Enchantment, 2) Disenchantment, and 3) Maturity.[1] There is something exciting and perhaps almost romantic in reaching out to help another human being. However, most helpers move before long to another stage in which the old helping process has little appeal anymore. They feel burned out and ineffective. The excitement and the romance are gone. It is at this point—making the transition from the disenchanted stage to the maturity stage—that both the marriage partner and the helper need assistance.

Many volunteer workers have been able to move into the maturity stage because of their participation in an Action Support Group. The concept of the Action Support Group is a very simple one. Several people who are involved in the same or a similar activity get together on a regular basis to encourage each other. This concept is an old, old concept, but the name is rather new.

Two of the concepts behind the evangelical movement known as "Key 73" were Awareness and Action Support. Since that time, the term Action Support Group has been used rather widely. Obviously, groups do not have to be called Action Support Groups to provide this function. Such groups as Bible Study groups, prayer groups, coffee groups, and many others provide an encouragement for those who meet.

As I mentioned earlier in this manual, we have in the city where I live a group of volunteers who staff a Personal Crisis Line, a telephone line that is kept available for anyone to call in anytime from 6:00 P.M. to 6:00 A.M. Although the average life of such lines is rather brief, this line has been open and staffed nightly for the last six years. During the 2,000-plus nights that the members of this group have staffed the line, they have responded to hundreds of persons in crisis situations. During these years hundreds of persons have experienced what it is to hear a warm, friendly voice on the other end of the line as they share their predicaments. One of the reasons it has continued to exist is that the volunteers have a monthly Action Support Group which gets together not only for in-service training, but to share how things are going for them as volunteers.

What happens in an Action Support Group? The members share not only their experiences but their *lives.* Therefore, there has to be a level of trust established. They discuss what they are doing—their failures as well as their successes. And together they find strength to go out and work again at their tasks.

FORMING AN ACTION SUPPORT GROUP

If you want to serve as a more effective helper to your friends, consider joining or forming an Action Support Group. Perhaps you are not a member of such a group and you want to get one going; one way to do this is to find three or four other persons with the same interest you have—people who want to be able to help a friend. This manual can be used as a resource guide for such a group. You can go through the manual at the rate of one chapter a week in less than a year. A different member of the group can be responsible each week for leading the discussion for a given chapter. You will probably find that you derive some help from the manual, but you will get a great deal more help from each other. In addition to working through the manual, you can also share how your own efforts to help are going, and you can find out how the others are doing as well. Sharing your failures and successes with others who care provides a great deal of support.

REFERENCES

1. Paul R. Welter. *Family Problems and Predicaments: How to Respond* (Wheaton, Illinois: Tyndale House Publishers, 1977), p. 101. This reference has a chart on these three stages of marriage, and an accompanying discussion of a couple who worked through the disenchantment stage.

43 Giving and Receiving

An important discovery came to me when I led an encounter group of registered nurses. They were a group of compassionate, skilled nurses who were doing an excellent job in their hospital setting. But I began to notice it was hard for them to share themselves. I wondered why this was. The trust level seemed to be good in the group, and they cared about each other. Why was it so hard for them to open up? Finally, it occurred to me that these nurses had spent all of their professional lives giving. They had never been trained to receive. They were not comfortable in sharing themselves because they weren't sure that it was all right to take up the others' time, and it was a new experience for some of them to open up to *receive* help from others. It was a fresh and worthwhile experience for them to begin receiving.

The purpose of this manual has been to provide you with some ways to give help to others. It is risky to do this, because once we begin to see ourselves as helpers, we tend to close ourselves off to receiving help from others. The occupational hazard of the helping profession is just that—the persons in these professions are identified as helpers. This raises a number of questions. Is it all right for the helper to receive help? Are there times when the helper *needs* help? Who helps the helper? The strain on professional helpers is very high. For example, the suicide rate among psychiatrists is about three times as great as among the general population.

Professional counselors and lay helpers will feel much less strain when we begin to realize that helping is a swinging door—we give help and we receive help from that person within a single conversation. One of the persons who was most helpful to me was a counselee of mine, a middle-aged, gentle, compassionate man. I think I helped him to function better at home and at work. I know I received help from him in my spiritual life. He had a very strong quest to serve God and to know him better, and he taught me something of what it means to be hungry and thirsty for spiritual growth.

As I think back over the relationships which I have had during the past years with scores of persons, I have come to a generalization; that is, when I have been most effective in giving—those were the times when I was also most open to receiving. So I have now come to think of all my helping relationships as always involving both giving and receiving.

This paradox is not unique to counseling. The best teacher is one who is learning. The teacher who thinks he has learned all that he needs to know has not only stopped learning; he has also stopped teaching.

So there is a rhythm in giving and receiving. Sometimes we give help; sometimes we receive help. Sometimes we may think we are doing one thing when really we are doing the other. But always we are *with* a friend in the predicament or crisis he/she is facing.

Appendixes

A TWENTY THINGS I LOVE TO DO— An Exercise in Value Clarification*

Think of twenty things you really love to do and write them in the space provided on the next page. Do all your writing to the right of the numbers. Just write them down in any way they come to your mind. They do not need to be rank-ordered. Think of activities that really excite you. Write in these things now. To learn the most from your work, do not turn to the next page for further instructions until you have completed writing all twenty.

*I have modified this exercise somewhat from the exercise, "Twenty Things You Love to Do," described by Sidney B. Simon, Leland W. Howe, and Howard Kirschenbaum in *Values Clarification* (New York: Hart Publishing Co., 1972), Strategy #1, pp. 30-34. This book has many exercises which are helpful in strengthening the choosing channel.

306 How to Help a Friend

TWENTY THINGS I LOVE TO DO

1	11
2	12
3	13
4	14
5	15
6	16
7	17
8	18
9	19
10	20

1. I learned that I

2. I learned that I

3. I learned that I

Now place coding marks to the left of the numbers of the twenty things you love to do.

1. Place a $ to the left of the number of each of the twenty things you love to do that require money—let's say $2.00 or more. Eating in a restaurant would be an activity that would be marked with a $. Going to Sunday school would not. Walking in the rain would not.

2. Place an M to the left of each of the things you love to do that your mother loves or loved to do. Do the same thing with an F for father, and an Sp for your spouse.

3. Place a PD in front of each of the things you love to do that your parents would disapprove of or would have disapproved of.

4. Place an SG before a spiritual growth activity such as prayer or Bible study.

5. Place a CH before any activity that involves your church.

6. Place an H before any activity in which you help others.

7. Place an RT before any activity that involves risk-taking, that is, it is either physically or psychologically dangerous.

8. Place a CR before any activity that requires creativity, for example, writing a poem or painting a picture.

9. Place an A in front of anything you love to do that you typically do alone.

10. Write Fam to the left of any of the things you love to do that you usually do with your family.

11. Write PS to the left of any of the things you love to do that require physical skills or physical strength.

12. Write RD to the left of any activity that involves reading.

13. Write 5 in front of any activity that you loved to do 5 years ago.

14. Write 65 in front of any activity that you will love to do at retirement. A common question here is, "But will I be able to?" The answer is usually, "Yes."

15. To find out how up to date you are on your values, write D in front of any you have done today, W to the left of those you have done in the last week but not the last day, Mn on those you have done in the last month but not in the last week, and Y on those you've done in the last year but not in the last month.

Now you are ready for the last step in this value clarification exercise. Go through the coding marks and look for patterns. For example, how many of the things you love to do, do you do alone? How many involve your family, your church? How many values do you share with your family and friends? After you have found several patterns, finish the "I learned" statements at the bottom of the page. These are three things you learned about yourself by working through this exercise—three areas of your personality and value system you have become more aware of.

B A PLAN for Helping Mark

In chapter forty you were given the practice situation described below and asked to plan how you would give help in this situation. It was mentioned there that the method we are trying to apply calls for us to determine three things about our friend: 1) What is his level of need? 2) What is his weak living channel? and 3) What is his strong learning channel? It was noted that you do not need all this information at the moment your friend comes for help. The first thing is to be sure you listen and resonate. You were asked to use the space at the right of the pages to jot down clues about life-style, learning style, level of need, ideas for your approach, and other reactions you have.

I've also worked at carrying out this assignment, so see the margin for some clues, ideas, and reactions I have. I suggest you look at my reactions not as the "right answers," but rather as possible approaches to add to your own helping methods.

SITUATION	NOTES
Mark is one of your good friends at work. You have noticed for the last couple of days that he seems preoccupied. Today as you eat together in the company cafeteria, he says to you, "It's been hard for me to keep my mind on my work the last few days. I've got a problem at home with my oldest boy, Phil. You know he's fifteen years old. And he's getting so he doesn't think he has to mind me anymore. It seems like we aren't as close as we used to be. When he was in elementary school we used to spend a lot of time together. Now, it's different. You know how it is here. I have to work some evenings and weekends. But in a way, it's not so bad working so much because if I were home I don't know what I'd talk about with him. It's uncomfortable for us to be together. He seems to get along OK with his mother and with the other kids, but he and I clash all the time. I don't know what to do."	*Concentration at work may be difficult for Mark unless he gets help soon.*
	Need Level?
	Deeper than a "problem." Does not appear to have the urgency of a crisis. Sounds like a predicament.
	Mark is not involved with Phil, and he's not sure how to build an involvement. Sounds a bit fearful.
Mark has always been a person who is task-oriented. If there is a job to be done, he can get it done. He has always been willing to take on more tasks at work. Work has a great deal of meaning for him.	*Mark may be a "product-oriented parent." In an effort to get Phil to "turn out" all right, he may be bypassing the present moment with him.*
Actually he is more at ease with work than he is with people. You are his only good friend at work. He seems generally to hold himself somewhat aloof from others. He doesn't seem to think he is better than other people; rather he just seems to feel uncomfortable in close relationships. The kind of work he does re-	*Life-style?*
	Apparently a lack of expressed warmth. Perhaps weak in the feeling channel.

quires excellent craftsmanship. He is well-coordinated, moves easily, and is good at games requiring physical skills.

Mark looks at you in an expectant sort of way after he has shared his "problem" with you. What would be the first thing you would say; how would you plan to proceed in the next few minutes; and what would be some of your long-range ideas for helping Mark?

NOTES

Learning Style?

Mark may be a touch/movement learner.

First Response: "I can tell from what you've said that you care for Phil a great deal, and you want to get more deeply involved in his life, even though it scares you to think about that."

The Next Few Minutes: During this conversation in the cafeteria my first goal would be to listen as intently as possible, and to respond to the deepest feelings that Mark expresses. I would not give "pat answers" or "easy advice." I need to understand him and his predicament more fully before I even *think* about action he should take.

Long-range Help: When Mark turns the corner from sharing feelings to exploring alternatives for action, I would ask him if he would like to make a plan which might result in greater involvement with Phil (Mark's influence with his son will be in direct proportion to their involvement with each other).

A plan for involvement could center on Mark's learning channel strength of touch/movement. Most fifteen-year-old boys like activities. Mark has many skills and abilities that may be used to build a greater involvement with Phil around an activity, once Mark has determined what Phil's interests are. One way he could do this would be to use a values clarification exercise at the family table, such as the one shown in Appendix A, "Twenty Things I Love to Do."

I would discuss with Mark ways he can begin to get in touch with Phil, e.g., back rubs, measuring Phil's height, and putting his arm around Phil's shoulder. These initiatives on Mark's part will strengthen his life-style by increasing his ability to express warmth. At the same time the relationship between Mark and his son will probably deepen. As the involvement between Mark and Phil grows stronger, the chances are Phil will "mind" his father better.

C A PLAN for Helping Carol

This is a follow-up from chapter forty-one in which you were given the practice situation described below and asked to plan how you would give help. You probably looked for clues concerning need level, life-style, and learning style. You were asked to jot down clues and possible approaches in the margin. I have carried out my own assignment by writing the notes that appear below. As with "A Plan for Helping Mark," I'm suggesting you view my responses simply as possible approaches to add to your own repertoire of helping methods.

SITUATION

NOTES

One of your neighbors is Carol, a young woman who now lives alone, and is getting a divorce. Her husband left her because of his involvement with another woman, and he is now planning to marry the other woman. Carol worked hard to bring about a reconciliation. Her husband refused to go for counseling with her. She has come over for coffee with you this morning.

After you have talked for awhile, she says, "Today we are going to work on a property settlement. I know in my head that it's all over, but I still love him. I have never felt so bad in my whole life as I do right now. There's not much for me to live for, but I know I have to go on living. I feel like quitting my job this afternoon when I go in to work, and moving out of town. I can't stand to see them together. What do you think I ought to do?"

You have learned how to appreciate the kind of person Carol is. She is warm and able to express her feelings easily and accurately. She enjoys talking and she listens well. It seems to help for her to talk through a situation she is in. You have also noticed some growth that she needs to make. She often fails to plan ahead, and when she does plan, she sometimes doesn't keep to her plan. She sometimes will act first, then not seem to be aware of the consequences of her actions until she encounters them later.

Based on what you know about Carol, and on what she has said to you in the above statement, jot down some notes in the right-hand column of these pages showing what would be your first response to her question, how you would proceed from there in the conversation, and some ideas you have for helping her today and during the next few weeks.

Need Level?

Deeper than a predicament, but does not seem to be at the panic stage. She appears to be in a crisis, with panic a possibility if she does not receive help.

Learning Style?

Carol may be strong in the auditory-vocal (hearing-talking) channel.

Life-style?

The evidences indicate a strong feeling channel, and a weak thinking channel, i.e., a tendency toward impulsiveness

My First Response: "I think you're doing exactly what you ought to do right at this moment. You're talking your situation over with a friend. Talking it over usually helps one to slow down. You're hurting very deeply right now, and you may be thinking that an impulsive decision to leave town will reduce your suffering."

The Remainder of the Conversation: I would listen deeply to Carol, and continue to respond to her intense feelings, e.g., her love for her husband, her loneliness, her feeling of rejection, and her anger. I would also ask questions focusing on the possible consequences of her decisions, e.g., "Do you think your supervisor will recommend you for another position if you quit your job without giving adequate notice?" "What is your plan for making a living if you quit your present job?" "Will escaping help reduce the loneliness you're feeling?"

Ideas for Helping: A supportive presence helps keep one from panicking. I think I would ask Carol if she would like to stop by later today after her time at the lawyer's discussing the property settlement.

A crisis usually lasts several weeks. Therefore, I would expect to make a heavy time investment in Carol for a month or so. I would affirm her as a person. Also, I'd use the guidelines mentioned in chapter thirty-eight, "Divorce—Finding a Way to Help," i.e., I'd expect strong emotions. I'd work to help Carol slow down, and I'd try to introduce her to a small, caring group—a redemptive community.

Her strong auditory-vocal learning channel suggests she needs many opportunities to "talk it over." Her relatively weak thinking (planning ahead) life-style channel indicates the advisability of helping her establish a *plan* prior to her making any important decisions.

Index